Take Your iPad® to Work, Second Edition

Brian Proffitt

Course Technology PTR

A part of Cengage Learning

COURSE TECHNOLOGY
CENGAGE Learning·

Australia • Brazil • Japan • Korea • Mexico • Singapore • Spain • United Kingdom • United States

COURSE TECHNOLOGY
CENGAGE Learning·

Take Your iPad® to Work,
Second Edition
Brian Proffitt

Publisher and General Manager,
Course Technology PTR:
Stacy L. Hiquet

Associate Director of Marketing:
Sarah Panella

Manager of Editorial Services:
Heather Talbot

Senior Marketing Manager:
Mark Hughes

Senior Acquisitions Editor:
Mitzi Koontz

Project and Copy Editor:
Marta Justak

Technical Reviewer:
Brown Partington

Interior Layout: Jill Flores

Cover Designer: Mike Tanamachi

Indexer: Sharon Shock

Proofreader: Sam Garvey

For product information and technology assistance, contact us at
Cengage Learning Customer & Sales Support, 1-800-354-9706
For permission to use material from this text or product,
submit all requests online at **cengage.com/permissions**
Further permissions questions can be emailed to
permissionrequest@cengage.com

iPad, iPhone, iPod, iPod Touch, iOS, and OS X are registered trademarks or trademarks of Apple Inc. BlackBerry is a registered trademark of Research In Motion Limited. Droid is a registered trademark of LucasFilm Ltd. Android is a trademark of Google Inc. Linux is a trademark of Linus Torvalds. Microsoft, Windows, and Internet Explorer are either registered trademarks or trademarks of Microsoft Corporation in the United States and/or other countries. PalmPilot, Palm, and webOS are either registered trademarks or trademarks of Palm, Inc., a subsidiary of Hewlett-Packard Company. Wite-Out is a registered trademark of the BIC Corporation. GTD and Getting Things Done are registered trademarks of David Allen and Co. Kindle is a trademark of Amazon Technologies, Inc.

All other trademarks are the property of their respective owners.

All images © Cengage Learning unless otherwise noted.

Library of Congress Control Number: 2012934298

ISBN-13: 978-1-133-68670-5

ISBN-10: 1-133-68670-2

Course Technology, a part of Cengage Learning
20 Channel Center Street
Boston, MA 02210
USA

Cengage Learning is a leading provider of customized learning solutions with office locations around the globe, including Singapore, the United Kingdom, Australia, Mexico, Brazil, and Japan. Locate your local office at: **international.cengage.com/region**

Cengage Learning products are represented in Canada by Nelson Education, Ltd. For your lifelong learning solutions, visit **courseptr.com**
Visit our corporate Web site at **cengage.com**

Printed in the United States of America
1 2 3 4 5 6 7 14 13 12

In memory of Frank and Martha Cook, who taught me that God has an awesome sense of humor. Because they sure knew how to laugh.

Acknowledgments

S o we meet again.

This is the second edition of *Take Your iPad to Work*, which means that the first edition did well enough to warrant another one. For that, I must thank all the readers who thought the book was good enough to pick up a copy. And thank you for following their example.

This book was completed on a very tight schedule, which meant my family helped support me through a slam-fest of work on *this* book and *all* the other projects that had to get done. I cannot thank the women of Team Proffitt enough—including our newest member, Elisabeth.

And then there are the professionals: great editors who have been the secret to my success. Mitzi Koontz, Marta Justak, Brown Partington, and Sam Garvey get thanks for taking my content and crafting it into something much better.

This book was unique in that it covered many different types of software applications. Several companies and developers generously donated copies of their apps so they could be reviewed and discussed. For all of the people who graciously responded to my requests for help, thank you.

About the Author

Brian Proffitt is a technology expert who blogs on ITworld.com on Open Source and Big Data technology and Twitters as @TheTechScribe on a wide range of technology sectors. Currently, he is an adjunct instructor at the Mendoza College of Business at the University of Notre Dame. But he won't let that go to his head.

Contents

Introduction

With the right applications, the iPad family of devices can become more than just content consumption devices for videos, music, and electronic books. An iPad device can be a content production device as well—generating documents, spreadsheets, and presentations for the workplace.

This ability to produce content, given the right applications, immediately shifts the iPad into a useful business device. Businesses that depend on fast, accurate business processes can utilize the iPad to quickly supply data, invoice customers, and manage vendors from a reliable, highly mobile platform.

The potential business use-cases for the iPad are limited only by your ingenuity:

◆ Restaurant owners can deploy iPads to wait staff to use as electronic devices to capture orders. The devices can, at the touch of an icon, double as colorful menus in any language the customer prefers.

◆ A traveling salesman can take orders, make presentations, and even demonstrate aspects of the product via video, all with the same iPad.

◆ A roving food vendor can use the iPad to announce his or her current location, handle sales, and track inventory from the truck, even as hungry food fans descend.

These, of course, are just a few possible scenarios for using the iPad in a business setting. While a computer could handle just about all of these tasks, such a device would be inconvenient to carry around, and the iPad's flat form greatly simplifies mobility.

Is the iPad right for every business situation? That's what this book will explore. By demonstrating the many types of business apps available for the iPad, you should be able to make the case for using the iPad effectively in your place of business.

Is This Book for You?

Take Your iPad to Work, Second Edition is for anyone who wants to get started using the iPad in a professional environment. Think of this book as a personal tutorial, a one-on-one class with an expert user of the iPad. You get to stay in the comfort of your own home or office and learn how to do the following things:

◆ Familiarize yourself with the iPad controls and interfaces

◆ Connect to the Internet with the iPad using WiFi or a cellular connection

◆ Add apps and multimedia content to your iPad

◆ Communicate with colleagues via email

◆ Create documents, spreadsheets, and presentations

◆ Print documents from the iPad

◆ Connect to an online storage service

◆ Remotely control your PC from the iPad

◆ Use the iPad as a point-of-sale and inventory tracking tool

◆ Use the power of social media to connect to customers

◆ Participate in online meetings with the iPad

◆ Manage your online blog sites

◆ Manage your professional tasks and projects

◆ Track customers with customer resource management tools

◆ Plug in to any SharePoint site

◆ Travel easily with the iPad

Chapter 1

First Step:
Introducing the iPad

- ◆ What Is the iPad?
- ◆ The Business Case for the iPad
- ◆ Choosing the Right iPad
- ◆ Getting an iPad
- ◆ Throwing in the Extras
- ◆ Setting Up the iPad
- ◆ Conclusion

Although it is not the first device of its kind, there is little doubt that the Apple iPad has revolutionized the consumer electronics market of the second decade of the 21st century.

While this may seem like a grandiose statement, the overwhelmingly positive consumer reaction (in the form of tens of millions of units sold to date) demonstrates that there must be *something* to this shiny little device that's making it such a hot commodity, beyond the hype generated by Apple.

Like many successful products, a combination of things are involved. Certainly, marketing and sales timing helps. The iPad was introduced at a time when smartphones were just hitting their stride in terms of general consumer adoption. Prior to 2007, the expense and usefulness of smartphones placed these handheld devices right within the bailiwick of business workers.

But as the decade drew to a close, more and more "regular" folks were entering the smartphone market, discovering the advantages of instant-on, highly mobile Internet and processing access. What changed? Perhaps the most notable catalyst was the introduction of iPad's ancestor, the original iPhone, in 2007.

With its sleek form factor, broad range of applications, and processing speed, the iPhone became a huge sales hit among consumers and business personnel alike. In that same year, Apple released what's considered to be the true predecessor to the iPad: the iPod Touch, an iPhone-like device without an on-board phone that connected to the Internet via wireless access points (WiFi).

Both of these devices also did something that paved the way for iPad acceptance: They introduced the concept of an on-screen keyboard to consumers and demonstrated that such a tool wasn't the anathema that it was originally thought to be. By gaining acceptance for on-screen keyboards, Apple knew consumers would be ready for a tablet with the same input method.

Today, the smartphone market is dominated by the iPhone and phones powered by Google's Android operating system. Microsoft has offerings in the smartphone market with its Windows Phone 7 software, although right now those offerings are few and far between. RIM's stalwart BlackBerry is still producing smartphones for business users, but the company is struggling to compete with the popular demand of iPhone and Android devices.

Faced with some stiff competition, Apple has continued to improve its iPhone product line, most recently with the release of the iPhone 4S model. But in 2010, Apple decided to raise the bar again, this time announcing a long-rumored tablet device scheduled for release in April 2010: the iPad.

In this chapter, you will discover:

◆ The business case for the iPad

◆ How to choose an iPad

◆ How to acquire an iPad

◆ What to do when you open the box

What Is the iPad?

When Steve Jobs announced the iPad in January 2010, the initial reaction was mixed at best. After the initial excitement died down, critics pointed out that this "new" device was hardly more than a giant iPod Touch. Sure, the screen was bigger, and the apps looked better, but other than that, what could such a device offer to consumers?

It turns out, plenty.

Perhaps the biggest draw to the iPad was the tablet form itself. In computer jargon, a tablet is any device that has a flat interface and a size that approximates a notebook tablet of paper. The size of the device is key: Digital readers such as the Amazon Kindle and Barnes & Noble Nook certainly have flat interfaces, but their smaller sizes and less robust screens can put them in a different category than tablets.

Other examples of tablet devices include the ASUS Eee Pad Transformer and the Samsung Galaxy Tab—both devices that have a touchscreen interface that directly competes with the iPad, although there are differences in available applications.

The iPad features that virtual keyboard mentioned earlier, and most applications don't even require a pen-like stylus to function. Just use your fingers to enter text and manipulate objects on-screen. With such a simple interface, and because the device itself is much lighter than laptops, notebooks, and even the ultra-light netbooks, it is a large-screen device that is much more portable for business travelers and general consumers.

Besides being large enough to get work done (and watch the occasional movie), the screen also features a multitouch interface, which is now becoming a common experience for many electronic device users. In the past, touchscreens on PDAs, smartphones, or even the occasional kiosk were primarily single-touch interfaces, meaning that one and only one touch at a time was registered by the application running on the screen.

Beginning with the iPhone, and continuing with the iPad family and other devices, the iPad has a multitouch interface, which allows users to touch and manipulate objects on the screen with more than one finger (or device) at a time. This interface enables users to shrink objects by "pinching" them or expand object by fanning out their fingers. Or they can type capital letters on-screen by virtually holding down the Shift key.

Applications are the biggest key to the iPad's success, if only by sheer numbers alone. Thousands of applications are available in the Apple App Store, free or otherwise, with a high percentage of them reviewed by other users. This social review system lets you find out quickly what's really going to work, and what may not. More than that, the stunning variety of apps available makes the iPad highly suitable for any number of use cases.

The Business Case for the iPad

With the right applications, the iPad can become more than just a content consumption device for videos, music, and electronic books. It can be a content production device as well, generating documents, spreadsheets, presentations, music, and video.

This ability to produce content, given the right applications, immediately shifts the iPad into a useful business device. Businesses that depend on fast, accurate business processes can utilize the iPad to quickly supply data, invoice customers, and manage vendors from a reliable, highly mobile platform.

The potential business use cases for the iPad are limited only by your ingenuity:

◆ Restaurant owners can give iPads to waitstaff to use as electronic devices to capture orders. The devices can, at the touch of an icon, double as colorful menus in any language the customer prefers.

◆ A systems administrator can log into a cloud-based administrative dashboard to monitor and control systems remotely.

◆ A traveling salesman can take orders, make presentations, and even demonstrate aspects of the product via video, all with the same iPad.

◆ A roving food vendor can use the iPad to announce his current location, handle sales, and track inventory from the truck, even as hungry food fans descend.

These, of course, are just a few possible scenarios to use in a business setting. While any portable computer could handle just about all of these tasks, such a device would be inconvenient to carry around (in the case of the wait-staff, nearly impossible!), while the iPad's flat form greatly simplifies transport.

Is the iPad right for every situation? Potentially, it is, although the design of the device itself should make you think about deploying it in certain instances. For example, this device has a large amount of glass, so using it in an environment where it's likely to be damaged is obviously not a good idea. Still, with the right accessory—namely, a good carrying case—even that problem can be mitigated.

If you see possibilities for using the iPad in your business, the first thing you need to do is get yourself an iPad, which sometimes can be easier said than done.

Choosing the Right iPad

Before you buy an iPad, you need to figure out first which iPad you're going to get, particularly now with the release of the third-generation iPad in March of 2012. While all iPads may look alike, there are two key differences found within all iPads that make it possible to choose between a total of nine different iPad models.

When choosing an iPad device, you may find yourself gravitating toward the new iPad, which is the latest in the iPad series of devices. The good news is that from a retail standpoint, the latest iPads are no more expensive than the first iPad or the iPad 2, and each model in the respective device families is similarly priced and put together.

An iPad by Any Other Name

Beginning in 2012, Apple decided to drop numbers from its product names for the iPad, which can be a bit confusing, since now the successive order of products is iPad, iPad 2, and (again) iPad. For more of the book, much of what will be described will apply to all the iPad devices, but if we have to point out a difference, we will call the latest device the "2012 iPad."

However, there are key differences between the first iPad, iPad 2, and 2012 iPad that should be taken into consideration.

First, the form factors of the iPad 2 and 2012 iPad are thinner and lighter than the original iPad. This is not a huge difference, but nonetheless it should be noted, because after holding the device for a while, you will notice the weight difference.

The two biggest differences between the devices are the faster processors in the 2012 iPad than the other two devices in the family and the onboard cameras in the iPad 2 and 2012 iPad.

The faster processors with each model do not change the nature of the apps that run on any version of the iPad, but it does increase the speed at which apps run on the iPad 2 and the new 2012 iPad. And the speed, like the lighter weight, is noticeable. iPad apps were never pokey, but when compared with performance on the iPad 2 and then the even faster performance of the 2012 iPad, they are indeed less responsive. Some apps, like Garage Band, can be used on the iPad, but they are recommended for the iPad 2 and 2012 iPad precisely because of the faster processors.

The cameras on the iPad 2, while not the greatest in the world, do afford the capability to run apps like FaceTime, a two-way videoconferencing app, and Photo Booth, a fun photo-morphing app. The 2012 iPad does an even better job, with a high-definition camera and an iPhoto app that will let you make edits on any picture you have on the 2012 iPad.

The one big advantage of the iPad and iPad 2 versus the 2012 iPad? Price.

While not officially sold by Apple anymore, first-generation iPads are being sold on the secondary market for big discounts from their original prices. Of course, this means buying an iPad used, with all the pros and cons of such a transaction. But, if you are on a budget, picking up an iPad on eBay or some other reputable vendor would be a great way to get started.

But Apple has decided to keep iPad 2s on the market for a while longer, as well, and it is offering the devices for exactly $100 less than their 2012 counterparts.

The first choice point for any iPad model is whether to get a WiFi or a WiFi+3G/4G device. All iPads have the capability to connect to the Internet using wireless access—the kind found in your home or many public businesses, like the coffee shop on the corner. This is usually pretty adequate, particularly within your own business, which should have its own wireless network.

WiFi+3G/4G models, on the other hand, can also tap into the AT&T cellular network and connect to the Internet anywhere the iPad can receive the AT&T network. iPad 2s and the 2012 iPads can use AT&T or Verizon as a cellular carrier. The iPad 2s can connect to these carriers' 3G networks, and the 2012 iPad can connect to the much faster 4G networks on AT&T and Verizon.

You should note that WiFi+3G/4G models uniformly cost $130 more than their WiFi-only counterparts, so using a WiFi-only device is a real cost saver.

The other differentiator across iPad products is the amount of solid-state storage each device has. All iPads are currently available with 16, 32, or 64 gigabytes of storage. The price of each model is directly proportional to the amount of memory. Table 1.1 displays the retail pricing of the 2012 iPad, and Table 1.2 shows the pricing for the iPad 2.

TABLE 1.1 2012 iPad Pricing (March 2012)

	16GB	32GB	64GB
iPad (WiFi)	$499	$599	$699
iPad (WiFi+4G)	$629	$729	$829

TABLE 1.2 iPad 2 Pricing (March 2012)

	16GB	32GB	64GB
iPad (WiFi)	$399	$499	$599
iPad (WiFi+3G)	$529	$629	$729

YOUR IPAD PRICE MAY VARY

Because first-generation iPads are now only available on the secondary market, pricing on the models can vary significantly depending on the seller.

The question of how much memory you need is one that plagues most iPad device users. While you may understand in the abstract that 16 gigabytes equates to 16,000 megabytes, which in turn represents 16,000,000 kilobytes, you may not know how that equates to real-world terms. (Not to mention, you may need a hobby.)

Table 1.3 puts together some numbers from Apple that do a better job of relating how big this storage is.

TABLE 1.3 iPad Storage Comparison

File (Average Size)	16 GB	32 GB	64 GB
Images (1.5 Mb)	10,922	21,844	43,688
Songs (5 Mb)	3,276	6,552	13,104
Movies (700 Mb)	23	46	92
TV Shows (325 Mb)	50	100	200
eBooks (1.2 Mb)	13,653	27,306	54,612
Documents (50 Kb)	335,544	671,088	1,342,176
Presentations (100 Kb)	167,722	335,544	671,088

Looking at Table 1.3, you might wonder why in the world you would ever need to store 1.3 million documents, and that certainly seems unlikely. But these sizes can give you a more practical idea of what kind of storage capacity we're talking about.

From a business standpoint, you need to factor in how you will use the device. If you are going to be based in one central location, and you plan to sync the device with a PC or Mac computer on a regular basis, then you will not need a lot of storage space. You can simply use your computer (and any storage device to which the computer has access) to handle storing files. In such a case, it is recommended you stick with one of the 16GB models.

If, however, you plan to be more mobile or otherwise be unable to sync on a regular basis, and will be handling a significant number of files, then consider purchasing one of the larger memory devices. It's likely that 32GB's worth of capacity is enough for most mobile use cases, unless you have an inordinate amount of multimedia files to carry around.

One good way for travelers to pin this down is to look at all the files you must have to do your job away from the office, calculate the amount of memory those files need, and then triple that number. This calculation should account for the original files' storage and the potential of creating twice as many files while away from your base PC.

As for the decision on WiFi-only versus WiFi+3G/4G, here the recommendation is not strictly along financial lines. It would be easy to say, for instance, that all stationary iPad users should be fine without plunking down an extra $130 for 3G or 4G cellular connectivity. You've got WiFi set up in your home or office, so why bother with 3G?

This is where you should ask a key question: What happens when your Internet connection goes down? If losing Internet connectivity would harm your experience on the device, then it may be worth it to spend the extra money and get the WiFi+3G/4G model. Most of the apps in this book, however, do not require always-on Internet connectivity, so you may want to consider that, too.

WHEN 3G OR 4G MAY NOT BE A GOOD IDEA

If you work in a region where AT&T or Verizon coverage is problematic or nonexistent, you may need to reconsider the 3G or 4G options. One possible workaround, for instance, would be to use a mobile WiFi device from another cellular carrier and connect to the Internet via that device's WiFi network.

The final determinate for buying a 2012 iPad or iPad 2 is color: You have a choice between a white or black screen border on these models. This is strictly a preference issue, but the choice will need to be made, nonetheless.

With these criteria in mind, you should be able to make an informed choice on getting the iPad device you need.

Getting an iPad

If you are fortunate enough to live near one of the hundreds of Apple retail stores, purchasing an iPad should be a relatively painless process. Just walk in, pick out the one you want, and then take it home. As of this writing, most U.S. Apple stores had caught up with the huge demand for these devices (especially the older iPad 2s), and usually had them in stock, though it is still sporadic. You may want to call ahead and see if the model you want is in stock before driving in to purchase it.

If you don't reside near an Apple store, you have two basic options: purchase the iPad online or through an Apple partner retailer, such as Target, Wal-Mart, or Best Buy. Be careful about expecting an iPad at a retail partner, though; these stores often only get a handful of devices at a time, which are usually snatched up very quickly.

The other route you might go is to check an AT&T or Verizon retail store, but here iPads are even more scarce—only the largest stores in a given region will actually have the device in stock, while a big majority of such stores will have to order them from Apple directly.

The good news about any of these options is that the cost of the iPad, either online or at another retail store, is always the same. There's no markup when you purchase the iPad somewhere other than an Apple store, and the online store will ship iPads free of charge, so there's no additional costs there.

If you choose to visit a partner retailer, if there's one near you, it should be just as convenient, though you should definitely call ahead and see if there's an iPad in stock. Be sure to specify which model—you don't want to get there and find out they have models that don't meet your technical or budgetary requirements.

If you are not in a hurry to receive the iPad, ordering it online is definitely recommended. You're working directly with Apple, and you won't have to dodge and weave past other shoppers to get the exact device you want.

Of course, getting a first-generation iPad is a little easier. If you find one at a reputable online vendor, you could have the device in your hands in a matter of days, at a much lower cost.

Throwing in the Extras

When you purchase an iPad device, you may be tempted by all the nifty-looking accessories you see around you in the actual or virtual store. You might be tempted to try one over the other, but here are some recommendations based on business-use cases.

◆ **Cases.** Available from Apple and a number of third-party vendors, a case is essential for anyone planning to transport the iPad device from one location to another. With a glass screen and a burnished metal exterior, the iPad device could easily be damaged without some sort of protective covering—not to mention that carrying the iPad device in full view in some public locations is an invitation to theft.

◆ **Smart Cover.** While not a full cover, Smart Covers are very useful for protecting the 2012 iPad and iPad 2 screens and, when folded correctly, serving as a portable stand. Magnets hold the cover in place, and also serve to turn the device off and on when the cover is used.

◆ **Apple iPad Camera Connection Kit.** If you plan to connect any USB camera or SD flash drive to your iPad, then this accessory is essential. The ability to transfer photos, videos, or other files to your iPad without using an iTunes-equipped computer is a real time-saver.

◆ **Apple iPad Dock.** This is a great stand to park your iPad in an upright position while you sync or charge the battery.

◆ **A Bluetooth-capable wireless keyboard.** Available from Apple and third-party vendors, a wireless keyboard is a very essential tool for the iPad. You might be tempted to purchase the Apple iPad Keyboard Dock and just get all-in-one functionality. This is not recommended, because the Keyboard Dock means that your screen and keyboard are mated and any change in position between the two will be impossible. Also, if you prefer a more ergonomic keyboard, the Keyboard Dock will be ill suited for you. Better to get the Dock and a wireless keyboard separately.

Setting Up the iPad

When the big day comes and you bring that white box home, you will be very tempted to turn the iPad on and start playing with it right away. Like all good things, you will need to put a little effort into your iPad before you can run it.

When iPads were first out, they had to be connected first to a PC or Mac computer that had iTunes installed.

With iPads that have iOS 5.0 installed, you no longer need to connect the iPad to any machine; it can set itself up directly over the air.

But there is one thing you can do to help set up your iPad faster. If you don't have one already, you need an Apple account. While many iPad applications are free, you may want to purchase some applications later or use the free iCloud storage service, so it's a good idea to get your Apple account set up first.

To set up iTunes and an Apple account:

1. Visit the iTunes Web page at www.apple.com/itunes/ (see Figure 1.1).

Figure 1.1

The iTunes home page.

2. Click the Free Download link. The Download page will appear.

3. Confirm the operating system you are currently running and click Download Now. The installation file will be downloaded and saved to your system.

4. Follow the normal installation procedures you use to install software on your operating system to install iTunes.

5. After iTunes is installed and running, click the iTunes Store link in the left column of the application. The iTunes Store page will open, as shown in Figure 1.2.

6. Click the Sign In link located in the upper-right corner. The account dialog box will open (see Figure 1.3).

Figure 1.2

The iTunes Store home page.

Figure 1.3

The account sign-in dialog box.

7. Click the Create New Account button. The Welcome page will appear.

8. Click Continue. The Terms and Conditions page will appear.

9. Click the I have read… checkbox and then Continue. The Store Account page, shown in Figure 1.4, will appear.

10. Enter the pertinent information and click Continue. The Payment Method page will appear.

11. Enter your credit card or iTunes gift card information, your billing address, and then click Continue. Your account will be created.

Once the iTunes account (which is the same as an Apple account) is created, you will now be able to set up your iPad device.

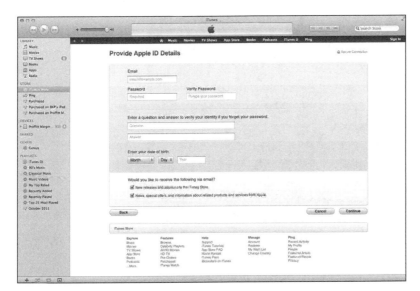

NO COMPUTER NEEDED

There's no need to have a computer to set up the Apple account; you can sign up for an Apple account ID directly from the iPad during set up, if you want. Setting it up beforehand, however, will save you a little time come the big day.

When you first press the Sleep/Wake button along the top edge of the device, you will see the special configuration lock screen that appears only at the very first startup. Tap and slide the gray lock switch at the bottom of the screen to begin the Setup Assistant, which starts at the language page (see Figure 1.5).

To set up the iPad:

1. Tap the desired language options and then tap the blue continue arrow. The Country or Region page will appear (see Figure 1.6).

2. Tap the correct country in which you reside (the iPad will make a reasonable guess) and tap Next. The Location Services screen will appear.

3. If you want your apps to always know where the iPad is, tap Enable Location Services and then tap Next. The Set Up iPad screen will appear (see Figure 1.7).

4. If this is a new iPad, tap the Set Up as New iPad option and then tap Next. The Apple ID screen will appear (see Figure 1.8).

Figure 1.5

The iPad setup language page.

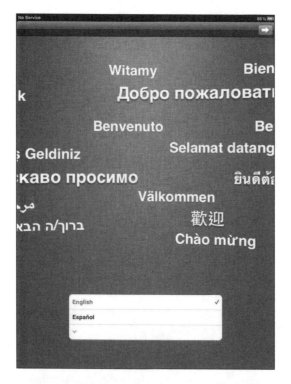

Figure 1.6

Define your location.

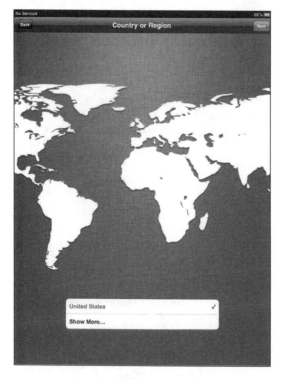

Figure 1.7
How will you want your iPad to be set up?

Figure 1.8
Have your Apple ID ready.

5. Tap the Sign In with an Apple ID option. A login dialog box will appear.

6. Enter your Apple account ID and the password you set up earlier and tap OK. The Terms and Conditions page will appear.

7. Read the legalese (if you want) and tap Agree. A dialog box confirming that you agree will appear.

8. Tap Agree in the dialog box. A pause screen will appear for a few moments as your ID is connected to this iPad. Then the Set Up iCloud screen will appear.

9. Since iCloud is free and we will review its operations in Chapter 11, "In the iCloud," tap the Don't Use iCloud option and then click Next. The Diagnostics screen will appear.

10. Tap the Automatically Send option so your iPad will send problem reports to Apple if it ever runs into trouble. Tap Next. The Thank You screen will appear (see Figure 1.9).

Figure 1.9

You're set to go!

11. Tap the Start Using iPad button. The iPad will be configured to your specifications and the home screen will appear.

It is important to note that this first configuration of the iPad could take a few moments. Be patient, and everything will set up smoothly.

Conclusion

In this chapter, you learned about the origins of the iPad family of devices and why the iPad has become so influential. You also were presented with the pros and cons of purchasing a particular iPad model. Finally, you learned how to set up iTunes, an iTunes Store Account, and the iPad itself.

While you're waiting for the iPad to finish its initial setup, grab a cup of coffee and come back for Chapter 2, "Second Step: Interfacing with the iPad." There, you'll learn about all of the iPad and iPad 2 controls and even some undocumented control features that may come in handy later.

Chapter 2

Second Step:
Interfacing with the iPad

◆ Touring the iPad Device

◆ Having the Right Touch

◆ Keying in the Keyboard

◆ Moving Text Around

◆ Configuring the iPad

◆ Conclusion

Like most iPad customers, you were probably already aware of quite a few of the iPad's capabilities. Apple's massive marketing plan has done a good job of highlighting the device so that by now most people know that the iPad is a touchscreen device, capable of connecting to the Internet and viewing a large variety of multimedia content.

When you first get to use the iPad, you will find a sleek, simple device that doesn't seem to belie that impression. A few buttons, a couple of switches—how hard can this be?

The simplicity is certainly there, but there's also a lot more going on with the iPad than you'd think. In this chapter, you will explore the following:

◆ The controls of the iPad

◆ The right way to use the touchscreen

◆ The virtual iPad keyboard

◆ The tools to configure the iPad

Touring the iPad Device

Take a look at the iPad. You hold in your hands a 9½ by 7½ inch, half-inch thick tablet with a grand total of four controls (not counting the screen itself, which is the iPad's main control). As you can see in Figure 2.1, three of the controls are located near the "upper-right" corner of the iPad.

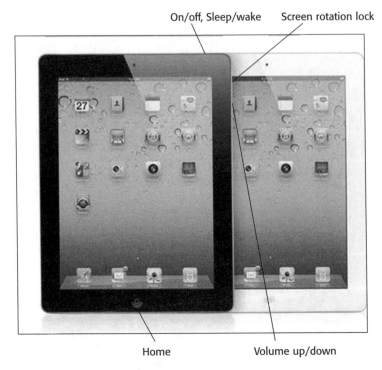

On/off, Sleep/wake   Screen rotation lock

Figure 2.1

The iPad's minimalist controls.

Home   Volume up/down

WHAT IS UP? WHAT IS DOWN?

The use of quotes in "upper-right" is a bit deliberate. Since the iPad can be oriented in any direction, there really isn't a "top" or "bottom" for the device. For the purposes of this section, when we will actually point out the position of controls, we will assume that the iPad is oriented as shown in Figure 2.1, with the Home button positioned at the bottom of the device.

The control you will use the most is the Home button, located on the front of the iPad, centered below the screen. Press the Home button, and you will be taken immediately back to the last home screen you were in. Since the iPad can use more than one application at a time, double-clicking the Home button will open the App toolbar and let you switch to any other open app.

The On/off or Sleep/wake button is something you'll also use often. Its dual name hints at its multifunction capability. If you simply press the button quickly, it will put the iPad to sleep, a very low-power state that will turn the screen off and prevent any other inputs until the Sleep/wake button or the Home button is pressed again.

The thing to remember about sleep mode is that, while the iPad appears to be powered down, it's actually not. The device will be waiting quietly for you to pick it up and start working again, ready to pop on the instant you wake it up. To come back so quickly, the iPad is in a state of readiness that uses a little bit of power as time goes by. Very little, to be sure, but the drain on the batteries is real. Leave the iPad asleep for too long (over a day or so), and it's possible you will find the batteries very weak or even drained when you come back to wake it up.

To prevent this unfortunate surprise, you can use the same button as an On/off control. To turn the iPad completely off, press and hold the On/off button for a few seconds. A red confirmation slide control will appear at the top of the window.

If you want to power down the device, drag the slide control to the right to power off, and the iPad will shut down. If you hold the Sleep/wake button down too long by mistake, you can tap the Cancel button on the bottom of the screen.

Once the device is all the way off, pressing and holding the On/off button is the only way to start the power-on sequence. (This is to prevent any accidental bumps from turning the iPad back on and thus start draining the batteries.) It takes a few moments to cycle all the way back on, so don't worry if it seems to take a while.

CAPTURE A SCREENSHOT

There's a cool little undocumented feature you can use with the Home and Sleep/wake buttons. Hold the Home key down and then press the Sleep/wake button at the same time. The screen will flash, and you'll hear the sound of a camera shutter. You've just taken a picture of your iPad's screen, which you will be able to view using the Photo app. In fact, all of the iPad pictures in this book were acquired using this method.

The Volume up/down control, located on the right side of the iPad, is pretty straightforward. Press the top of the control to turn the volume of the iPad's speaker up, and press the bottom of the control to bring the volume down. This control is the master volume control for the iPad. Some applications, such as the Music and Video apps, have their own on-screen volume controls that handle output volume just for those apps. This is something you should be aware of, as you might see sound amplitude differences as you use different apps.

The Mute or Screen Rotation Lock switch is just above the Volume up/down control. It may seem like this is confusing, but actually it's not. When the initial iPad was released, this switch only controlled the screen rotation. But Steve Jobs is rumored to have insisted on making the switch a mute control, just as a similar switch does on the iPhone. A software upgrade on the iPad changed the function of the switch to just mute.

That decision, however, was met with consumer outcry, because many iPad users liked the screen rotation switch just fine, thank you. So, when the iPad 2 was released, Apple gave users the capability to decide for themselves. The switch can be used for one or the other function, based on a setting users can change. (More on that later in this chapter.)

As a rotation lock, when the switch is in the up, or off, position, the screen will rotate freely based on the orientation of the device or the sound will be on. Flip the switch to the on position, and the orientation of the screen will stay right where it is, no matter how you hold the device. This is useful, should you be reading something and don't want the contents of the screen to shift every time you move in your chair or set the iPad down.

As a mute switch, the up position enables sound, and the down position mutes the device.

There are other notable elements on the iPad about which you should know. Figure 2.2 displays the top and bottom of the iPad device, where these important features lie. The locations of these hardware features are identical on the iPad 2 and 2012 iPad.

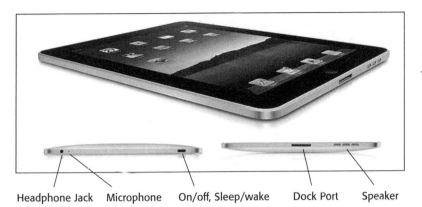

Figure 2.2
Other iPad hardware features.

Headphone Jack   Microphone   On/off, Sleep/wake   Dock Port   Speaker

We've already reviewed the Sleep/wake On/off button, so here are more details about the other features:

◆ **Headphone Jack.** This is a standard 3.5-mm stereo headphone jack, into which you can plug your favorite headphones.

◆ **Microphone.** This tiny hole is actually the microphone for the iPad. It does work well for everyday applications, but for higher-quality work, you may want to get a better microphone.

◆ **Dock Port.** This port is the primary way to connect the iPad to a PC or Mac, a power adapter, or to an iPad Dock or Keyboard Dock.

◆ **Speaker.** This is where the sound comes from if headphones are not in use. Try not to cover this up, so you get better sound.

Now that we've looked at the other controls of the iPad, let's examine the most important control: the iPad screen itself. Most of the work you will do and content you will view will be done on the screen, so it's a good idea to get the lay of the land.

When you press the Sleep/wake or On/off button for the first time, you will initially see the Lock screen (shown in Figure 2.3). This screen will stay visible until you slide the Slide to Unlock control or about seven seconds have passed—in which case the iPad will go back to sleep.

To slide the control, place your finger on the gray arrow button and drag your finger to the right. This will open the home screen, as shown in Figure 2.4.

Figure 2.3

The iPad lock screen.

Connection status   Clock   Status Bar   Battery status   Apps

Figure 2.4

The iPad home screen.

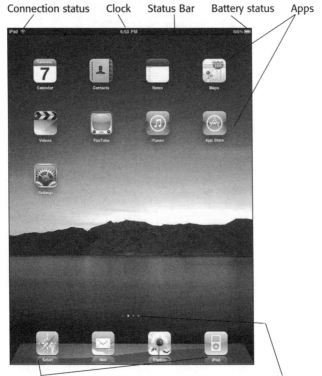

Favorite apps   Home Screen status

Here's a rundown of the different components of the home screen:

◆ **Status Bar.** This area on the top of the screen is home to various status messages the iPad or its apps may display.

◆ **Connection status.** Displays the status of the WiFi connection the iPad is currently using. In 3G or 4G models, the connectivity to AT&T or Verizon is also displayed.

◆ **Clock.** Displays the current time.

◆ **Battery status.** Shows the strength of the current battery charge. Also displays when the battery is being charged.

◆ **Apps.** Icons that, when tapped, start the various applications that run on the iPad.

◆ **Home Screen status.** Displays which home screen the iPad is currently showing, and the number of available home screens. The iPad can accommodate up to 11 home screens.

◆ **Favorite apps.** This is an area that houses your favorite apps. This area is displayed on all the home screens.

The look and feel of any of the home screens will remain the same, regardless of how many or how few apps are displayed. Each home screen can display 20 apps or folders and the Favorites section can hold up to six applications or folders. As you can see in Figure 2.5, the same components are visible when the iPad is in landscape mode.

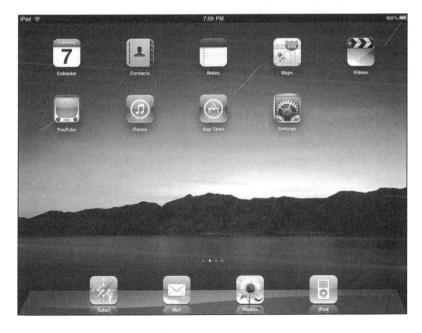

Figure 2.5

The iPad home screen in landscape.

Another available screen on the iPad is the Search screen (see Figure 2.6), which is always located to the left of the home screen. The Search screen enables you to find files and applications quickly on the iPad.

Figure 2.6

The iPad Search screen.

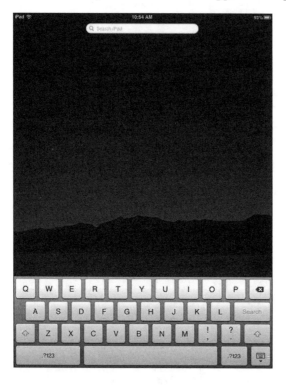

Having the Right Touch

Using an iPad is not like using a "typical" PC or Mac, where a mouse is used to move a cursor around a screen and clicking the mouse once or twice brings up menus, windows, and dialog boxes. No, the iPad has a different interface, but one that mirrors the now-familiar actions many people are used to on their computers.

The most useful gesture is the tap. Tapping once on the screen will start an app, "press" a button, type a letter, or select an option on a list. The results of the tap vary from application to application, but it is directly analogous to a single click of a mouse.

A related gesture is the double-tap, which can also perform useful actions. In Maps, for instance, a double-tap will zoom in on that area of the map.

Pinching the screen on a given spot can zoom out from that spot. This may not be intuitive when you read it, but try it (Maps is a good app for this example), and it will make sense. Pinching acts to bring the edges of the area "in," thus creating the zoom-out effect. The farther away your two fingers (or finger and thumb) are when starting the gesture, the more dramatic the "zoom." To get the opposite effect, you can pinch out, which is how Apple refers to the motion of starting with two fingers together on the screen and moving them apart to zoom in. This is also referred to as "fanning," since you can fan your fingers out to achieve the zoom.

Panning, also known as dragging, is done by placing your finger on the screen and moving it around to display the area you want, or you can move an object or text around the screen. A related move is two-fingered dragging, which will scroll any window within a window.

Swiping, as you've seen in the previous section, is done by quickly pressing and dragging a control across the screen. Swiping is also how you can move from one home screen to another. Flicking is a similar gesture: If you have a long list of items to scroll through, flicking a finger across the screen will simulate a quick scroll with some inertia behind it.

Some objects, particularly in iWorks applications, will contain objects that can be rotated. A special two-fingered move known as *rotating* will handle this. The best way to describe it is like grabbing an imaginary radio knob and twisting your fingers in opposite directions to rotate the object.

Finally, some applications will call for a long-press, also known as the "touch and hold." This gesture is pretty self-explanatory, and it can be done by pressing a part of the screen for over one second.

Keep in mind, not every application will use every gesture. It varies from application to application. But these are the basic moves that will help you navigate the iPad when needed.

BUSINESS GESTURES

All of the gestures that are unique to the iPad give the applications a common trait: Many functions are done with an economical use of gestures and touches, with a minimum of input. You will see these traits recurring in many of the applications in this book.

Keying in the Keyboard

The most noticeable lack of hardware on the iPad is, naturally, the keyboard. Like the iPhones and smartphones that are penetrating the consumer markets, the iPad relies on what's known as a *virtual keyboard* for users to enter text. That means the keyboard is driven only by software and appears directly on the screen, as displayed in Figure 2.7.

Shift key   Backspace key

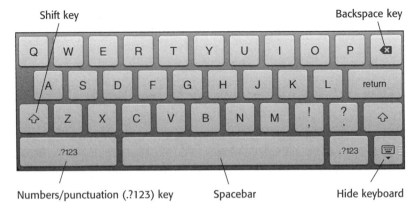

Numbers/punctuation (.?123) key   Spacebar   Hide keyboard

If you are using the iPad's Dictation feature, the keyboard will look a little different. For apps that have Dictation support, the keyboard will have a small microphone key, shown in Figure 2.8.

Dictation key

Not every app will support Dictation, but if an app does, it can be a great way to enter text without typing. To use Dictation, tap the key and speak normally into the iPad microphone near the top of the screen. Tap the Dictation key again, and after a few seconds, your words will be transcribed on the screen.

Keyboards appear whenever the user taps a field or area of the screen where text needs to be entered or changed. Yes, it's "keyboards," plural, because as software, the keyboard can self-configure itself to meet the needs of the environment in which you are typing.

The keyboards in Figure 2.7 and 2.8, for instance, are the keyboards that display when using the Pages app (depending on whether Dictation is turned on). But tapping on the URL field (where Web addresses are entered) in the Safari Web browser shows some key differences (shown in Figure 2.9).

Figure 2.9

The iPad keyboard in Safari.

Note the presence of the .com key, which is a nice shortcut for typing what falls at the end of most Web addresses. The Return key has been changed to Go, and common Web address punctuation has been added to the bottom row of keys.

Because each application developer may require a different set of common keystrokes, the variations of keyboards are potentially limitless. And that's just in English (more on that in a bit).

Referring back to Figure 2.7, note the .?123 key. Tapping this key will display the numbers and punctuation keyboard, shown in Figure 2.10.

Figure 2.10

The numbers and punctuation keyboard.

Symbols (#+=) key   Main Keyboard (ABC) key

If you tap the symbols key, denoted as #+=, the symbols keyboard will appear (see Figure 2.11).

To return to the main keyboard, tap the ABC key at any time. If you want to remove any keyboard from the screen, tap the hide keyboard key. The keyboard will be hidden until the next time you tap in a text-entry area.

Typing with the iPad keyboard is just like typing with a regular keyboard, but with some slick differences. For instance, if you find yourself typing a word that needs accented characters (such as résumé), then press and hold the "e" key and a pop-over menu containing several variations of the vowel will appear, with different accents and umlauts. Slide your finger to the correct variant (in this case, "é"), release the key, and the letter will appear in your text.

Not every key in a keyboard has these variant keys available, so you will need to explore. Two very useful variant keys include:

◆ Hold and slide the comma key to access an apostrophe without tapping the .?123 key.

◆ In the Internet keyboard in Safari, hold and slide the .com key to view the .org and .net variations.

Another hold-and-slide trick, which will take a little practice, is to type a letter, then slide your finger over to the .?123 key, and—without lifting your finger—slide to the number or punctuation mark you need and then let go. This will insert the character and return you right back to the ABC keyboard without having to tap the ABC key.

But the iPad keyboard has a few more surprises in store for users. Beginning with the release of the latest major update to the iPad's operating system, iOS5, the keyboard can be moved around the screen... and even split in two to enable "thumb typing."

Splitting the keyboard is very simple: Just touch the keyboard in two places and drag your fingers in opposite directions, left and right. The keyboard will immediately split, and undock from the bottom of the screen, as seen in Figure 2.12.

To move the keyboard up and down the screen, touch and drag the hide keyboard key on the right side of the keyboard, under the right Shift key. The keyboard will move to wherever is most convenient for your hands.

To merge the keyboards, just touch each side of the separate keyboards and drag the sides back together.

Figure 2.12
The split keyboard.

You can also long-press the Hide Keyboard key to view a pop-over menu that displays the Dock/Undock and Split/Merge commands (see Figure 2.13).

Figure 2.13
The keyboard control menu.

Moving Text Around

Most of us who have used computers are familiar with the word processing capabilities of our machines when it comes to creating documents. We even take these features for granted, especially the cut, copy, and paste text functions.

But in the iPad, the question immediately becomes, how to cut, copy, or paste text without a mouse? Or a Control key?

The answer is actually quite simple, and it's just a few taps away.

To cut or copy text, double-tap the word you want to edit. The word will be selected and an Edit menu will appear immediately above it (see Figure 2.14).

Tap Cut, and the word will immediately be removed from the document, but held in storage on the iPad's "clipboard," which is a temporary storage area for text and objects that have been cut or copied. If you tap Copy, the word will be stored on the clipboard, but not removed from the document.

Figure 2.14

The Edit menu.

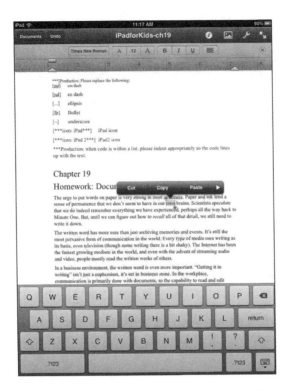

Long-press the location in the document you want the cut or copied word to appear. The Edit menu will appear again. Tap Paste, and the cut or copied term will appear at the desired location.

CLIPBOARD FUNCTIONALITY

Text or objects in the clipboard can be pasted indefinitely until another set of text or another object is cut or copied.

SELECTING PARAGRAPHS

To cut, copy, and paste an entire paragraph, triple-tap the paragraph to select all of it.

Configuring the iPad

Now that you have a good idea of the layout of the iPad, it's time to start customizing it to meet your personal needs. You can customize many things about the iPad, but for now we will focus on some of the more popular settings.

One of the first things users want to do is change the wallpaper on their iPad. While this seems trivial, let's face it—we all want to give things our own identifier.

To change the wallpaper:

1. Tap the Settings icon on the home screen. The Settings split view app will open, as seen in Figure 2.15.

Figure 2.15

The Settings app.

2. Tap the Brightness & Wallpaper setting. The Brightness & Wallpaper pane will open.
3. Tap the Wallpaper control. The Wallpaper pane will open (see Figure 2.16).

Figure 2.16

The Wallpaper pane.

4. Tap the Wallpaper control again. A gallery of wallpaper options will appear.

5. Tap an image you like. The wallpaper will appear full size with an Options bar on top. You can use this wallpaper for the Lock Screen, the Home Screen, or Set Both (see Figure 2.17).

6. Tap the option you prefer. The sample wallpaper will close, and the Settings app will appear.

7. Press the Home button. The new wallpaper will be visible.

Figure 2.17
Choosing where to use the wallpaper.

Users for whom English is not their native language will very likely want to make a more significant change—the addition of a keyboard more suited to their own language.

To change the language of a keyboard:

1. Tap the Settings icon on the home screen. The Settings split view app will open.
2. Tap the General settings. The General pane will open.
3. Tap the Keyboard option. The Keyboard pane will open.
4. Tap the International Keyboards option. The International Keyboard pane will open.
5. Tap Add New Keyboard. The Add New Keyboard pane will open.
6. Tap an option. The option will be added to the International Keyboards pane.

To use an added keyboard, enter an app that uses a keyboard. Immediately, you will see a globe key in the keyboard (see Figure 2.18). This is the International Keyboard key.

Figure 2.18

The International Keyboard key.

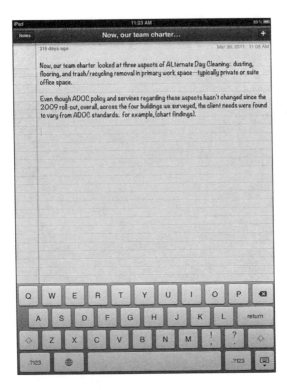

To activate the new keyboard, tap the globe icon to cycle through the available options. The name of the keyboard will appear in the spacebar as you type. Or long-press the globe icon to see an action menu of the available options (see Figure 2.19). Slide your finger to the desired International option and release. The keyboard will be set.

To remove an International Keyboard:

1. Tap the Settings icon on the home screen. The Settings split view app will open.
2. Tap the General settings. The General pane will open.
3. Tap the Keyboard option. The Keyboard pane will open.
4. Tap the International Keyboards option. The International Keyboard pane will open.
5. Tap the Edit key. The pane will appear in Edit mode.
6. Tap the red delete icon for the keyboard you want to remove. The Delete button will appear (see Figure 2.20).
7. Tap the Delete button. The option will be removed.

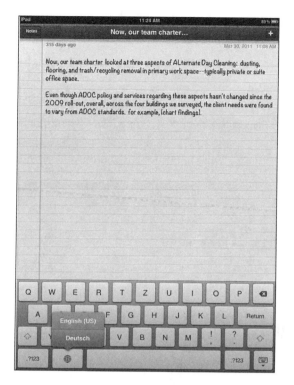

Figure 2.19
The International Keyboard options.

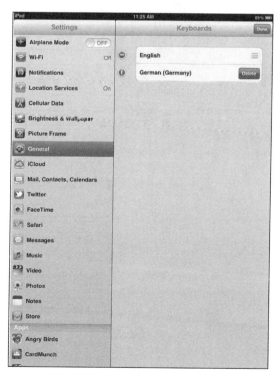

Figure 2.20
Removing a keyboard.

For English users, there are additional keyboard enhancements that you may want to explore.

To explore additional keyboard options in English:

1. Tap the Settings icon on the home screen. The Settings split view app will open.

2. Tap the General settings. The General pane will open.

3. Tap the Keyboard option. The Keyboard pane will open (see Figure 2.21), and the following options will be displayed.

Figure 2.21

General keyboard settings.

◆ **Auto-Capitalization.** Capitalizes the first letter after the end of a sentence.

◆ **Auto-Correction.** Displays suggested words from the iPad dictionary when iPad thinks you have made a spelling error.

◆ **Check Spelling.** Checks spelling within an opened document.

◆ **Enable Caps Lock.** Lets you start Caps Lock typing by double-tapping the Shift key.

◆ **"." Shortcut.** Double-tapping the spacebar will insert a period followed by a space.

4. Select the options you want to activate or deactivate by sliding the appropriate control.

5. Press the Home button. The changes will be made.

Finally, as mentioned earlier in this chapter, you can specify whether you want the iPad's side switch to control muting the sound or locking screen rotation.

To change the side switch action:

1. Tap the Settings icon on the home screen. The Settings app will open.

2. Tap the General settings. The General pane will open.

3. In the Use Side Switch to: section, tap the option you prefer.

4. Press the Home button. The changes will be made.

Conclusion

In this chapter, you learned about the various hardware and software controls available on the iPad. You discovered the basic gestures needed to navigate the iPad interface and learned some handy shortcuts along the way.

In Chapter 3, "Third Step: Connecting with the iPad," you'll learn how to really tap into the iPad's power by getting connected to the Internet, and you'll be that much closer to doing your work while using the iPad.

Chapter 3

Third Step:
Connecting with the iPad

- ◆ Connecting to iTunes
- ◆ Using the WiFi Connection
- ◆ Using the Cellular Connection
- ◆ Troubleshooting Connectivity
- ◆ Conclusion

On its own, the iPad is a great device to edit documents, view videos, or even listen to music. All you need to perform these and other tasks is the iPad itself—you don't even need a connection to a computer anymore.

But because the iPad doesn't need to be connected to a PC or Mac to acquire this great content, it's more important than ever to be able to connect to the Internet.

Apple's approach to the Internet is different than that of other computer or mobile device companies. Since the opening of the Internet to the public in the early 1990s, the basic approach that software developers took to Internet software like browsers and email applications was this: Show the users everything and let them figure out what's good.

In the last decade of the 20th century, that was not much of a problem, since content on the Internet was scarce, and what content there was, was such a novelty, it could not help but be interesting. That didn't last long. As PCs and Macs got better and networks got faster, content shifted from static text and images to dynamic applications and multimedia experiences. The nature of the content grew much more diverse, ranging from the very good to the very ugly.

"Ugly" is not just a judgment on the taste or aesthetics of the content; it also means the content can be actively unsafe for you and your data. Viruses, Trojans, and other forms of computer malware can lie hidden on even the most reputable of websites, if they've been hacked.

Apple, particularly with their iPhone and iPad devices, has decided to leave the one-window-on-the-Internet approach behind and shift to a more managed content approach. Safari, the traditional browser, is still available, of course, but other apps on the iPad family (and iPhone) present Internet content in a very managed, "clean" environment.

You may or may not agree with this "walled garden" approach, but the good news is that you can opt to use this approach or surf the Internet traditionally with the Safari browser. And there is some evidence to suggest that because Apple screens applications before they are posted to the iTunes store, the iOS platform could be safer for business environments.

This approach also means that how the iPad processes business data is also segmented into defined channels. Instead of one-size-fits-all applications that manage different types of data, iPad apps work well on smaller data sets and data types.

Before we get to the Internet, it's important to connect to a more local computer, your iTunes-based PC or Mac. You don't have to do this anymore, since iPads can now perform any updates or backups over the Internet, without a computer. Still, you may find it's easier to manage your iPad with iTunes on a local machine, so we'll cover it here. This was already done in Chapter 1, "First Step: Introducing the iPad," when you first configured your iPad, but now it's time to learn more about what iTunes can do for you.

In this chapter, you will learn how to:

◆ Connect to and sync with iTunes

◆ Connect to the Internet with WiFi

◆ Connect to the Internet via 3G service

◆ Troubleshoot Internet connectivity

Connecting to iTunes

Because of the connectivity the iPad has to the Internet, it is possible to use iTunes with the iPad just once in its operational life—at the very first configuration described in Chapter 1. Many people do this, since applications, data, and multimedia content can all be purchased and downloaded "over the air."

You could make the case that for personal use only, this approach is fine. But from a business standpoint, it is very important that you connect to and synchronize your iPad with an iTunes computer on a regular basis. Even if you don't download a lot of content, syncing with iTunes will give you the very important benefit of backing up all of your iPad's data.

iCloud Backups

You can, in the Settings app, choose to back up your iPad to Apple's iCloud service. If you travel extensively, this is recommended, but if you are always near a base computer, it's faster to back up to that machine.

As nice as the iPad is, the truth is that things can (and will) go wrong. Your iPad could be dropped. Or damaged. Or lost. Even less drastic problems might happen—a poorly put-together app could freeze the iPad and the only way to stop the problem might be to restore the device back to its original factory state. When that happens, having a backup of your iPad's data and settings is a great thing because you can direct iTunes to restore your data and put you right back where you were, with no loss of data.

For this reason alone, business users should regularly sync their iPad with iTunes. Personal users should do so as well.

Auto and Manual Syncing

Synchronizing the iPad with iTunes is very simple, as demonstrated in Chapter 1. Just plug one end of the USB/docking cable into the Dock port and the other end into the PC or Mac with iTunes installed. This will immediately start iTunes and begin the syncing process, as shown in Figure 3.1.

Figure 3.1

Syncing the iPad.

Depending on how long it's been since you last synced your iPad, this operation could take anywhere from one to several minutes. As it is syncing, you can still perform tasks on your iPad, but this will slow down the syncing process.

After the sync operation is complete, you can disconnect the iPad from the computer. If you leave it connected, you can use iTunes to configure the iPad and the synchronization process.

With the iPad still connected to your iTunes-equipped computer, click the name of the iPad in the Devices section. The iPad's configuration pages will appear, as shown in Figure 3.2.

In Figure 3.2, the Summary page is displayed. This page reveals a lot of information about the status of your iPad, particularly the capacity of the device. If you are wondering if your iPad is running low on memory, this is the page to check.

Figure 3.2

iTunes' iPad pages.

The buttons along the top of the iPad window will navigate to other pages that will let you configure various aspects of the iPad directly from within iTunes. Click the Info button, for instance, and you will find a page that will enable you to configure how the contacts, calendar, and email apps will collect their data (see Figure 3.3).

If you make any changes to your iPad configuration anywhere in iTunes, then the Sync button in the iPad window will change to two buttons: Apply and Revert (see Figure 3.4).

Figure 3.3

The iPad Info page.

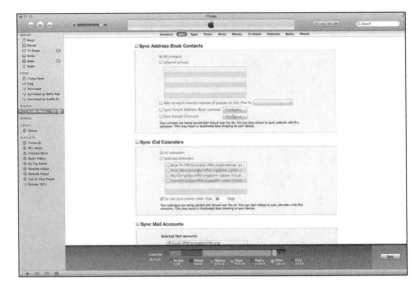

Figure 3.4

Applying your iPad settings changes.

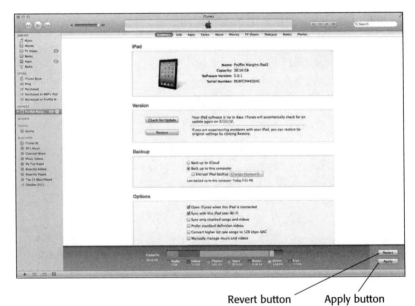

Revert button   Apply button

To manually sync the iPad with the new changes, click Apply.

To manually sync the iPad at any time, regardless of changes that may or may not have been made, simply click the Sync button in iTunes.

Choosing What to Sync

The iPad window not only lets you configure the iPad and its apps (which will be more thoroughly reviewed in Chapter 4, "Fourth Step: Using the iPad Apps"), but it also synchronizes files from the iTunes computer to the iPad. This is important, especially if you have a very large collection of music or video files. Even at a maximum of 64GB, the iPad may not have the capacity to hold your entire multimedia collection. Or, if it does, it may not leave you enough room for apps or other data.

To specify which music files will move to the iPad:

1. With the iPad still connected to your iTunes-equipped computer, click the name of the iPad in the Devices section. The iPad's Configuration window will appear.

2. Click the Music button. The iPad Music page will appear (see Figure 3.5).

Figure 3.5

The iPad Music page.

3. Click the Selected playlists, artists, albums, and genres option. The Options window will appear, as shown in Figure 3.6.

Figure 3.6

Choose the music you want to sync.

4. In the Genres window, select the option you desire.

5. Click Apply. The music on your iPad will now include only the songs in this genre (see Figure 3.7).

Figure 3.7

Chasin' those naughty blues.

MIXING YOUR IPAD MUSIC

You can select music to sync to the iPad based on individual artists or any playlists you've created on the iPad or in iTunes.

Restore the iPad

As mentioned earlier in this chapter, you can use iTunes to restore your iPad to either completely new factory settings (useful if you're going to sell the iPad and want no personal or business data on the device) or to the last backup you made.

Care must be taken that you only perform a restore operation when absolutely needed. This is a last-ditch solution for resolving issues with the iPad, mainly because it can take a very long time to restore the iPad.

Still, if all other options are exhausted, restoration can greatly help put your iPad to rights.

To restore the iPad:

1. With the iPad still connected to your iTunes-equipped computer, click the name of the iPad in the Devices section. The iPad's Configuration window will appear.

2. In the Summary window, click Restore. A confirmation dialog box will appear (see Figure 3.8).

Figure 3.8

Confirm that you want to restore the iPad.

3. Click Restore. The confirmation dialog box will close, and the restoration process will begin.

DO NOT DISCONNECT

Do not disconnect the iPad from the iTunes computer during restoration. An incomplete restoration could create more problems on your iPad.

4. Once the restoration process reaches the halfway point, you will be asked to restore the device to factory new settings or from your last backup. Click the From backup option and then click Restore.

At the end of the lengthy restoration process, your iPad should be restored to its last backed-up state.

Using the WiFi Connection

After you have gotten the hang of connecting to iTunes, you should complete the connection circuit and get your iPad out on the Internet.

For iPad WiFi users, there is only one way to connect to the Internet—joining an 802.11 wireless network. Luckily, such networks are rather common.

In many Western nations, high-speed Internet access is provided by Internet Service Providers (ISPs), such as telephone, cable, or satellite companies. These large ISPs provide broadband Internet connectivity to businesses and home customers at relatively affordable rates, usually based on usage. Most of these broadband consumers have wireless access by default, as the routers provided by the ISPs usually have connections for network cables ("wired") to your computer(s) *and* 802.11 wireless service.

All wireless service in the 802.11 spectrum works something like this: A router in your business or home is connected to the ISP's network (and from there out to the Internet). Your computers and other devices accessing the Internet communicate to the router only, either through wired or wireless connections. This configuration (if all is secure) hopefully means that your devices are protected from the pitfalls and malware of the Internet, since the router also acts as a firewall, keeping the "fire" of the Internet safely at bay.

If your router supports wireless, it will broadcast a radio signal at a range of about 100 yards in the clear or throughout a typical two-story home, depending on the composition of walls, layout, and so on. The signal is identified by a unique label, known as the *SSID*. The SSID is the name of the router's wireless network; think of it as the call letters of your favorite radio station. Knowing the SSID of your wireless network is important, although most of the time it will be pretty obvious what the SSID is.

That's because when devices like laptops and the iPad detect a wireless network, the device's software will also see the strength of the network and whether it's an open or protected network. If you are using your iPad in your local coffee shop, for example, you may detect a few nearby wireless networks, but the strongest one has the SSID "Cup_O_Joe," so it isn't hard to tell in this case.

MAKE SURE THAT YOU KNOW THE NETWORK

If you are at all unsure what the right network is, do not connect to it—even if it looks right. The author was once in a major bookstore chain and noted the right SSID was accompanied by one that had a similar name, but not as strong and not protected. A little walking around found a teenager sitting in the stacks with his own router, trying to catch unsuspecting customers to log on to his network and thus have their data intercepted. If you're not sure, ask the manager. If you *are* the manager, periodically check for the presence of SSIDs that look like your own establishment's network.

For some networks, you may also need the key to the network. Public networks or some business networks will provide a completely open network for citizen or customer convenience. You might find the network to which you want to connect is protected (or locked) by a password, also known as a *key*. Before you can connect to the Internet through such a network, make sure that you have the key.

SAFETY FIRST

Unless you are on your own home or business wireless network, do not conduct any business or financial transactions on a wireless network—even if it's protected. Radio signals can still be received by malicious individuals and potentially decrypted. *Under no circumstances should you conduct any private business over an open network.* Ever.

Once you have the SSID and key in hand, you can quickly connect the iPad to the Internet.

To connect to the Internet:

1. Tap the Settings app. The Settings screen will open.
2. Tap the Wi-Fi setting. The Wi-Fi Networks pane will appear (see Figure 3.9).
3. Tap the network you want to join. If the network is protected, the Enter Password form will appear (see Figure 3.10).

Figure 3.9

The detected nearby wireless networks.

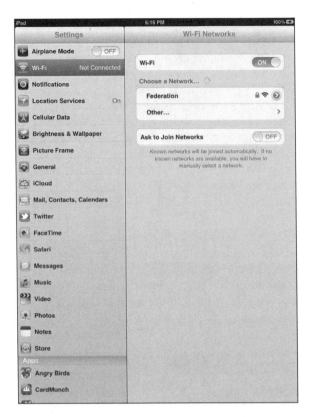

Figure 3.10

Protected networks will need a password.

4. Type the password and tap the Join key. If the password is entered correctly, the network will be joined, as indicated by the check mark next to the network name.

One great feature of the iPad is that it will remember networks as you join them. So once you join networks in various businesses and locations, the iPad will keep track of them and auto-join them when you return.

Now that you're connected to the wireless network, you can start to use any iPad application that uses Internet connectivity.

Using the Cellular Connection

iPad WiFi+3G owners will have the added advantage of being able to connect to the Internet via a 3G or 4G cellular network, just like the one used by your mobile phone.

Older iPads will connect to a 3G cellular connection, while the 2012 iPad model will be able to connect to 4G (and faster) networks as well.

There are some caveats to keep in mind when deciding to use the 3G/4G connection. First, cellular connections will rarely let you work as fast as a solid WiFi connection (and 3G connections never will). If you never work away from WiFi, then don't just activate the 3G or 4G for the sake of turning it on.

That said, the very nice thing about using the iPad's cellular connection is that it's strictly pay as you go—no contracts needed. You sign up for the service, and you're set for the next 30 days. At the end of the 30 days, the plan will automatically renew, but you can cancel the plan at any time.

In the U.S., 3G and 4G are provided by two carriers, AT&T and Verizon. Verizon is only available on the iPad 2 and 2012 iPad, and you have to choose between the two carriers when you first buy these two later models. The pricing plans get a little tricky to compare, because AT&T has two payment options: up front (pre-paid) or at the end of the month (post-paid), while Verizon is paid after the month is over (post-paid). So how do they compare?

AT&T 3G service is available for the original iPad and iPad 2 and comes in one of two plans:

◆ 250MB for 30 days: U.S. $14.99

◆ 2GB for 30 days: U.S. $25

If you sign up for the 250MB plan and end up transmitting more data over the network than you planned, you will be asked to pay for the 2GB option. If you use 2GB up before the end of 30 days, you will have the opportunity to purchase one of the plans again for another 30-day period.

Under the pre-paid option, if you used 251MB in 30 days, it would cost $29.98 and 2.1GB would cost $50. But if you use post-paid, AT&T tacks on a $10/GB overage charge per gigabyte. This means 251MB would still run you about $30, but 2.1 GB would only be $35.

Just looking at AT&T alone, which original iPad users will have to do, the post-paid option is definitely better if you run over your monthly traffic limit. AT&T 3G plans include unlimited WiFi at all AT&T hotspots, too.

How does this compare to Verizon? All 3G Verizon plans, as mentioned, are post-paid at:

◆ 1GB for 30 days: U.S. $20
◆ 3GB for 30 days: U.S. $35
◆ 5GB for 30 days: U.S. $50
◆ 10GB for 30 days: U.S. $80

You can see that for just $5 more than the base AT&T plan, you can get four times the traffic allotment. Add $5 a month to the next level of AT&T, and you can get 50 percent more than the upper-level AT&T plan. If you plan on doing a lot of 3G network surfing, Verizon may be a better deal for U.S. citizens.

Canadian residents have similar plans in place through Rogers:

◆ 250MB for 30 days: C $15
◆ 5GB for 30 days: C $35

iPad 3G options tend to be affordable in every country where they are implemented. Note that these are plans for residents of these nations: These are not roaming charges for, say, U.S. residents traveling abroad, which are far more expensive.

Pricing May Vary

All cellular prices were valid when this book went to press in the spring of 2012.

With the introduction of the 2012 iPad, the capability to connect to the faster 4G cellular networks for both AT&T and Verizon were added. Here, the pricing is very similar in cost and structure.

The AT&T plans for 4G are:

◆ 250MB for 30 days: U.S. $14.99
◆ 3GB for 30 days: U.S. $30
◆ 5GB for 30 days: U.S. $50

Verizon plans for 4G are only slightly different than their 3G counter-part plans:

◆ 1GB for 30 days: U.S. $20
◆ 2GB for 30 days: U.S. $30
◆ 5GB for 30 days: U.S. $50
◆ 10GB for 30 days: U.S. $80

Again, for just $5 more than the base AT&T 4G plan, you can get four times the traffic allotment. But, for $30 a month, AT&T offers 50 percent more than the second-level Verizon plan.

So, which to choose? Again, I recommend you start at the lower end for your cellular needs. Most of the time, you won't even need the cellular connection, and unless you are pulling down a lot of big files (like movies), then 2–3GB a month is likely more than enough. Most people don't sign up for cellular access on a monthly basis, instead only using it for just the month in which they are traveling, and then not renewing it the next month when they are back at the office.

To sign up for cellular access in the U.S.:

1. Tap the Settings app. The Settings screen will open.
2. Tap the Cellular Data setting. The Cellular Data pane will appear (see Figure 3.11).
3. Slide the Cellular Data setting to On.
4. Tap the View Account button. The Cellular Data Account form will open (see Figure 3.12).
5. Type in the appropriate information, providing an email address and a password that you will use to log in to the cellular network.
6. Tap the desired data plan. The selection will be denoted by a check mark.
7. Enter your credit card and billing information.
8. Tap Next. The Terms of Service page will appear.
9. Read the terms and then tap Agree. A Summary page will appear.
10. Confirm your information and then tap Submit. A notification message that your account will be updated will appear. Tap OK.

Figure 3.11

Configuring cellular access.

Figure 3.12

Sign up for a data plan.

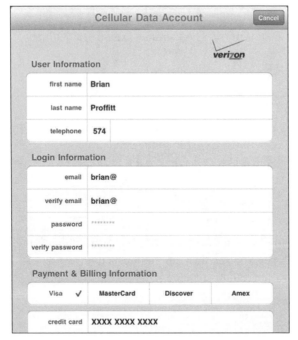

In a few moments, you will receive an Alert message indicating that your data plan has been activated. Tap OK to close the Alert box.

If you want to cancel or change your plan, return to the Settings app, tap Cellular Data, and then View Account to see the options available to you (see Figure 3.13).

Figure 3.13

You can always return to the Cellular Data Account form to change or cancel your plan.

Troubleshooting Connectivity

There will be times where connectivity may not quite work as hoped. Different WiFi routers can be configured incorrectly or have some problems in the network that might limit your connection. These types of things are usually beyond your control.

But there are some things you can try if you are experiencing unexpected WiFi issues.

◆ **Be sure you're on the correct network.** If you have joined a network that's really far away, try joining one that's closer.

◆ **Look around.** If you are in a public place with lots of laptops and Internet devices going, the wireless router may simply be overworked. You may need to wait for some machines to drop off the network.

◆ **Interference is present.** Radio signals can fall victim to any kind of electromagnetic interference. Metal objects, exposed cables, microwave ovens… these can all degrade your WiFi signal.

◆ **The router dropped you.** Sometimes wireless routers can be flaky. Try tapping the Settings app, then WiFi, and then the network you're currently on. Tap Forget this Network and then follow the steps to rejoin the network.

Your iPad is pretty adaptive for WiFi conditions, so if you are having problems, it's likely the router and not your device. If WiFi problems are consistent no matter where you try to join, it could be a hardware issue. Seek out your local Apple service specialist for help.

Conclusion

In this chapter, you found out how to connect your iPad to a local iTunes-installed computer and how iTunes can help you manage your device. You also learned how to connect to the Internet quickly and easily using WiFi access or cellular connectivity.

In Chapter 4, "Fourth Step: Using the iPad Apps," you'll delve into how iPad apps can be acquired, managed, and configured.

Chapter 4

Fourth Step:
Using the iPad Apps

- Opening and Arranging Apps
- Acquiring Apps
- Updating Apps
- Configuring Apps
- Removing Apps
- Conclusion

Since the popularity of the iPhone, the ubiquitous advertising catch phrase "there's an app for that" has become synonymous with the iPhone and now the iPad. From games to productivity to content—with the thousands of apps available, and more coming every day, there almost is an app out there for any solution you may need.

As part of the "walled garden" approach that Apple has toward content, all applications for the iPad are only available through the iTunes Store. This central-store method means that ideally all applications will be checked for stability, appropriateness, and malicious behavior before they are ever exposed to the general public. By and large, that has been true to date, although not every app is necessarily checked for quality and usability.

This is where customer feedback comes into play. Users are able to quickly rank applications based on a five-star system, as well as provide detailed reviews on what they like (and don't like) about the app. This review system is a great way to narrow down the quality applications for your iPad.

In this chapter, you will discover how to:

◆ Open and rearrange apps on your home screen

◆ Switch between apps

◆ Close apps that are having problems

◆ Download free and purchase commercial apps from iTunes

◆ Configure app settings

◆ Remove an app from the iPad

Opening and Arranging Apps

Apps come in all shapes and sizes, but they all share a common feature: How they are started. From any home screen, just tap the app's icon once. No matter what app you are using, that one action will get the application started.

The presentation of app icons on the home screens is initially determined by the iPad, but you can quickly shuffle them around to any configuration you want.

To move app icons, long-press any icon on any home screen. In a brief moment, you will see the icons start to shake in their positions (see Figure 4.1).

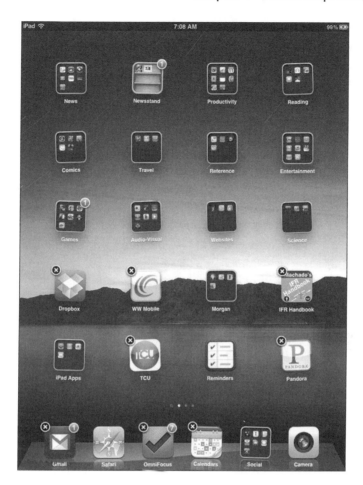

Figure 4.1
Shaky apps, ready to move.

Look again at Figure 4.1, and you will note that some apps now have black X icons. These are apps that can be removed from the iPad. Note that in this example configuration, some apps cannot be removed. That's because they are system apps, put on the iPad by Apple, and are not able to be deleted.

Regardless of their removability, all apps can be moved to any part of the screen.

To move an app to a different screen location:

1. Long-press any icon on the home screen. The icons will begin to shake.
2. Tap and drag the icon you want to move to another part of the home screen.
3. Click the Home button. The apps will stabilize, and the app will reside in its new position.

Moving an app icon to another home screen is just as easy. In fact, when you long-press an icon, notice the home screen status indicator: It will add another empty home screen to your collection as a potential destination for any moved app. If you don't make use of the empty home screen, the home screen indicator will display the same number of screens you had before the move operation.

To move an app's position on the home screens:

1. Long-press any icon on the home screen. The icons will begin to shake.
2. Tap and drag the icon you want to move toward the edge of the home screen, adjacent to the home screen to which you want to move the icon. After a pause, the next home screen will slide into view.
3. Drag the app icon to the desired spot on its new home screen.
4. Click the Home button. The apps will stabilize, and the app will reside in its new position.

You can also store apps within folders on the iPad screen. This feature lets you store more apps on a particular screen and, even better, organize your apps into something that makes a bit more sense. For instance, if multiple children are using the iPad, you can store each child's set of apps within a folder with their name, so the apps are easy to locate and use.

To create a new folder and name it:

1. Long-press any icon on the home screen. The icons will begin to shake.
2. Tap and drag the icon you want to store in a folder so it is on top of another icon you want to store in the same folder. After a pause, the icons will superimpose, and a new folder pop-over window will appear (see Figure 4.2).
3. Drag the app icon to the desired spot within the folder window, as seen in Figure 4.3.
4. The iPad will attempt to guess at a suitable folder name, but if it needs to be changed, tap the name field and use the keyboard to enter a new name.
5. Tap Done on the keyboard and then press the Home button. The Folder will be renamed, as seen in Figure 4.4.

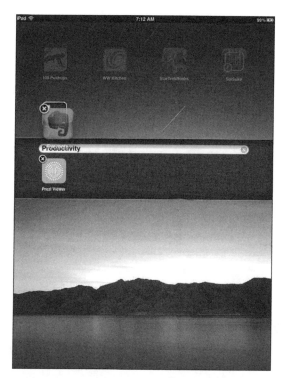

Figure 4.2

Creating a new folder.

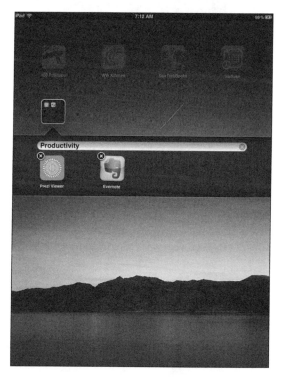

Figure 4.3

Positioning apps in the folder window.

Figure 4.4

A new folder, set and named.

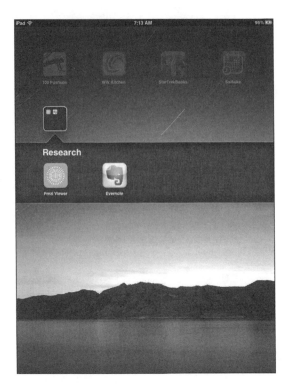

Folders, like app icons, can be moved around to any iPad location, including the Favorites area, located on the bottom of every home screen. The Favorites area will house up to six app icons or folders. Move any icon to the Favorites by long-pressing it and dragging it to the Favorites area.

You can also, should you want, use iTunes to move your app icons or folders around. This is especially useful if you want to do a lot of reorganizing.

To reorganize folders or app icons:

1. With the iPad connected to your iTunes-equipped computer, click the name of the iPad in the Devices section. The iPad's Configuration window will appcar.

2. Click the Apps button. The Apps page will be displayed (see Figure 4.5).

Figure 4.5

The iTunes Apps configuration page.

3. Click the home screen you want to modify. The home screen will appear.

4. Click the app or folder icon you want to move. The icon will be selected, and the X icon will appear.

MOVE MORE THAN ONE ICON AT A TIME

To click multiple icons, hold the Ctrl key on your keyboard and click.

---

5. Click and drag the icon(s) to the destination home screen.

6. Click and drag individual icons to the desired locations on the new home screen.

7. Click Apply. The iPad will be synced with the new changes in place.

Acquiring Apps

Getting apps for the iPad, whether free of charge or something you pay for, is always done through the iTunes Store. Fortunately, you can get to the iTunes Store through your iTunes application on your computer or over the air using the App Store app on your iPad.

The real trick to getting an app in the first place is finding the right one. While Apple has vetted the apps in the App Store as free of malware and relatively stable, don't assume that every app in the App Store will be the greatest thing since sliced bread, even if it's in a featured spot within the App Store.

When you hear about a new app on the Internet, read more than one review about the app from reputable sources. Use your favorite search engine to locate such reviews or blog entries about the app.

If you still want to try the app, or you're looking for apps in the App Store itself, the next place to check is the review section of the app itself. Look at the number of positive versus negative ratings, but also read the reviews. Sometimes disgruntled users will blast an app for some feature (or lack of feature) you don't even need. "It won't scramble eggs!," they cry. Okay, that's notable, but you're just looking for an app to help in your business, so the lack of scrambled eggs is not a problem.

If there is a free version of the application available, definitely try that one first. It may have limited features, but it should give you a feel for how the app is put together and if (with the added features) the paid version will be a good fit.

One thing to watch out for is the iPhone apps that can run on the iPad. It doesn't take too much coding to get an iPhone app to run on the iPad, but such quick changes will result in an application that's clearly not configured for the iPad (see Figure 4.6).

Figure 4.6

Google Plus: Great social media app, but not quite ready for the iPad.

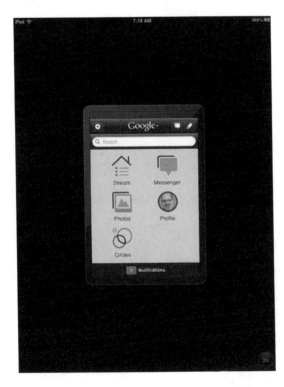

Figure 4.7 displays the 2X effect applied to the Google Plus app. More readable, but still not great quality. For this kind of app, the issue is not a major concern, but for an important business-specific app, iPhone-specific apps can be a little off-putting.

Figure 4.7

Google Plus in 2X view.

You may like the app so much that you will live with this configuration (at least until the developers come out with a true iPad version). One way to know if you are getting an app like this is to look for a small "+" symbol in the app's download button. This symbol indicates that the app was developed for the iPad *and* the iPhone. Look at the screenshot of the app on the app's download page—many of these dual-platform apps are getting configured properly for iPad display, even if they will also run on the iPhone.

Each version of the App Store (whether in iTunes or the App Store app) will have different categories to organize apps. Most of these categories overlap, but if you are having trouble finding something, try browsing both stores.

Finally, the Search bar in both versions of the App Store is a powerful tool for locating apps. This tool will search app titles, keywords, and descriptions to help you find the appropriate application.

Given all of these avenues, it's going to be relatively simple to find your app.

Using the iTunes Application

Though the content of the iTunes version of the App Store is identical to its iPad counterpart, the iTunes application is best to use when you are planning on finding and installing a lot of apps. It's not a question of speed, but rather organization. You can find, download, and install apps with the iTunes application and then use the same application to quickly organize the apps on your iPad.

To use the iTunes application to find the Netflix app:

1. Start iTunes on your PC or Mac; then click the iTunes Store link. The iTunes Store window will appear.

2. Click the App Store tab. The App Store window will appear.

3. Click the iPad button to shift the App Store to iPad apps (see Figure 4.8).

Figure 4.8

The iPad section of the App Store in iTunes.

4. Click in the Search Store field, type Netflix, and press Enter. The results will be displayed, as shown in Figure 4.9.

5. Click the Netflix app. The Netflix app page will open (see Figure 4.10).

6. To read more about the app, click the More link below the Description paragraph.

7. To find out how other users liked the app, read the Customer Ratings section.

8. When satisfied you want to download this app, click the Free App button. A login dialog box will appear (see Figure 4.11).

Netflix app

Figure 4.9
Tracking down Netflix.

Figure 4.10
The Netflix app page.

Figure 4.11

You must log into the iTunes Store for every app, even the free ones.

9. Enter your ID and Password information for the iTunes Store and click Get. The app will be downloaded.

10. The next time you sync with the iPad, the new app will be loaded onto the iPad.

REDEEM YOUR GIFT CARDS

If you have an iTunes Gift Card or Gift Certificate, click the Redeem link on the home page of the iTunes Store; then provide your gift card information. If you purchase an app, you will be given the choice to use the redeemed gift card amount or the payment method associated with your iTunes account.

Using the App Store App

Finding and installing an app from the iPad is just as easy as using the iTunes application. Let's track down the Square app, which is a great app to convert your iPad into a point-of-sale device.

To find and install an app:

1. Tap the App Store icon to start the App Store (see Figure 4.12).

2. Tap the Search bar, type Square, and tap Search. The results will be displayed, as shown in Figure 4.13.

3. Tap the Square app. The Square app page will open (see Figure 4.14).

Figure 4.12
The App Store app.

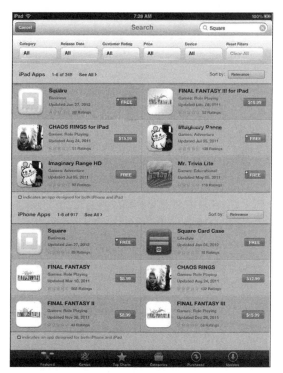

Figure 4.13
Tracking down Square.

Figure 4.14

The Square app page.

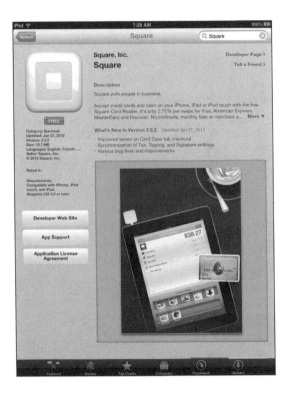

4. To read more about the app, tap the More link below the Description paragraph.

5. To find out how other users liked the app, read the Customer Ratings section.

6. When satisfied you want to download this app, tap the Free button below the large app icon. The button will change to a green Install App button.

7. Tap the Install App button. A login dialog box will appear.

8. Enter your iTunes Password information for the iTunes Store and tap OK. The app will be downloaded and installed.

Updating Apps

As improvements and fixes are made to the applications installed on your iPad, the App Store will keep track of any new versions for your installed software, and when they arrive, the App Store app will notify you with a red numeric indicator on the App Store icon (see Figure 4.15).

Numeric indicator

Figure 4.15
The number indicates the number of apps to be updated.

To update an app:

1. When such an indicator is visible, tap the App Store icon. The App Store will open.
2. Tap the Updates icon on the tab bar. The Updates page will open.
3. Tap the Update All button. The App Store will close, and any apps in the Updates list will be downloaded and installed.

Configuring Apps

Applications in the iPad vary in how they can be configured. Some apps have just a few configuration settings, if any, so the tools to configure them will be found in the App itself.

But some iPad apps will follow iPad convention and plug their configuration settings in the iPad Settings app. If you can't find configuration settings in your app, check the Settings app. For this example, let's configure the Keynote app, which will let you create slide presentations on the go.

To configure an app:

1. Tap the Settings app icon. The Settings app will open.

2. Tap the Keynote setting. The Keynote setting pane will open (see Figure 4.16).

Figure 4.16

An example of an app's configuration settings.

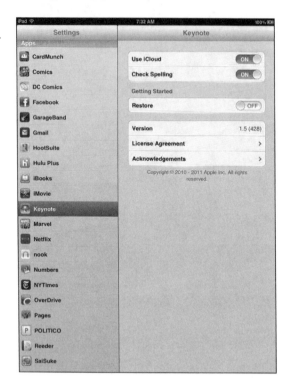

3. Slide the settings switch you would like to change in Keynote. The setting will be activated or turned off.

4. When your configuration is complete, click the Home button. The settings will be made in Keynote.

Removing Apps

If you find you're not using an app, you can easily opt to remove it from your iPad. In this example, let's remove the Netflix app because you're too busy working to use this cool service.

To remove an app:

1. Long-press the app you would like to remove. The apps will begin to shake, and removable apps will be indicated by a black X indicator.

2. Tap the Netflix app. A confirmation dialog box will appear (see Figure 4.17).

Figure 4.17
Confirm you want to delete an app.

3. Tap Delete. The app will be removed from your screen.
4. Click the Home button. The app icons will stabilize.

GONE, BUT NOT FORGOTTEN

When an app is removed from the iPad, it will still be maintained in the iTunes Library on your computer. To completely remove the app, click the Apps link in iTunes, select the app, and press Delete. You will be asked to confirm the action, and whether or not you want to keep the app's files or move them to the Recycle Bin. Select the option you want, and the app will be completely removed from your Library.

Conclusion

In this chapter, you've learned how to acquire, manage, and configure new apps for the iPad.

In Chapter 5, "Work the Web: Safari," you'll explore the Internet with the iPad's powerful Safari browser.

Chapter 5

Work the Web:
Safari

- ◆ Navigating Websites
- ◆ Managing Bookmarks and History
- ◆ Managing Tabbed Browsing
- ◆ Searching for Content
- ◆ Customizing Your Browser
- ◆ Conclusion

Browsers have actually been around for a long time, but were never really called browsers. Instead, they were called *text readers* or *read-only applications*, because what these programs did was open simple files of text and let someone read them—like a book. These programs were on computers called *dumb terminals*.

It seems odd to call a computer dumb, but compared to the computers used today, these computers weren't very smart. All they did was display information from monster servers called *mainframes* that were the size of an average living room. These servers weren't all that smart either, but they were good enough to take a lot of information and help business-people make sense of it.

The problem was that all these dumb terminals could only talk to the servers they were connected to. There was an Internet back then, but there was no World Wide Web. Internet traffic was mainly limited to messaging and file transfers, using tools such as Usenet, Archie, or Gopher.

Then, in 1990, a scientist in Switzerland, Sir Tim Berners-Lee, got a brilliant idea. What if you could read files on any computer connected to the Internet anytime you wanted? You could put those files on a special server that had one job—showing those files to anyone who asked for them. Sir Berners-Lee, who was knighted for his work at the CERN institute, knew this idea would only work if all of these files were made readable by any computer.

So Sir Berners-Lee suggested that people use HyperText Markup Language (HTML) files. Because they are essentially ASCII text files, HTML files could be read by any computer, would let people create any content they wanted, and would have hyperlinks—something that would revolutionize the way people absorbed material.

Browsers came about as instruments to read all of these new HTML files. As with the dumb terminals, Sir Berners-Lee just wanted people to read information quickly in files—not change their content. So he and his colleagues figured out a way to make a program that did nothing but read and display HTML. Other people got involved and made the application read more complicated HTML code.

People began calling the information on the Web *pages* and calling the process of reading those pages *browsing*—and that's where the *browser* name comes from. Later, when the general public started using the Web, the verb *browsing* got morphed into *surfing*. The name *browser* stuck, though, because it still describes more accurately what this type of application does. You can call any program like this a browser, of course. A program that does nothing but show pictures could be a picture browser. But these days the name is more synonymous with Web browsers, such as iPad's Safari.

As the Web grew more popular, businesses were quick to see the value of the Web—first, as a way to communicate more robustly with customers; then as a platform to get work done. Web browsers became useful not just for looking at the Web, but also as tools to conduct business across every industry.

In this chapter, you will find out how to:

◆ Navigate websites

◆ Manage bookmarks and history

◆ Use multipage browsing

◆ Search for content

◆ Customize your browser experience

Navigating Websites

Browsing is more than just tapping through a collection of hyperlinked files. What really makes the whole thing work is the Uniform Resource Locater (URL). URLs are pseudo-English labels that make it possible to find and retrieve resources across the Internet in a consistent, predictable, well-defined manner. Every Web server has an IP address, but URLs make it easy for regular folks to type an address into the Address Bar of Safari and bring up a page.

Of course, when you look at URLs such as www.llanfairpwllgwyngyllgogerychwyrndrobwllllantysiliogogogoch.co.uk/, using the IP address might actually be a blessing, but for the most part, URLs are easier.

WE CAN'T MAKE THIS STUFF UP
Llanfairpwllgwyngyllgogerychwyrndrobwllllantysiliogogogoch is a village on the Isle of Anglesey in North Wales that currently holds the Guinness record for the longest English place name. The village's website holds the record for the longest valid URL.

You can begin browsing with Safari as soon as you start the app. If the iPad is not connected to the Internet yet, Safari will prompt you to make that connection.

To browse with Safari:

   1. Tap the Safari icon. Safari will start (as shown in Figure 5.1).

Back   Forward   Bookmarks/   Add   Address bar   Reload   Search bar
History   Bookmark

Figure 5.1
The Safari
browser.

2. Tap the Address bar and then the clear field icon so the URL in the field is removed and the keyboard appears.

3. Type the URL for the website you want to visit in the Address bar.

A HELPING URL HAND

You do not have to type the URL identifier http:// before the website address. Safari will fill it in for you.

4. Tap Go to visit the new page.

5. Long-press a highlighted or underlined hyperlink. An action menu will appear, giving you the options to open the link, open the link in a new tab, add the link to your browser's Reading List, or copy the link (see Figure 5.2).

Figure 5.2

A hyperlink action menu.

6. Tap Open to go to the new page.

You don't have to type in the full address every time you visit a website, thanks to the AutoFill feature in the Address bar. Just start typing the URL, and Safari will display a list of similar URLs for you to choose from.

After you have been browsing for a while, you may need to go back to a Web page you visited earlier in your current browser session. Two controls, the Back and Forward icons, will enable you to navigate through the pages you have visited.

Note, however, that navigation through Web pages is not tracked for every Web page you visit during a session. Safari uses a sequential navigation method that tracks only the pages along a particular path. For instance, assume you were browsing Page A, then Pages B, C, and D. On Page D, you found a hyperlink back to Page B and clicked it to visit that page. Now, from Page B again, assume you went off and visited Pages

E and F. If you were to use the Back icon in this session, the order of pages that would appear for each click of the Back icon would be F to E to B to A. Pages C and D, because they were on another "track" of browsing, would no longer be a part of the browser's navigation, even if you were to cycle forward through the same pages again using the Forward icon.

One of the nicer features of the iPad is its capability to call up Safari whenever any hyperlink or Web page shortcut is clicked—in any app. That capability is particularly handy when using the Mail app, where you often receive URLs from colleagues.

Another useful feature in Safari is its capability to zoom in on any Web page. There are two ways to go about this while browsing.

The first method is the reverse pinch, or fanning, technique. To zoom in, simply tap the section of the page you want to enlarge and move your fingers apart. The page will zoom in as long as you move your fingers out. Reverse the move to a pinch and zoom back out.

The second method is double-tapping on a particular section of the page. Safari will automatically zoom in to have that section of the page fill the screen. This is particularly useful when visiting a page with a section of useful content surrounded by images and ads. To zoom back to the full-page view, double-tap again.

Managing Bookmarks and History

Human beings are creatures of habit, and often we find ourselves clinging to the familiar as we move through our workday. Safari accommodates this trait with its Bookmarks feature. Bookmarks are markers that, when selected in a menu or clicked in the Bookmark toolbar, will take you directly to the Web page you want—without typing the URL address.

You can create a bookmark very easily in Safari. Then, when you need to, you can open up a page with just a couple of taps.

To open a bookmark, tap the Bookmark icon and select the bookmark you want from the action menu (see Figure 5.3). If there is a bookmark within the Bookmark bar, all you need to do is tap it.

When you find a page you want to save, you can bookmark it and add it to your bookmark collection.

To add a bookmark:

1. From a page you want to save, tap the Add Bookmark icon. The Add Bookmark action menu will open (see Figure 5.4).

2. Tap Add Bookmark. The Add Bookmark pop-over will appear (see Figure 5.5).

Figure 5.3
The Bookmark action menu.

Figure 5.4
The Add Bookmark action menu.

Figure 5.5

The Add Bookmark pop-over.

3. Confirm or edit the name of the bookmark you want to use.

4. Tap the Bookmarks control if you want the bookmark to appear somewhere other than the main Bookmark menu and then tap a new location.

5. Tap Save. The bookmark will be added to the desired location (see Figure 5.6).

As time goes on, you may find your collection of bookmarks has grown quite a bit. Safari includes a way to organize bookmarks in a way that makes the best sense for you.

Figure 5.6

The new bookmark in the Bookmarks bar.

To organize bookmarks:

1. From any page, tap the Bookmark icon. The Bookmark action menu will open.
2. Tap the Edit button. The action menu will shift to Edit mode.
3. Tap and drag the Move icon on any item to move it up or down the list of bookmarks. The Move icon is denoted by three horizontal lines.
4. Tap the New Folder button. The New Folder pop-over will appear.
5. Type a Title for the new folder and tap Bookmarks. The new folder will appear in the Bookmarks action menu.
6. Tap a bookmark's Delete icon; then tap the Delete button. The book-mark will be removed.
7. Tap Done. The menu will reflect the changes you made.

You can also put bookmarks on any of the home screens. When they appear on a home screen, bookmarks are referred to as *Web clips*.

To add bookmarks to a home screen:

1. From a page you want to save, tap the Add Bookmark icon. The Add Bookmark action menu will open.

2. Tap Add to Home Screen. The Add to Home pop-over will appear (see Figure 5.7).

Figure 5.7

The Add to Home pop-over.

3. Edit the name of the Web Clip icon and tap Add. The Web Clip icon will be added to a home screen.

If you've been browsing around a while, and just can't seem to remember that site you visited a couple of days ago (and naturally forgot to bookmark), you can use Safari's history feature to track that site down.

To use Safari's history feature:

1. From any page, tap the Bookmark icon. The Bookmark action menu will open.

2. Tap the History folder. The History action menu will open (see Figure 5.8).

3. Tap the page you want to revisit. The page will open in Safari.

Figure 5.8

*The History
action menu.*

If you want to clear the history in Safari, the fastest way to accomplish this is through the History action menu.

To clear a history in Safari:

1. From any page, tap the Bookmark icon. The Bookmark action menu will open.

2. Tap the History folder. The History action menu will open.

3. Tap the Clear History button. The Safari history will be erased.

Managing Tabbed Browsing

Many PC and Mac-based browsers have a feature known as tabbed browsing, which enables the user to access multiple pages at once.

As of iOS5, Safari on the iPad now features tabs, which is a useful way to handle many pages at the same time.

To manage tabbed browsing:

1. From any page, tap the Add Tab icon (the + at the upper right of the screen). A new Untitled tab will open, as shown in Figure 5.9.

Figure 5.9

A new tab, ready to load.

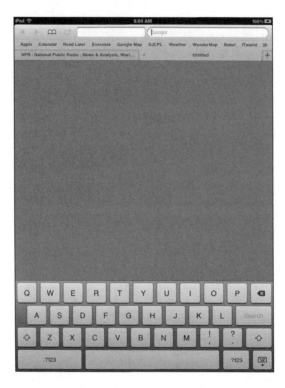

2. Type any URL. The tab will open to that page within Safari.

3. To move a tab, press and drag the tab across the screen to a new location in the tab bar.

4. To close the tab, tap the small close icon on the left side of the tab. The tab will close.

If you tap the Multiple Page icon, you will see the page displayed as one of the minipages. To remove a page, tap the black X icon to remove the page.

Searching for Content

Finding information on the Web used to be very easy—with only 500 or so websites in existence in the early 90s, you could almost index them by hand. Today, there are billions of Web pages and finding useful content can be daunting sometimes. Safari has a search tool that not only uses the most powerful search tools around, but also allows you to choose the search engines you prefer.

Using the Search bar is easy: Just type in what you are looking for and press Enter. By default, the Search bar connects to the Google search engine, and it will display the results of your search in a new tab.

SUGGESTIVE SEARCHES

Safari will suggest search terms similar to what you type in an effort to save you time. If you see the term you were looking for in the menu, tap it to start the actual search.

To change search engines using the Settings app:

1. Tap the Settings app icon. The Settings app will open.
2. Tap the Safari setting. The Safari settings pane will open (see Figure 5.10).

Figure 5.10

The Safari settings.

3. Tap the Search Engine setting. The Search Engine pane will open.
4. Tap one of the three available options. The selected search engine will be indicated by a check mark.
5. Click the Home button. The new search engine will be used in Safari.

Customizing Your Browser

Whenever you travel extensively on the Internet, you're bound to run across a few common bumps in the road that could slow you down. Fortunately, Safari has some settings that will smooth out the ride.

One such feature is the AutoFill tool. AutoFill's job is to help you fill in those registration or payment information forms you might run into while surfing the Web. AutoFill uses your own contact information to provide information for those forms when you come across them.

> **IDENTITY ALERT**
>
> Using AutoFill is handy, but be aware that if your iPad falls into someone else's hands, Safari could fill in your personal and corporate information, including passwords for sensitive data. It's something to keep in mind.

To activate AutoFill:

1. Tap the Settings app icon. The Settings app will open.
2. Tap the Safari setting. The Safari settings pane will open.
3. Tap the AutoFill option. The AutoFill pane will appear.
4. Slide the Use Contact Info control to On. The My Info control will activate.
5. Tap the My Info control. A menu of your contacts will appear.
6. Tap the contact that represents you. That contact will appear in the My Info control.
7. Slide the Names and Passwords control to On. This will keep track of any login names and passwords as you enter them.
8. Click the Home button. The changes will be saved.

Pop-up windows can be the bane of your Web experience or a vital tool. Disreputable sites can use them as forced advertising, but legitimate sites also have a use for them. Depending on your Web habits, you may or may not want pop-ups blocked, which is Safari's default setting.

To turn blocking off:

1. Tap the Settings app icon. The Settings app will open.
2. Tap the Safari setting. The Safari settings pane will open.
3. Slide the Block Pop-ups control to Off.
4. Click the Home button. The change will be saved.

Cookies are another piece of Web technology that can help or hinder your Web experience. Cookies are little bits of tracking code that websites will "hand" you when you visit. They can enhance your surfing, because when you return to the site, it will "remember" you and your preferences because of the cookie your browser has received from the earlier visit.

The problem is that cookies can represent a security threat because any site can use a cookie to track where you have been on the Web even after you leave the site. Cookies can also be used as delivery mechanisms for some pretty nasty malware. Safari will give you the options not to accept cookies, pick them up just from sites you've visited, or pick them up from any site at all.

Of all of these options, the visited site option is probably the best compromise, but it's a matter of personal preference.

To change the cookie setting:

1. Tap the Settings app icon. The Settings app will open.
2. Tap the Safari setting. The Safari settings pane will open.
3. Tap the Accept Cookies control. The Accept Cookies pane will open.
4. Tap the option you prefer. The selected option will be denoted by a check mark.
5. Click the Home button. The change will be saved.

Conclusion

In this chapter, you learned some of the finer points of operating the Safari browser, a flexible and fast window to the Internet.

In Chapter 6, "Get the Word Out: Mail," we will examine how to use the other most-used aspect of the Internet: email, and how the iPad's Mail app handles this important job.

Chapter 6

Get the Word Out:
Mail

- ◆ Setting Up an Account
- ◆ Organizing Mail
- ◆ Conclusion

It is not entirely clear when the use of email began to be so indispensible to the business world, but it was a fast adoption. When the Internet was opened to the general public in the mid 1990s, businesses were relatively quick to adopt email. The prospect of being able to send messages of virtually any length instantaneously to anyone in the world with an email address was simply too great a communications tool to ignore.

The iPad is endowed with a built-in email app, cleverly named *Mail*. Don't let the simple name fool you—this is a robust and versatile application.

If you've used any email application in Windows, OS X, or Linux, there's a lot about Mail that you are going to recognize. If you are in an office that uses Microsoft Exchange Server, Mail is one of the non-Microsoft clients that can connect to Exchange and pull email messages.

In this chapter, you will learn how to do the following:

◆ Create an email account

◆ Download your messages

◆ Organize your email

Setting Up an Account

Getting an email account these days is a pretty simple thing. Most employers have them for their employees, universities have them for students and staff, and private Internet service providers often provide multiple email accounts per Internet connection—one for each member of the family.

Most emails (especially away from internal business accounts) are delivered over the Internet via the Post Office Protocol (POP) or Internet Mail Access Protocol (IMAP). A POP or IMAP account works something like this—someone sends you an email. The Internet's control servers route that message to your email server, which can be located anywhere in the world. There your message will sit until you come along and download it (and any other messages) into Mail. Unless you have an email server in your home or cubicle, emails never come directly to you. This is actually good, because this two-step process gives your mail server a chance to clean out spam and junk mail.

Outbound mail is a little different. You type a message, address it, and tap Send. The message is immediately sent out to the destination server via the Simple Mail Transfer Protocol (SMTP) server. It doesn't stay there long; the SMTP server has one job to do, and it does it very quickly. It checks the address in your message and makes sure there's actually a mail server ready to receive messages at the other end. If there is, boom! Off your message goes. If there isn't, the SMTP server will immediately bounce your message back to Mail and tell you what went wrong.

RETURN TO SENDER

Note that the SMTP server on your end only checks for valid mail servers. If the username in the address is incorrect, or that user no longer has an account, it's the job of the receiving POP server to figure that out and send you the bounce message. It's a fine line, but if you do get a bounce message, knowing from where it was sent will help you figure out what went wrong.

Whenever you set up a new email account, your Internet service provider will provide you with some important information that you need to memorize or store in a safe place somewhere.

For a POP mail account, you need:

◆ Your new email address
◆ Your user name for the POP server
◆ Your password for the POP server
◆ The Internet address of the POP server
◆ The Internet address of the SMTP server

For other accounts, such as iCloud, MobileMe, or Gmail, Mail only needs your username and password. Microsoft Exchange users will also need to know their domain name, as well as the username and password.

When you first start Mail, you will immediately be given the opportunity to set up an email account. You can set up as many accounts as you would like, but you should have the complete set of information for at least one of your accounts configured when you start Mail for the first time. Here's how to set up an account on Gmail, the popular email service from Google.:

To set up an account on Gmail:

1. Tap the Mail app icon. The Welcome to Mail screen will open (see Figure 6.1).
2. Tap the Gmail option. The Gmail form will open (see Figure 6.2).
3. Type the appropriate information in the fields. It is important that you fill out all the fields.
4. Tap Save. After verification, the Mail app will open, download your messages, and display the latest message (see Figure 6.3).

Figure 6.1

Welcome to Mail.

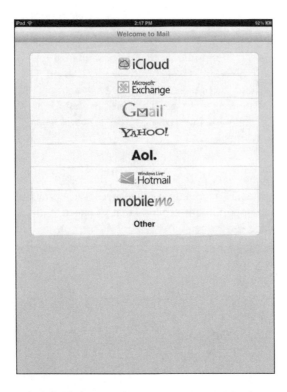

Figure 6.2

Provide your Gmail account info.

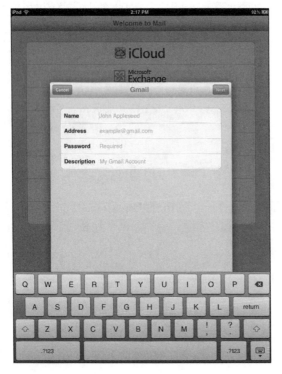

Figure 6.3

Your email, displayed.

If you don't have an account at one of the major provider types listed on the Welcome to Mail screen, you can still use your POP or IMAP server information to get your account set up.

To use your POP or IMAP server information to get your account set up:

1. Tap the Mail app icon. The Welcome to Mail screen will open.

2. Tap the Other option. The New Account form will open.

3. Type the appropriate information in the fields. It is important that you fill out all the fields.

4. Tap Save. Mail will determine if your mail server uses IMAP or POP. If it does, the Enter your account information form will open, as shown in Figure 6.4.

5. Tap the POP or IMAP button, depending on the type of account you have.

6. Type your account information into the appropriate fields.

7. Click Save. After verification, the Mail app will open, download your messages, and display the latest message.

Figure 6.4

Provide your POP or IMAP account info.

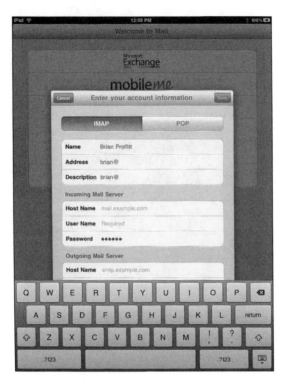

Your account is set to manually download email by default, which means email will be downloaded only when you specify or when you first start Mail.

To set Mail to download email automatically:

1. Tap the Settings app icon. The Settings screen will open.

2. Tap the Mail, Contacts, Calendars setting. The Mail, Contacts, Calendars setting pane will open (see Figure 6.5).

3. Tap the Fetch New Data setting. The Fetch New Data pane will open (see Figure 6.6).

4. Tap the interval option you want. The selected option will be denoted by a check mark.

5. Click the Home button. The options will be saved.

Figure 6.5
The Mail, Contacts, Calendars setting pane.

Figure 6.6
Configure how often you want to get email.

> **TAKING IT EASY ON THE POP SERVER**
>
> You can set Mail to download email automatically at a certain interval. The fastest interval is 15 minutes, so you don't overload your POP server. That's a good idea if you're connecting through 3G. If you can control the timing of email downloads, you can manage the flow of traffic through your wireless connection.

If you want to add another email account to Mail, you will need to use the Welcome to Mail tool again.

To access the Welcome to Mail tool:

1. Tap the Settings app icon. The Settings screen will open.
2. Tap the Mail, Contacts, Calendars setting. The Mail, Contacts, Calendars setting pane will open.
3. Tap the Add Account setting. The Add Account pane will open (see Figure 6.7).
4. Tap the type of account you want to add and follow the steps you used in the Welcome to Mail screen to complete the task.

Figure 6.7

Adding an additional account.

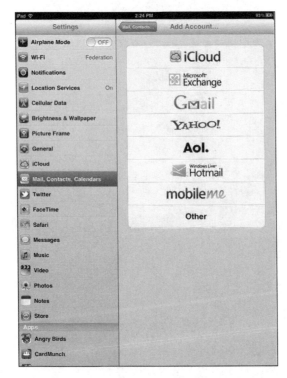

Receiving and Sending Email

Once you have one account set up in Mail, you are free to send and receive email as long as you are connected to the Internet.

CHECKING FOR NEW EMAIL

If you did not set Mail to download messages automatically (or just want to see what's out there before the next scheduled download occurs), tap the Inbox button and then the Reload icon at the bottom of the Inbox menu. Your messages will be downloaded.

As you can see in Figure 6.8, the Mail app is very simple.

Mailboxes   Message   Reading   Mailboxes   Archive   Reply/   Compose
            list   window   Forward

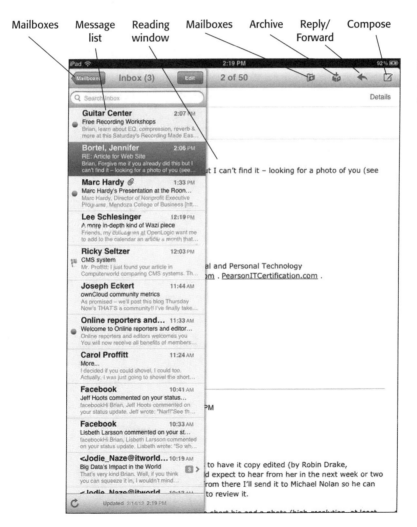

Figure 6.8

The vertical Mail interface.

Reading a message is simple: Just tap the Inbox folder; then tap a message in the Message list, and its contents will be displayed in the Reading window.

After you have read an email, you will note that the blue dot icon next to the message in the Message list will be removed.

If you want to always see the Message list, turn the iPad 90 degrees until the Mail app is displayed horizontally (see Figure 6.9). You can tap messages in the Message pane and read them in the Reading pane.

Figure 6.9

The horizontal Mail interface.

Of course, you can do more with an email than just read it. In fact, more often than not, a message will warrant a reply.

To reply to the sender of the message only:

1. Open a message to which you want to reply. The message will be displayed in the Reading window.

2. Tap the Reply/Forward icon. The Reply/Forward action menu will open.

ONE REPLY, OR MANY?

Mail is clever enough to notice when you have received an email sent to just you or to other people, too. If the message has multiple recipients, the Reply to All option will be visible on the Reply/Forward action menu.

3. Tap Reply. A preaddressed Compose window will open (see Figure 6.10).

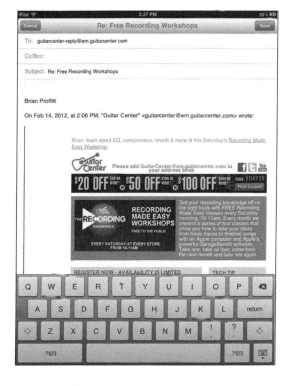

Figure 6.10

Replying to a message.

4. Type your reply in the body of the message.

5. When finished, tap Send. The Message window will close, and with a whoosh sound effect, the message will be sent.

If the message was sent to you and other people, you can send a reply to all the recipients and the sender.

To send a reply to all the recipients and the sender:

1. Tap a message to reply to all recipients. The message will be displayed in the Reading window.

2. Tap the Reply/Forward icon. The Reply/Forward action menu will open.

3. Tap Reply to All. A preaddressed Compose window will open.

4. Type your reply in the body of the message.

5. When finished, tap Send. The Message window will close, and with a whoosh sound effect, the message will be sent.

To forward a message to someone else:

1. Tap a message to reply to forward. The message will be displayed in the Reading window.

2. Tap the Reply/Forward icon. The Reply/Forward action menu will open.

3. Tap Forward. A preaddressed Compose window will open.

4. Type an additional message in the body of the message.

5. When finished, tap Send. The Message window will close, and with a whoosh sound effect, the message will be sent.

To send a new message to a single or multiple recipients:

1. Tap the Compose icon. A Compose Message window will open (see Figure 6.11).

2. Type an email address in the To field.

Figure 6.11

A new Message window.

CONTACT CONNECTION

If you use the Contacts tool on the iPad, tap the blue + icon on the right end of the To:, Cc:, or Bcc: fields to open the All Contacts list. Tap the addresses you need without typing a single ampersand.

3. If you need to blind carbon copy a recipient, tap the Cc/Bcc: field to open separate Cc: and Bcc: fields and type the address in.

4. Type a Subject.

5. Type a message in the body.

6. Tap Send. The Message window will close, and with a whoosh sound effect, the message will be sent.

Organizing Mail

After you have read your messages and sent your replies, what next? You don't want to leave your Inbox cluttered, and unless it's junk mail, you don't want to delete everything, either.

Mail is very good about handling lots of email at once. Let's take some steps to organize the Inbox first.

If you tap the Inbox button and then tap the Mailboxes control, you will see a list of mailboxes with which to filter the Message list (see Figure 6.12). Usually, these mailboxes are folders or categories imported from your email account. Tap these mailboxes, as desired, to see the results on your Message list.

The mailbox is a really useful tool in Mail for organizing your information. Using mailboxes, you can essentially treat messages as files, which is what they are. Mail cannot create or change mailboxes—this has to be done directly within your account.

To move messages into folders:

1. Tap a message to organize. The message will be displayed in the Reading window.

2. Tap the Mailboxes icon. The Mailboxes list will open (see Figure 6.13).

3. Tap the mailbox into which you want to move the message. The message will "fly" into the mailbox, and the latest message in your Inbox will be displayed.

Figure 6.12

*Viewing your
mailboxes.*

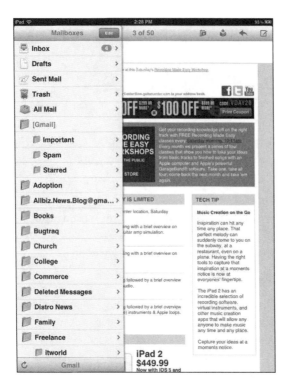

Figure 6.13

*Organizing with
mailboxes.*

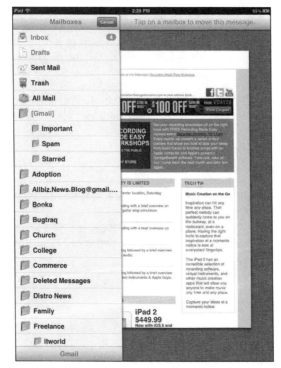

To move a number of messages into a folder:

1. Tap the Inbox button. The Message list will open.

2. Tap the Edit button. The list will shift into Edit mode (see Figure 6.14).

Figure 6.14

Editing the Inbox.

3. Tap the messages you want to move into a mailbox. The messages will be selected by red check mark icons and "stacked" in the Reading window (see Figure 6.15).

4. Tap the Move button. The Mailboxes list will open.

5. Tap the mailbox into which you want to move the messages. The messages will "fly" into the mailbox, and the latest message in your Inbox will be displayed.

Figure 6.15

Selecting multiple messages.

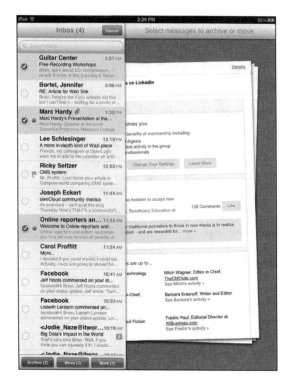

To delete individual messages:

1. Tap a message to delete. The message will be displayed in the Reading window.

2. Tap the Delete icon. The message will be deleted.

To delete multiple messages (just like organizing multiple emails):

1. Tap the Inbox button. The Message list will open.

2. Tap the Edit button. The list will shift into Edit mode.

3. Tap the messages you want to delete. The messages will be selected by red check mark icons and "stacked" in the Reading window.

4. Tap the Delete button. The messages will be deleted.

If, perchance, you happened to delete a message that shouldn't have been trashed, don't panic because you can still get the message back.

To get a message back that you've deleted:

1. Tap the Inbox button. The Message list will open.

2. Tap the Mailboxes button. The Mailboxes list will open.

3. Tap the Trash mailbox. The Trash list will appear.

4. Tap the Edit button. The Trash list will shift into Edit mode.

5. Tap the messages you want to recover. The messages will be selected by red check mark icons and "stacked" in the Reading window.

6. Tap the Move button. The Mailboxes list will open.

7. Tap the mailbox into which you want to move the messages. The messages will "fly" into the mailbox, and the latest message in your Inbox will be displayed.

Conclusion

There is a lot more to email these days than just reading and writing. With this medium becoming so integrated in our daily lives, it's good to see that there are excellent tools in the iPad that can make email use easy.

In Chapter 7, "Get to iWork: Documenting with Pages," you will learn how to start creating content and managing numbers for your business, using the tools found in the iWork suite of apps: Keynote, Numbers, and Pages.

Chapter 7

Get to iWork:
Documenting with Pages

◆ Creating a Pages Document

◆ Exploring the Pages Interface

◆ Editing Documents

◆ Configuring a Document

◆ Sharing Pages Documents

◆ Conclusion

The urge to put words on paper is very strong in most cultures. Paper and ink lend a sense of permanence that we don't seem to have in our own brains. Scientists speculate that we do indeed remember everything we have experienced, perhaps all the way back to Minute One. But, until we can figure out how to *recall* all of that detail, we still need to write it down.

The written word has more uses than just archiving memories and events. It's still the most pervasive form of communication in the world. Every type of media uses writing as its basis, even television (though some writing there is a bit shaky). The Internet has been the fastest growing medium in the world, and even with the advent of streaming audio and video, people mostly read the written works of others.

In a business environment, the written word is even more important. "Getting it in writing" isn't just a euphemism, it's set in business stone. In the workplace, communication is primarily done with documents, so the capability to read and edit documents on the iPad is very important.

Pages, one of the three apps in the iWork suite, is a great tool to get your words on paper or on computer screens around your company. In this chapter, you will learn how to:

◆ Get around the Pages interface

◆ Create a Pages document

◆ Edit a Pages document

◆ Share Pages documents

Creating a Pages Document

Even though the three iWork components are completely separate apps, the developers at Apple have built these applications to share the same content management system. This lends a consistency to the iWork apps, which makes it easy to navigate content with these apps.

In Pages, this content management system is accessed by the Documents button.

Tapping on any of these buttons, located in the upper-left corner of Pages, will open up the Documents screen, which is shown in Figure 7.1.

To view the documents on your iPad, flick through the documents that appear in the Documents screen. When the one you want is centered and highlighted, tap the document to open and begin editing it.

The Documents screen also has an Edit mode that will reveal more controls for managing your documents, as shown in Figure 7.2.

New document   Sort By controls   Edit

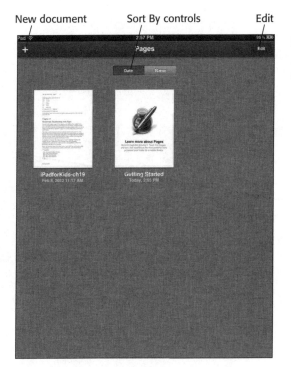

Figure 7.1

The Documents screen.

Share   Duplicate documents   Trash

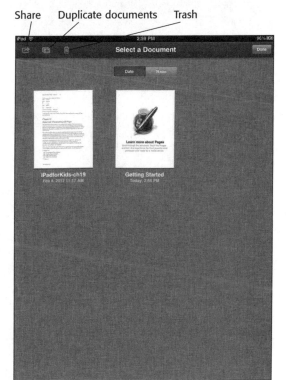

Figure 7.2

Managing your documents in the Documents screen.

When you create a new document, you can create a blank document or choose from the available templates provided by Pages.

To create a new document from the Documents screen:

1. Tap the New Document button. The Create Document action menu will open (see Figure 7.3).

Figure 7.3

The Create Document action menu.

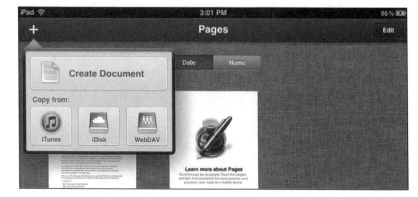

2. Tap the Create Document button. The Choose a Template screen will open (see Figure 7.4).

Figure 7.4

The Choose a Template screen.

3. Flick through the template gallery until you locate a document template that fits your needs and tap it. Or tap the Blank document option. The document will open for editing.

If there is a document on your iPad that has many style or content features that you need in a new document, you can make a copy of the document.

To make a copy of an existing document:

1. Flick through the documents in the Documents screen until the one you want to copy is highlighted.

2. Tap the Edit button. The Edit mode of the Documents screen will appear.

3. Tap the Duplicate Document icon. A copy of the document will appear.

If you would like to change the name of the copied (or any other) document, long-press and release the name of the document on the screen. The Rename Document screen will appear (see Figure 7.5).

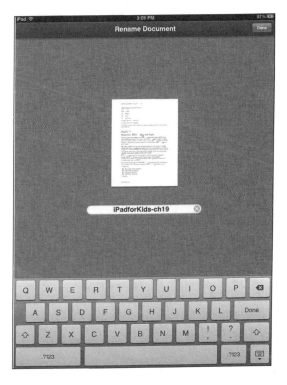

Figure 7.5

The Rename Document screen.

Type a new name in the document name field and tap Done. The new name will be applied.

Besides creating new documents, Pages can open existing documents that you can import to your iPad using iTunes.

To open an existing document to import to your iPad with iTunes:

1. With your iPad connected to your iTunes-equipped computer, click the device listing to view the iPad window.

2. Click the Apps tab. The Apps page will open.

3. In the File Sharing section of the Apps page, click the Pages app. The app's file window will open (see Figure 7.6).

Figure 7.6

The File Sharing window.

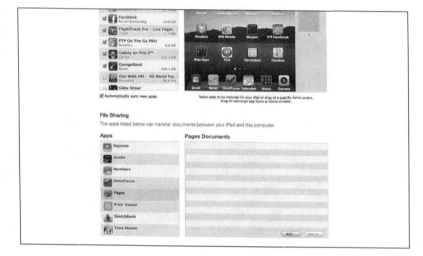

4. Click the Add button. The Open dialog box will appear.

5. Navigate to the file(s) you want to add, click to select, and then click Open. The files will be added to the file window.

6. Click Apply. iTunes will add the files to Pages.

7. In Pages, tap the Add Document button. The Create Document action menu will appear.

8. Tap the Copy from: iTunes button. The Copy from iTunes form will appear (see Figure 7.7).

9. Tap the document you want to import into Pages. The document will be imported to Pages (see Figure 7.8).

10. Tap Done to dismiss any Document Import Warnings. The document will appear in the Documents page.

Now that you understand the basics of creating new files or importing content to Pages, let's start looking at how to use Pages.

Figure 7.7

The Copy from iTunes form.

Figure 7.8

Pulling in a document.

BUMPS ON THE IMPORT ROAD

Sometimes, particularly when importing Microsoft Office documents, iWork apps may bring up an Import Warning about missing fonts. They're not missing; they're just a font the iWork app doesn't use. Typically, the iWork app will substitute another font that's similar in appearance.

Exploring the Pages Interface

Part word processor, part desktop publisher, Pages has plenty of tools and functions to put a document together. This section will detail the tools that make up the Pages app.

When you work with a document in Pages, you will see a clean and simple interface (see Figure 7.9).

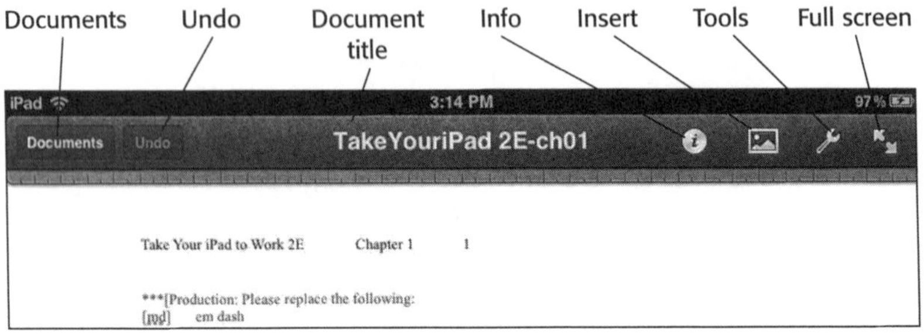

Documents   Undo   Document   Info   Insert   Tools   Full screen

title

Figure 7.9

The Pages interface.

iPad	3:14 PM	97%
Documents Undo	TakeYouriPad 2E-ch01	ℹ 🖼 🔧

Take Your iPad to Work 2E   Chapter 1   1

***[Production: Please replace the following:
[rp]   em dash

This interface seems almost too simple, but it contains a lot of power.

◆ **Documents.** Opens the Documents screen, where documents can be created, opened, and shared.

◆ **Undo.** Undoes the last edit performed in the document.

◆ **Document title.** Shows the file name of the document.

◆ **Info.** Opens the Style, List, and Layout menus, which handle paragraph-level formatting.

◆ **Insert.** Opens the Media, Tables, Charts, and Shapes menus, which enable you to insert photos and other objects into your document.

◆ **Tools.** Accesses the Document Setup screen, as well as Find and Help functions. Controls for edge guides and spell check are here as well.

◆ **Full screen.** Hides this toolbar when tapped.

This is not the end of the tools available in Pages. Tapping within any document will immediately open the Ruler toolbar, shown in Figure 7.10.

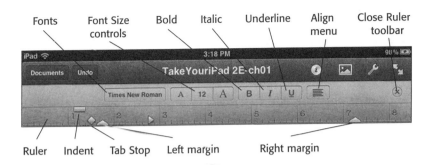

Figure 7.10

The Ruler toolbar.

The Ruler toolbar primarily focuses on the manipulation of text and paragraph styling:

◆ **Fonts.** Applies the selected font to selected text.

◆ **Font Size controls.** Applies the selected size to selected text.

◆ **Bold.** Applies the bold style to selected text.

◆ **Italic.** Applies the italic style to selected text.

◆ **Underline.** Underlines selected text.

◆ **Align menu.** Contains options to align selected paragraphs to left or right margins, centering text, and justified text.

◆ **Close Ruler toolbar.** Hides the Ruler toolbar.

◆ **Ruler.** Enables accurate positioning of text.

◆ **Indent.** Sets position of paragraph indentation.

◆ **Left margin.** Sets position of left margin.

◆ **Tab stop.** Sets position of tabs.

◆ **Right margin.** Sets position of right margin.

Editing Documents

When you work with a Pages document, you will do more than just type in text. You will also need to do what's known as *word processing*, a technology that's been around so long that most users have forgotten what life was like before word processors came along. Two words: typewriters and Wite-Out.

Word processing enables users to edit text at any point in a document. If you make a mistake, you just go back and fix it. If there's a body of text to be moved, you just cut and paste it somewhere else (harkening back to the days when text was literally cut and pasted with scissors and hot wax or paste).

This functionality has been around for PC and Mac users for a long time, but there weren't many powerful tools available on a mobile platform, until Pages.

Navigating Documents

Before learning about word processing with Pages, it's important that you know how to move around within a document.

To scroll within a document, the easiest way is to tap and drag up and down on the screen. If you have a lot of pages to cover, you can also flick up or down to move through the document more quickly. This method is a little less accurate than the tap and drag technique.

If you want to have a higher degree of navigational control, tap and hold the right edge of the document screen to see the visual scrolling tool known as the Navigator (see Figure 7.11).

Figure 7.11

The Navigator.

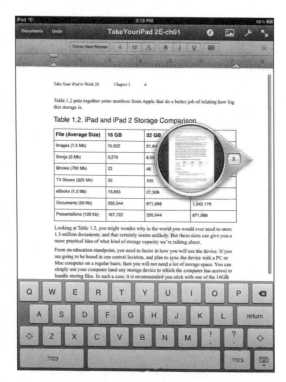

Drag the Navigator up and down the screen until you find the page you want to view. Release the Navigator, and the page will be displayed.

Selecting Text

Of all of the available menus in Pages, the Edit menu is perhaps the most useful. It contains the most helpful commands in Pages.

In the Edit menu, you'll find the ubiquitous Cut, Copy, and Paste functions, as well as the Copy Style, Replace, and Definition commands.

To use the Edit menu, you first need to select some text in the document. There are two ways to select text in Pages:

◆ Double-tap will select a single word in the document.

◆ Triple-tap will select a paragraph in the document.

When you perform one of these tapping actions, the Edit menu will also appear adjacent to the selected text. But the Edit menu changes with the amount of text selected. For instance, as you can see in Figure 7.12, when a single word is selected, more commands are available.

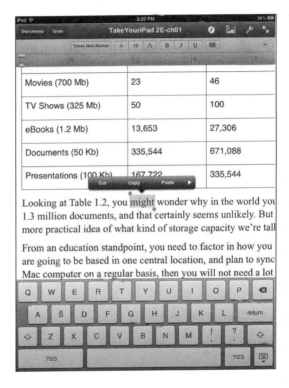

Figure 7.12

The Edit menu for a selected word.

When more than one word is selected, such as when you triple-tap to select a paragraph, another command, Style, is made available (see Figure 7.13).

You can select more than just a single word or an entire paragraph. Double- or triple-tap to select text in the document; then carefully tap and drag one of the blue selection handles to position the selection to a new location. The useful thing about changing a selection is that while you'd think you would need to zoom into the document to see the selected text better, dragging a selection handle actually brings up a magnification tool to assist you in placing the handle accurately (see Figure 7.14).

Figure 7.13

The Edit menu for multiple words.

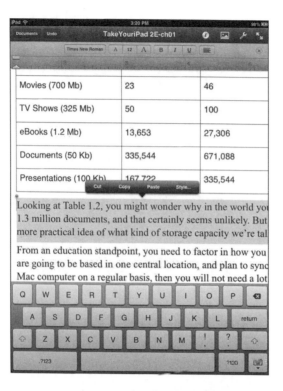

Figure 7.14

Moving a selection handle.

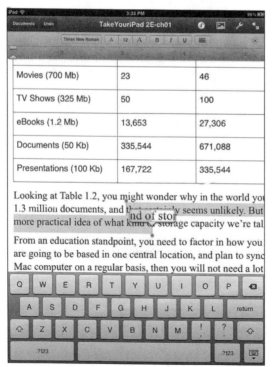

After the text is properly selected, you can use the Edit menu command to manipulate text, such as cutting and pasting.

To manipulate text:

1. In an open Pages document, select a passage of text.
2. On the Edit menu, tap Cut.
3. Long-press the destination point for the cut text in the document. The Edit menu will reappear.
4. Tap Paste. The cut text appears in the new spot.

To create copies of text:

1. To copy text, select the text.
2. On the Edit menu, tap Copy.
3. Long-press the destination point for the cut text in the document. The Edit menu will reappear.
4. On the Edit menu, tap Paste. A copy of the text appears in the new spot.

Defining Words

Another useful tool in the Edit menu is the Definition tool. If you select a single word, you can have Pages define that word for you.

To define a word:

1. Double-tap a word to select it.
2. On the Edit menu, tap the more arrow. Additional tools will appear.
3. Tap Define. A Dictionary pop-over will appear with a definition of the word (see Figure 7.15).

Spell-Checking Your Work

As you type words into Pages, you may notice that every once in a while a suggested word will appear underneath the word you are typing. This word is what Pages thinks is the correct spelling of what you're typing. Most of the time, this is a useful suggestion, and when you tap the Spacebar, the word you typed will be replaced with the correctly spelled word.

If you want to ignore this suggestion, tap the X icon in the suggested word to remove it.

When you import existing documents, you may find existing misspelled words. Fixing these words, indicated by a red dashed underline, is quick and painless. Tap the word, and a menu of one or more alternatives will appear (see Figure 7.16).

Tap the correct word, and Pages will replace the misspelled word.

Figure 7.15

Defining the iPad.

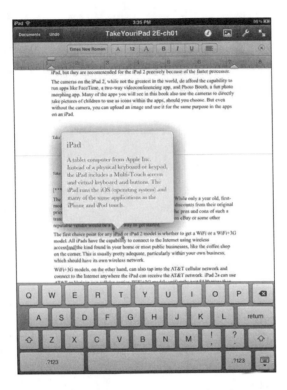

Figure 7.16

Getting the spelling right.

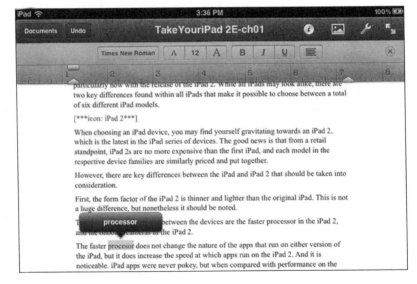

Applying Styles

Formatting a document is essential in today's world. No longer are readers content to see a page with plain-looking letters. Even a large fiction novel, which is nothing but words, has been formatted with the font that the publisher feels is most attractive and at the same time most legible.

Pages has three levels of formatting: characters, paragraphs, and pages.

When you format these items, you apply new fonts, change font sizes and colors, set tab stops, indent lengths, and page margins—and that's just for starters.

The following two examples will guide you through the basics of formatting at the character and paragraph levels.

To format characters in a document:

1. In an open Pages document, select a passage of text.

2. Tap the Italics button. The text will appear in an italicized font.

3. With the text selected, tap the Info icon. The Info action menu will appear (see Figure 7.17).

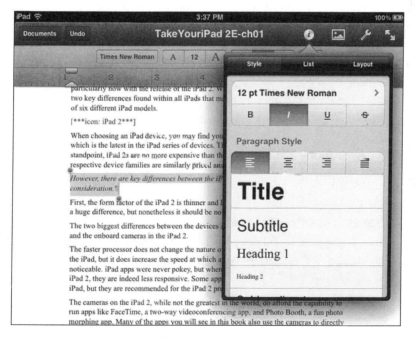

Figure 7.17
The Info action menu.

4. Tap the font information field at the top of the action menu. The Text Options action menu will appear, shown in Figure 7.18.

Figure 7.18

The Text Options action menu.

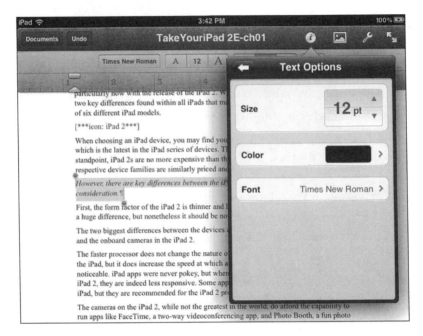

5. Tap the Size control up or down to select a new size.

6. Tap the Color control. The Text Color action menu will appear.

7. Tap a desired color. The selected color will be represented by a check mark.

8. Tap the Back button to return to the Text Options menu.

9. Tap the Font control. The Fonts action menu will appear (see Figure 7.19).

10. Tap the desired font. The selected font will be represented by a check mark.

WORKING WITH MORE FONT OPTIONS

In the Fonts action menu, many of the fonts have a blue options icon. Tap the icon to find more variants of the font from which to choose.

---

11. Tap the Back button to return to the Text Options menu.

12. Tap the Info icon to see the results of your setting changes.

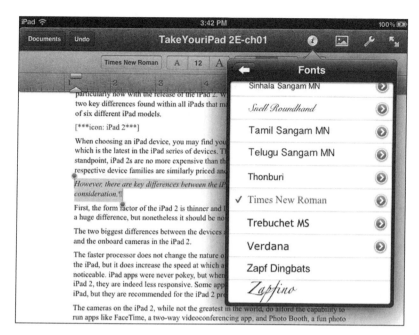

Figure 7.19

The Fonts action menu.

To restyle a paragraphs:

1. Triple-tap a paragraph to select it.
2. Tap the Paragraph styles button on the Rulers toolbar. The Styles action menu will appear.
3. Tap the desired style. The selected style will be represented by a check mark.
4. Tap the Paragraph styles button to see the results of the changes.

ANOTHER PATH TO PARAGRAPH STYLING

You can also tap the Info icon and change styles in the Style window of the Info action menu.

If a paragraph or word has a specific style you would like to apply elsewhere in your document, you don't have to reformat text all day. Just copy the style you want and paste it somewhere else.

To copy a specific style to a new document:

1. Select the text with the style you want to duplicate. The Edit menu will appear.

2. Tap the Copy Style option. (If a single word has been selected, tap the More option to make this option available.) The style will be copied.

3. Select a new passage of text. The Edit menu will appear.

4. Tap the More option.

5. Tap Paste Style. The style will be applied to the selected text.

Making Lists

Lists in documents are commonplace. Two major types of lists include numbered lists and bulleted lists.

To create a list in Pages:

1. Type a four- to five-item list, pressing Enter after each item.

2. Select the entire list.

3. Tap the Info icon. The Info action menu will appear.

4. Tap the List option. The List page will appear.

5. Tap any of the available options. The selected option will be denoted by a check mark.

6. Tap the right indent control to indent the list by an increased amount

7. Tap the Info icon to see the results of the changes.

Working with Objects

In the early days of electronic document creation, there was text. That was it. Things got rather exciting when italic text came on the scene. Underlining caused a huge ruckus. But then things sort of calmed down.

That lasted for a few years (eons in computer time), until someone got the idea to put real-time artwork in documents. Today, if you don't have graphics in your document, people look at you funny.

Pages enables you to insert artwork quickly and easily into your document.

To insert artwork:

1. In an open Pages document, tap the Insert icon. The Insert action menu will appear (see Figure 7.20).

2. Tap the Photo Album where your image is stored. The contents of the album will be displayed.

3. Tap the desired image. The image will be inserted in the document.

4. Tap the Insert icon to see the results of the changes.

In the document, the image appears surrounded by a box comprised of blue circles (see Figure 7.21). These are the graphic handles.

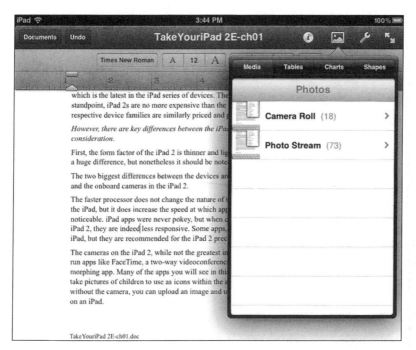

Figure 7.20

The Insert action menu's Media page.

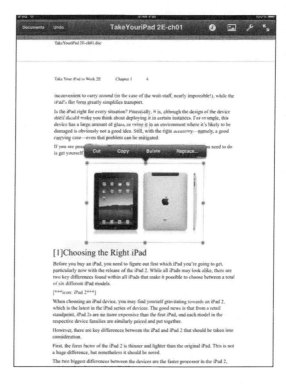

Figure 7.21

An inserted image, ready for placement.

To size and move the image in your document:

1. Tap and hold the left-center handle. Drag the handle to the right to make the image smaller. You can repeat this action with any of the graphic handles, sizing the image as you desire.

2. Tap and drag the image across the screen. The image will move where you point it.

You can also rotate any image by using the special rotating gesture. Tap an image to select it. Using two fingers as if rotating a dial or knob, slowly rotate the image until you get it to the angle you want. Release the image and tap anywhere else on the screen to see the results, as seen in Figure 7.22.

Figure 7.22

It's a topsy-turvy world.

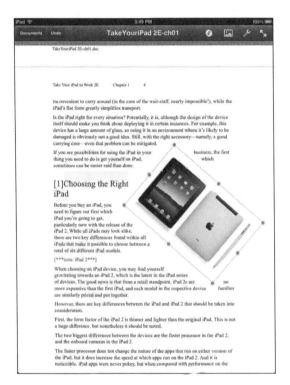

You can also insert tables into a Pages document. More complete than lists, tables provide a fast, compact way of getting information across to readers.

To create a table in pages:

1. In an open Page document, tap the point where you want to insert the table.

2. Tap the Insert icon. The Insert action menu will appear.

3. Tap the Tables button. The Tables window will appear (see Figure 7.23).

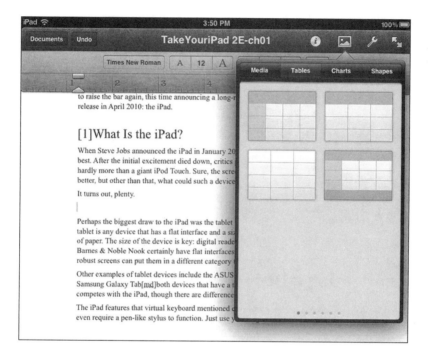

Figure 7.23

Begin building a table.

4. Flick to the left and right to find a table design that appeals to you.

5. Tap the option you want to use. A placeholder table will appear in the document (see Figure 7.24).

6. To add rows to a table, tap the row handle. A number control will appear.

7. Tap the number control up or down to set the number of desired rows.

8. Repeat to add columns, using the column handle.

9. To resize a table, tap and drag a table handle to bring the table to the size you want.

10. Double-tap any cell to insert text.

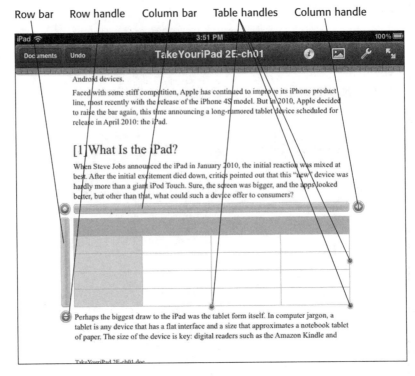

Row bar   Row handle   Column bar   Table handles   Column handle

Figure 7.24

A placeholder table.

Configuring a Document

Most documents you will create will be configured for letter-sized paper, with standard margins. If you need to create a different type of document, it's a simple process to set that up.

To create a different type of document:

1. Tap the Tools icon in Pages. The Tools action menu will appear.
2. Tap the Document Setup option. The Document Setup screen will appear (see Figure 7.25).
3. Tap and drag any of the margin handles to resize the margins.
4. Tap the folded corner. The page will flip up to reveal the Paper Size options (see Figure 7.26).
5. Tap the size option you want. The page will flip back down, and the new option will be displayed.
6. Tap Done. The main Pages screen will appear with the new options in place.

Figure 7.25

The Document Setup screen.

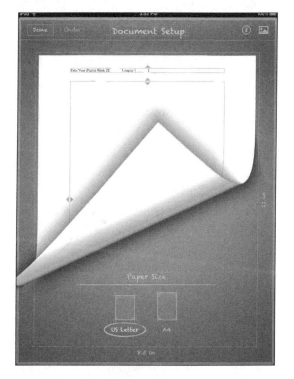

Figure 7.26

Viewing the Paper Size options.

> **PERSISTENT OBJECTS**
>
> If you want to insert an image (such as a corporate logo) or other object on every page of your document, tap the Object icon in the Document Setup screen to insert the object on the page just as you would an individual page.

Sharing Pages Documents

You may have wondered where the option is to save your work. You might be surprised, and even alarmed, to learn that Pages doesn't have a button or control for you to save a document.

There is nothing to worry about. Pages, and the other iWork apps, will automatically save your work as you go. This enables you to click the Home button to leave the Pages app at any time, or just click the Sleep/Wake button to put down the iPad and come back to it later.

Instead of saving a document, Pages gives you the option to share your document. This can be done through one of three options:

◆ **Send via Mail.** The document will be sent to a specified recipient via the Mail app.

◆ **Share via iWork.com.** The document will be sent to Apple's iWork.com site, where you and other permitted users can access the document and collaborate on it online.

◆ **Export.** The document will be sent back to your iTunes computer so it can be saved there.

Of the three options, it is likely you will use the Export option most, as saving your work on a local computer is a more typical function for a business.

To export your document:

1. When ready to export a document, tap the Documents button. The Documents screen will open.
2. Tap the Edit button. The Documents screen will shift to Edit mode.
3. Tap the document you want to export. The document will be selected.
4. Tap the Share icon. The Share action menu will appear.
5. Tap the Copy to: iTunes option. The Choose Format form will appear (see Figure 7.27).

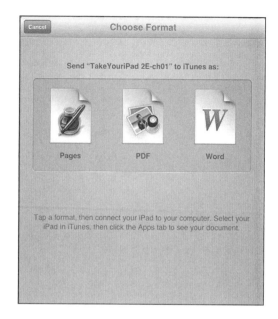

Figure 7.27

The Choose Format form.

6. Tap the format you want to use. The document will be exported.

7. Sync your iPad.

8. Click the device listing in iTunes and then click the Apps tab. The Apps page will open.

9. In the File Sharing section of the Apps page, click the Pages app. The app's file window will open.

10. Click the file you exported. The file will be selected.

11. Click the Save to button. A Save dialog box will open.

12. Save the file to the desired location.

Conclusion

This introduction to Pages and its many functions covered a lot of material, but there is more to the iWork suite than just using a word processor.

Chapter 8, "Get to iWork: Analyzing with Numbers" will focus on the spreadsheet app for iWork, the Numbers app.

Chapter 8

Get to iWork:
Analyzing with Numbers

- ◆ A Spreadsheet Primer
- ◆ Exploring the Numbers Interface
- ◆ Editing Spreadsheets
- ◆ Adding Charts
- ◆ Conclusion

ccountants aren't the only ones using spreadsheets these days. With online banking, online trading, and online loan applications available to the average consumer, more and more people are using spreadsheets to track their rapidly changing finances.

This new demand, coupled with the already present needs of the business world for clearer, faster reporting, requires a spreadsheet program that is pretty powerful. Numbers, the iWork spreadsheet app, delivers the spreadsheet power you need from your iPad. This app delivers many of the same functions found in Microsoft Excel or Numbers on OS X, and it maintains interoperability with these applications and the rest of the iWork suite.

In this chapter, you will learn how to:

◆ Use the basic interface of spreadsheets and Numbers

◆ Build basic spreadsheets

◆ Format data in Numbers

CREATING AND SHARING SPREADSHEETS

All of the iWork apps share the same file management tools, so creating, importing, and sharing spreadsheets in Numbers is functionally identical to performing these actions in Pages and Keynote. Refer to the appropriate sections in Chapter 7, "Get to iWork: Documenting with Pages," for details on these actions.

A Spreadsheet Primer

You have likely used a spreadsheet before at one time or another. Many spreadsheet users, however, often do not create or modify the basic workings of the spreadsheets they use. They just plug in the numbers and print the assigned reports like they're supposed to.

There comes a time in computer users' lives when they need to create a spreadsheet for themselves. At that time, it's a good idea to know how these spreadsheet doodads work.

It all comes down, more or less, to cells. A familiar type of cell is the basic building block of your body. There are many different types of cells: muscle cells, skin cells, liver cells—the list goes on and on. But no matter what kind of cell you look at, they all have pretty much the same basic structure: nucleus, plasma, cell wall, mitochondria, and other hard-to-pronounce components. Even though they have the same overall structure, cells can have vastly different jobs because of the specialized way they have been put together.

The same theory applies to spreadsheet cells. They are all rectangular, and they all can contain data. But each cell in a spreadsheet can have a different task. One cell may sit empty, filled in with an attractive shade of purple. Another cell may contain the number 42. Still another may contain a formula that refers to the number 42 in another cell and displays something completely different.

Cells are all the same, but they can be used in many different ways.

Cells are typically positioned and referred to in rows and columns. By universal convention, spreadsheet rows are denoted with numbers, and columns are denoted with letters. Because spreadsheets sometimes need more than 26 columns, the columns after the letter Z move to a two-letter notation (AA, AB, AC, and so on).

You can identify cells by their row and column position in the spreadsheet. The cell that's five rows down and three columns across is identified as cell C5, as seen in Figure 8.1.

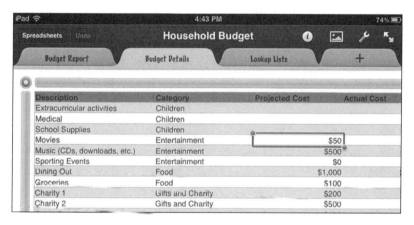

Figure 8.1

A selected cell.

Multiple cells are called *ranges*. A selection box denotes a selected range of cells. The coordinates of a range include the cell in the upper-left corner of the range and the cell in the lower-right corner of the range. Thus, you would reference the range selected in Figure 8.2 as A5:E7.

Numbers is unique among spreadsheet applications because it does not usually deal with cell data in a coordinate fashion, like Microsoft Excel. Instead, data is contained within a table format, which means that on a given sheet within a spreadsheet, Numbers only manipulates data as a table.

Now you've got the basics down. As you progress through the chapter, you will start to see how the cells of a spreadsheet fit together to make a body of data.

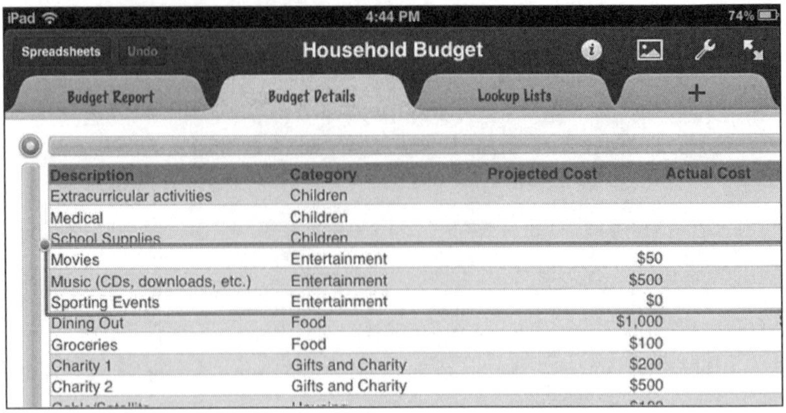

Figure 8.2

A Numbers range.

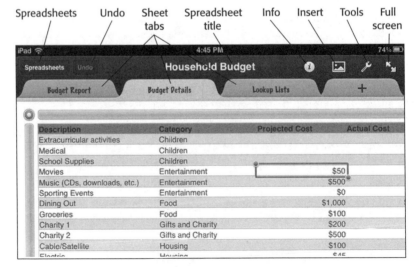

Exploring the Numbers Interface

When you start cooking, you want to have all of your ingredients out on the counter before you begin. Nothing is so frustrating as having to stop to find the jar of saffron when your hands are covered in flour. Even better, have your ingredients chopped, cut, and measured before you begin for true speed.

The same concept applies when building a spreadsheet. You need to have all of your tools before you begin. In this section, the Numbers interface will be examined.

When you open a spreadsheet in Numbers, you will see a clean and simple interface (see Figure 8.3).

Figure 8.3

The Numbers interface.

This interface seems almost too simple, but it contains a lot of power.

◆ **Spreadsheets.** Opens the Spreadsheets screen, where spreadsheets can be created, opened, and shared.

◆ **Undo.** Undoes the last edit performed in the spreadsheet.

◆ **Spreadsheet title.** Shows the file name of the spreadsheet.

◆ **Info.** Opens the Table, Headers, Cells, and Format menus, which handle cell and table formatting.

◆ **Insert.** Inserts photos and other objects into your spreadsheet by using the Media, Tables, Charts, and Shapes menus.

◆ **Tools.** Accesses the Print, Find, and Help functions. The controls for edge guides and spell check are here as well.

◆ **Full Screen.** When tapped, hides this toolbar and enters the full-screen mode, which can display summary data.

◆ **Sheet tabs.** Opens any single sheet within the spreadsheet document.

There are more tools available in Numbers. Double-tapping within any cell will immediately open what Apple refers to as an "intelligent keyboard" to edit cell data, as shown in Figure 8.4.

Number keyboard   Date & Time keyboard   Text keyboard   Formula and Functions keyboard   Cell value

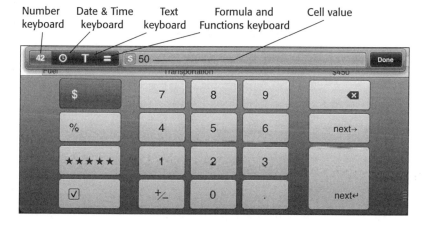

Figure 8.4
The Number keyboard.

The keyboard will adjust to the type of data found in the cell. Double-tapping a cell with text, for instance, will bring up the Text keyboard shown in Figure 8.5.

Figure 8.5

*The Text
keyboard.*

By tapping on any of the keyboard control buttons, you can switch to a
new keyboard, such as the Date & Time keyboard or the Formula and
Functions keyboard.

The Full Screen view does more than hide the toolbar and keyboard. Tap
the Full Screen icon, and these elements will indeed be hidden, but if
you long-press a cell you will see a summary window for the data in the
cell pop up. Drag across a range of cells, and you will see a summary of
the data in that range, as seen in Figure 8.6.

Figure 8.6

*A summary of a
data range.*

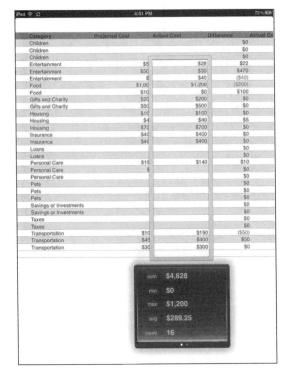

Swipe the summary window to the left, and you will see a graph of the same data, generated on the fly.

Editing Spreadsheets

When you work with Numbers spreadsheets, you will notice that many of the tools resemble the table editing tools in the Pages app. That's because Numbers organizes data in tables, which is a little different from the traditional spreadsheet model. Fortunately, this model makes a lot of sense for a device where you're using a touch screen and virtual keyboards.

Navigating Spreadsheets

Before learning about spreadsheet work, it's important that you know how to move around within a spreadsheet.

To scroll within an individual sheet, the easiest way is to tap and drag up and down the screen. If you have a lot of data rows to cover, you can also flick up or down to move through the sheet more quickly. This method is a little less accurate than the tap-and-drag technique. Most sheets don't contain that much data, so this is usually all that is going to be needed.

Spreadsheets can contain any number of sheets. To get from sheet to sheet, simply tap the sheet's tab on top of the Numbers screen. If a tab is not visible, tap and drag (or flick) the tabs left or right to scroll to the proper tab.

If you need to add a sheet to the spreadsheet, scroll to the far right of the tabs and tap the Add Sheet tab, denoted by a "+" sign. A blank sheet called Sheet 1 will be added to the end of the sheet tab row.

To rename the new sheet, quickly double-tap the sheet label in the tab. A cursor and keyboard will appear, enabling you to rename the sheet.

To move the sheet, tap and drag the tab across the tab row to the new location and release.

If you want to remove a sheet, you will need to perform a slightly modified gesture. Tap the tab to be deleted once, pause, and then tap again. The Edit menu will appear. Tap the Delete option, and the sheet will be removed.

Manipulating Content

Like all iWork apps, replicating or moving content around can be done with the Edit menu, using the Cut, Copy, and Paste functions. In Numbers, you can also select cells or a range of cells to move them.

To use the Edit menu, you need to select cells in a table first. This is done by tapping on a cell once. To select a range of cells, tap and drag one of the cell selection handles so the selection box encompasses the cells you want.

To see the Edit menu, you need to tap once more on the selected cell or cell range. This will bring up the Edit menu shown in Figure 8.7.

Figure 8.7

The Edit menu in Numbers.

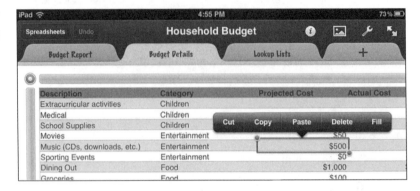

If you want to select content within a cell and access the Edit menu, double-tap the cell to bring up its associated keyboard. Then double-tap the value of the cell in the keyboard to see its Edit menu, as seen in Figure 8.8.

Figure 8.8

A Value's Edit menu.

Table rows and columns can also be changed with the Edit menu. Tap a cell in a table to see the table bars. To select an entire row, tap the row bar next to the row you want to select. Then tap the row handle once to see the row's Edit menu (see Figure 8.9).

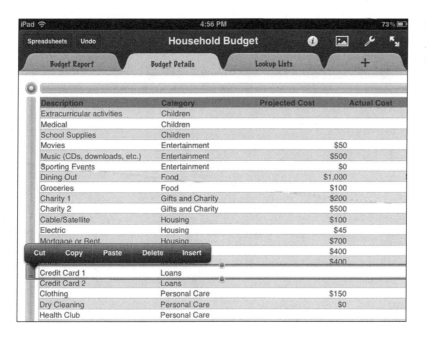

Figure 8.9

A row's Edit menu.

Once the cell, value, row, or column is properly selected, you can use the Edit menu command to cut and paste these items, just as you would in any iWork app.

Numbers also has an even easier way to move content around—just tap and drag.

To move content the easy way:

1. In an open Numbers spreadsheet, tap a single cell once to select it.

2. Long-press the cell and drag it to a new location in the table.

3. Release the cell. The cell appears in its new spot.

Any selected item can be moved this way. The trick, which takes a little practice, is not to double-tap the item. Select it, pause, and then long-press the object or its handle if it's a row or column to start moving it.

Table handles can be used to add rows or columns quickly. Tap and drag the row handle down the screen, and you will add rows to the table, as seen in Figure 8.10.

Figure 8.10

Resizing a Numbers table adds rows or columns to the table.

Working with Cell Content

There is no one way to display data values. One dataset may project a significant value to the hundredths place, while another projects it to the thousandths place.

Even in the English-speaking cultures, numbers carry different names. In the United States, citizens refer to 1,000,000,000 as a billion. In the United Kingdom, a billion is officially 1,000,000,000,000,000,000. Advocates of the Queen's English refer to this as yet another example of the insidious U.S. corruption of the English language. Quite.

Within a spreadsheet, it may not be obvious to users what is a data value and what is text. Is that 1999 indicative of a year, one short of 2,000 items, or the brand-name of a new company?

In Numbers, the easier way to tell is to double-tap the cell to see which keyboard appears. You can also use the keyboard to reformat a cell's value.

To reformat a cell:

1. In an open Numbers spreadsheet, double-tap a numeric cell once to select it. The Number keyboard will appear.
2. Tap the Currency button. The format for the cell will change to currency, which will be reflected in the keyboard and in the cell.

If you want to get more refined formatting, or you need to format a range of cells, you can use the Info action menu to format the data.

To format the data with the Info action menu:

1. In an open Numbers spreadsheet, select a range of cells.

2. Tap the Info icon. The Info action menu will appear (see Figure 8.11).

Figure 8.11

The Info action menu in Numbers.

3. Tap the Format button to open the Format window.

4. Tap the Currency option control. The Currency Options window of the action menu will appear (see Figure 8.12).

5. Tap the Currency option. The Currency Symbol window will appear.

6. Tap the desired currency symbol option. The format will be applied.

Using the Info action menu, you can format the values of a cell and the look and feel of the cells as well.

To format the value of a cell or the look and feel:

1. In an open Numbers spreadsheet, select a range of cells.

2. Tap the Info icon. The Info action menu will appear.

3. Tap the Cells button to open the Cells window (see Figure 8.13).

Figure 8.12

Detailing the currency format.

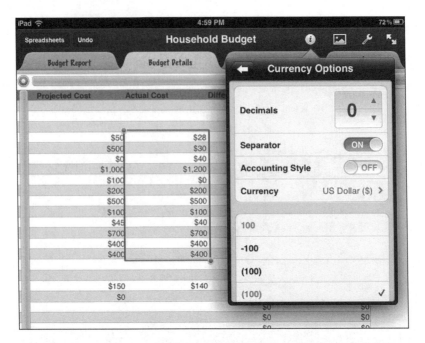

Figure 8.13

Formatting cells.

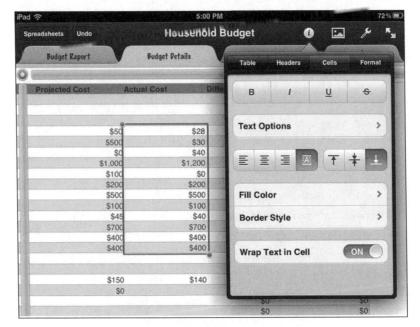

4. Tap the Fill Color option. The Fill Color window will appear.

5. Tap the desired color. The selected color will be denoted by a check mark and applied to the selected range in the table.

Creating Formulas

A key function of any spreadsheet app is performing calculations on your data. Otherwise, your spreadsheet will be nothing more than a nice-looking collection of words and numbers.

Numbers has hundreds of functions to apply to your data, ranging from accounting to engineering to trigonometric. Whichever one you use, it's not hard to use these functions to create simple or advanced formulas for your work.

To create a formula (in this case, a straightforward SUM function):

1. In an open Numbers spreadsheet, double-tap the cell to which you want to add the formula. The keyboard for the cell will appear.

2. Tap the Formulas and Function control. The Formulas and Functions keyboard will appear (see Figure 8.14).

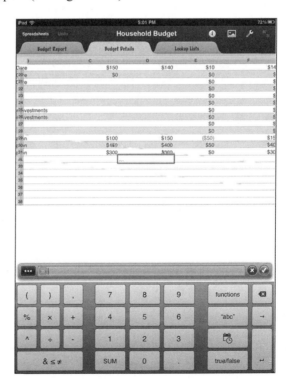

Figure 8.14

Prepping to add a formula.

LEARN YOUR FUNCTIONS

If you want to learn more about the functions in Numbers, tap the functions key on the Formulas and Functions keyboard. Navigate to the function you want to learn and click the blue advanced icon next to the listing to reveal a detailed explanation of the function's purpose and how to implement it.

3. Tap the SUM key. The function will be inserted with Numbers guessing the data range you want summed.

4. To change the range to be summed, tap and drag the range handles to encompass the correct range.

5. Tap the green check mark to submit the formula to the cell. The value of the formula will be displayed in the cell.

Adding Charts

They say a picture is worth a thousand words, and rarely is that more true than when working with a bunch of data. Envisioning the impact of rows and rows of information can be challenging, to say the least.

To help convey the meaning behind the numbers, spreadsheet applications like Numbers use charts to display data in a format that enables users to grasp the data immediately.

To create a chart:

1. In an open Numbers spreadsheet, tap the Insert icon. The Insert action menu will appear.

2. Tap the Charts button. The Charts window will appear.

3. Tap the chart type you want to use. A placeholder chart will appear on the sheet (see Figure 8.15).

4. Tap the placeholder chart. The chart will be readied for adding references.

5. Tap the table from which to pull the chart data.

6. Select the range of data to chart.

7. Tap Done. The new chart will be configured with the data.

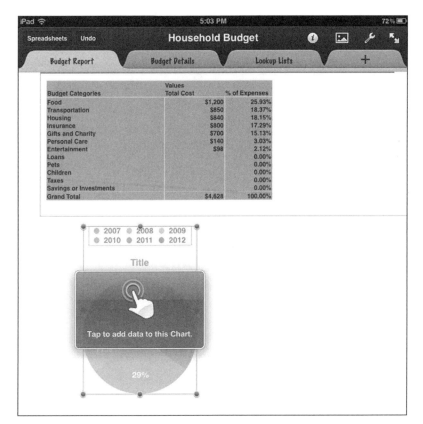

Figure 8.15
A placeholder chart.

Conclusion

Numbers is an effective tool for the creation and management of data spreadsheets for your company. This chapter reviewed many of the basic tools of Numbers, and as you explore this application in your continued use of the iPad, you will find it to be a very powerful tool in the office.

Chapter 9, "Get to iWork: Presenting with Keynote," will review the iWork app that will enable you to present your ideas to the world in new and attractive ways: Keynote.

Chapter 9

Get to iWork:
Presenting with Keynote

◆ Exploring the Keynote Interface
◆ Creating a Presentation
◆ Conclusion

Some people are good at presentations. They stand up in front of everyone else and mesmerize us with their logic, charisma, and charm. No notes, no slides—just the person and his or her vision.

The rest of us may require a little assistance. In a public speech, the power of the speaker's words is the only thing that can help people remember the speaker's message. Have you ever noticed how politicians always work some sort of catch phrase into their speeches? They are not trying to be trite—they're trying to give their audiences something to remember, because our memory and sense of hearing do not always work well together.

In a private business setting, where a lot of detail may be required, entirely verbal presentations would be impossible for others to remember later. So speakers have two choices: reduce the presentation to its mere essence to get the overall points across, or rely on some other form of communication to convey the finer points of the message to the audience.

Since many people fear public speaking second only to death, most would rather not become fiery orators in order to get their points across. Which leaves the second option: Use another way to communicate. We simply remember things better if we have seen them with our own eyes.

Thus, the corporate slide show was born.

It started off with placards at first, showing charts created by people whose job was to do nothing but show the charts. Overheads were used next, lending presenters the ability to support their points on the fly. Then came slides, which added color and speed to presentations. Finally, the slides were created directly on a computer and projected from there, as well.

Which brings us to the component in iWork that gets this job done for you: Keynote.

In this chapter, you will:

◆ Explore the Keynote interface
◆ Learn how to organize ideas for a presentation
◆ Create a Keynote presentation

CREATING AND SHARING PRESENTATIONS

All of the iWork apps share the same file management tools, so creating, importing, and sharing presentations in Keynote is functionally identical to performing these actions in Pages and Numbers. Refer to the appropriate sections in Chapter 7, "Get to iWork: Documenting with Pages," for details on these actions.

Exploring the Keynote Interface

The makers of Keynote have loaded it with quite a few interesting tools that help you build great-looking presentations with ease. This is readily apparent when looking at the Keynote interface (see Figure 9.1).

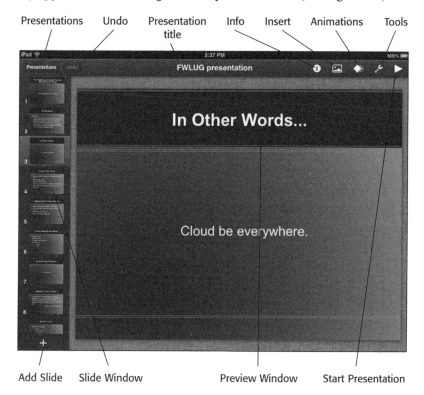

Figure 9.1

The Keynote interface.

While it shares some similarities with the other iWork apps, Keynote is immediately different from Pages and Numbers in that there is only one orientation available: horizontal. You can pivot your iPad all you want, but Keynote will always stay in this orientation, since that's the most optimal for Keynote to use.

The main tools that Keynote uses are:

◆ **Presentations.** Opens the Presentations screen, where presentations can be created, opened, and shared.

◆ **Undo.** Undoes the last edit performed in the presentation.

◆ **Presentation title.** Shows the file name of the presentation.

◆ **Info.** Opens the Style, Text, and Arrange menus, which handle formatting for slide text.

- **Insert.** Inserts photos and other objects into your presentation by using the Media, Tables, Charts, and Shapes menus.
- **Animations.** Starts the Animations tool to create slide transitions.
- **Tools.** Accesses the Find and Help functions. The controls for guides, slide numbering, and spell check are here as well.
- **Start Presentation.** Starts the presentation when tapped,.
- **Add Slide.** Adds slides based on the current theme or a blank slide.
- **Slide Window.** Displays slides for your presentation.
- **Preview Window.** Shows the editing and display window for individual slides in your presentation.

Creating a Presentation

After you have figured out what to say, there are two opposing schools of thought as to how to create a new presentation in Keynote:

- Outline your presentation content first and worry about the design later.
- Create a blank design and fill in the text later.

There is no right way to do this, really. Each method has an equal number of pros and cons. It basically comes down to personal preferences. Do you like to organize your text first or your slides first?

If you are new to using Keynote or a similar application, I recommend that you use the "Create a new presentation from scratch" to get things started. It's simple and quick. Plus, it's much easier to build a base of slide design and add content as needed.

To create a presentation from scratch:

1. Tap the Keynote app icon. Keynote will start.
2. Tap Presentations. The Presentations screen will appear.
3. Tap the Add Presentation button. The Add Presentation action menu will appear.
4. Tap the Create Presentation option. A gallery of presentation templates will appear on the Choose a Theme page (see Figure 9.2).
5. Tap the Modern Portfolio option. The template will appear in the Preview window (see Figure 9.3).

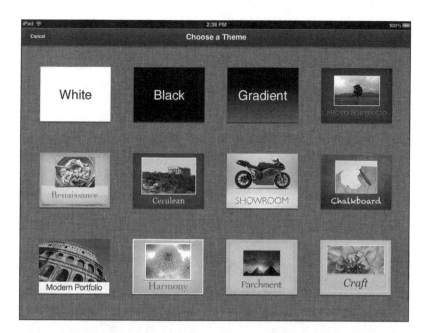

Figure 9.2
Keynote has some nice themes with which to work.

GET MORE THEMES

There are many third-party vendors who have themes for Keynote for iPad available. Some are free, and some come with a small cost. One such vendor is KeynoteStage.com.

Figure 9.3
The first slide in your presentation.

Editing Text

When you create any new slide in Keynote, it will usually have what's known as placeholder text (or dummy content) on the slide to get you started. You can use the position and format of the text that's there and just replace the dummy content with your own. Or you can get creative and move things around.

To replace presentation placeholder text with your own content:

1. In a new slide, double-tap the placeholder text you want to replace. The cursor and keyboard will appear.

2. Type your text in. When finished, tap somewhere else on the slide.

3. To change the position of the text, long-press the text block and drag the text to a new position on the slide (see Figure 9.4).

Figure 9.4

Repositioned text.

4. To change the text format, tap the text block once to select it and then tap the Info icon. The Info action menu will appear.

5. Tap the Text button. The Text action menu will appear.

6. Tap the text information field at the top of the action menu. The Text Options action menu will appear, shown in Figure 9.5.

Figure 9.5

The Text Options action menu.

7. Tap the Size control up or down to select a new size.

8. Tap the Color control. The Text Color action menu will appear.

9. Tap a desired color. The selected color will be represented by a check mark.

10. Tap the Back button to return to the Text Options action menu.

11. Tap the Font control. The Fonts action menu will appear.

12. Tap the desired font. The selected font will be represented by a check mark.

WORKING WITH MORE FONT OPTIONS

In the Fonts action menu, many of the fonts have a blue options icon. Tap the icon to find more variants of the font from which to choose.

13. Tap the Back button to return to the Text Options menu.

14. Tap the Info icon to see the results of your setting changes.

Handling Images

Images are an important part of any presentation. They can be abstract images designed to entertain and intrigue the audience or images of specific things, such as new products.

To insert and manipulate images:

1. In a Keynote slide, tap the Insert icon in the toolbar or tap the Insert icon on any placeholder image. The Insert action menu will appear (see Figure 9.6).

Figure 9.6

The Insert action menu's Media page.

2. Tap the Photo Album where your image is stored. The contents of the album will be displayed.

3. Tap the desired image. The image will be inserted in the document (see Figure 9.7).

In the document, the image appears surrounded by a box comprised of blue circles (refer to Figure 9.7). These are the graphic handles.

To size and move the image in your document:

1. Tap and hold any handle. Drag the handle toward the center of the image to make the image smaller. You can repeat this action with any of the graphic handles, sizing the image as you desire.

2. Tap and drag the image across the screen. The image will move where you point it.

You can also rotate any image using the special rotating gesture. Tap an image to select it. Using two fingers as if rotating a dial or knob, slowly rotate the image until you get it to the angle you want. Release the image and tap anywhere else on the screen to see the results.

Figure 9.7

The new image is auto-sized to the same size as the placeholder text.

Adding Slides

It's easy to build an individual slide, but unless you're planning on just having a single placard behind you on the screen, you might want to add more slides to your presentation.

To add slides to your presentation:

1. In Keynote, tap Add Slide icon. The Add a slide action menu will appear (see Figure 9.8).

2. Tap a slide sample. The slide will be added to the end of your presentation and displayed in the preview window.

3. Repeat these steps as needed.

As you add slides, you may want to edit text and images as you go or continue to add slides now and come back to edit these objects later.

Figure 9.8

The Add a slide action menu.

Changing Slide Order

Sometimes, as you're creating slides on the fly, you may decide to change your mind about the order of your slides. Maybe it's a good idea, for instance, to talk about last fiscal year's results *before* you project the coming fiscal year.

You can change the order of the slides with just a single gesture. In the Slide window, long-press the slide thumbnail you want to move and drag it to the new position in the presentation. Release the thumbnail, and the slide is in the new position.

Another useful presentation trick is hiding an individual slide in your presentation. A good use case for skipping a slide is a presentation you make in three different offices that will share most of the same material, but has at least one slide with unique information about each respective office. You could make three separate presentations for each office, but why waste the storage? Make one slide for each office and then have Keynote skip the two slides that don't apply to the office where you are making your presentation.

To skip slides in a presentation:

1. In Keynote, tap a slide thumbnail to select it and tap it again. The Slide Edit menu will appear (see Figure 9.9).
2. Tap the Skip option. The slide will be compressed to a line, and the Slide window will renumber the "visible" slides (see Figure 9.10).

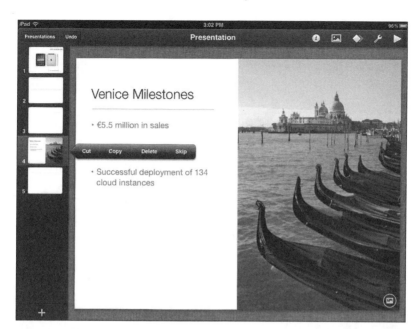

Figure 9.9
The Slide Edit menu.

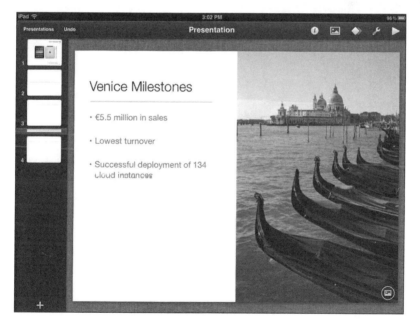

Figure 9.10
Skipped slides aren't deleted, just hidden.

3. To stop a slide from being skipped, tap the skipped slide thumbnail to select it and then tap it again. The Slide Edit menu will appear.

4. Tap the Don't Skip option. The slide will be expanded and made visible again.

Animating Transitions

If you were to show your slides now, they would simply flash from one slide to the next, with no transition between them. What you need is an animation, which will transition your presentation smoothly from one slide to the next.

To animate a transition:

1. In Keynote, tap a slide thumbnail to which you want to add a transition; then tap the animation icon. The Animation tools will appear (see Figure 9.11).

Figure 9.11

The Animation tools.

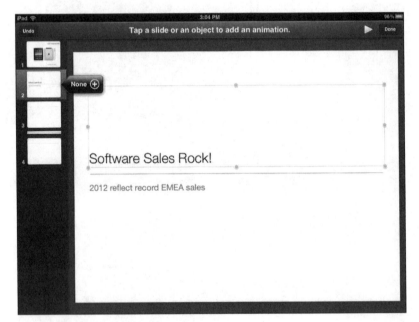

2. To add an animation to the entire slide, tap the plus icon on the slide thumbnail. The Transitions action menu will appear (see Figure 9.12).

3. Tap the transition option you want. The slide thumbnail will be marked with a transition icon, and the animation will be previewed once in the Preview window.

4. To change the animation effect, tap the Options button in the Transitions action menu. The Effects page will appear (see Figure 9.13).

5. Slide the duration slider to adjust the length of time for the animation effect.

6. Dial the orientation tool to change the direction of the animation.

7. Tap Done. The transition will be added to the slide.

Figure 9.12

The Transitions action menu.

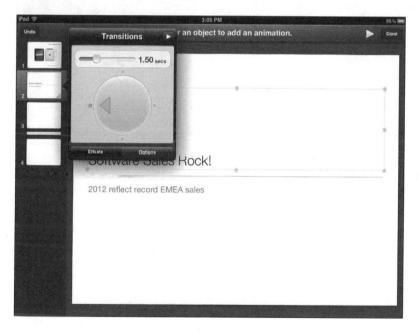

Figure 9.13

The Effects page in the Transitions action menu.

You can also add transitions to items in a slide, such as a list that will display only one item at a time.

To animate items in a list:

1. In Keynote, tap a slide thumbnail to which you want to add a transition; then tap the animation icon. The Animation tools will appear.

2. To add an animation to a list, tap the text block with the list. The Transitions Edit menu will appear (see Figure 9.14).

Figure 9.14

The Transitions Edit menu.

3. Tap the + icon in the Build In option. The Build In action menu will appear (see Figure 9.15).

4. Tap the option you want to use for building in the list items. An animation of the effect will appear in the Preview window.

5. To apply the effect to individual list items, tap the Delivery button in the Build In action menu. The Delivery page will appear (see Figure 9.16).

6. Tap the By Bullet option.

7. Tap Done. The animation will be added to the list items.

Presenting Your Ideas

Presenting your Keynote presentation can be done by either exporting the file to another computer or exporting directly from your iPad, using the optional iPad VGA to Dock adapter, which will allow you to connect the device directly to a slide projector.

Figure 9.15
The Build In action menu.

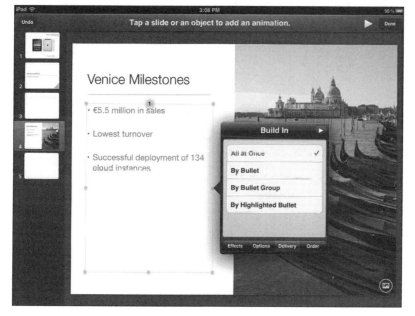

Figure 9.16
The Delivery page in the Build In action menu.

EXPORTING PRESENTATIONS

If you export your presentation as a PowerPoint file, you should note that you will likely lose many of the transitions you built into the file. Exporting to Keynote is a better option, if you can.

To run a presentation, all you have to do is tap the first slide in the presentation and then tap the Start Presentation icon. This will expand the slides to full screen, and as you keep tapping, the presentation will advance through its slides.

Conclusion

In this chapter, you reviewed the wealth of tools contained within the Keynote app. You can create slick-looking presentations in very little time and can present them directly from your iPad with some additional equipment.

In Chapter 10, you will discover how to put all of your ideas on paper by exploring the printer options available from the iPad—even if you don't have a compatible printer.

Chapter 10

From iPad to Paper: Printing

When the iPad was first introduced, many industry watchers immediately noticed the lack of a USB port, and wondered aloud, "How will users be able to print from the iPad?" (There are people who actually get paid to think up questions like this.) Surely, they thought, Apple will provide a utility for wireless printing. But when the iPad was first announced, imagine their surprise when no such utility was available.

It would not be long, though, before third-party vendors would step up to provide solutions that would provide printing functionality from nearly every iPad app that could utilize it. The best of these, to date, is PrintCentral by EuroSmartz.

With the release of iOS 4.2, Apple itself added AirPrint functionality to the iPad (and the later-released iPad 2). AirPrint will seamlessly connect to any AirPrint-compatible printer on your network, without any configuration steps.

In this chapter, you will find out how to:

◆ Print from most apps with AirPrint functionality

◆ Connect to printers on your local network

◆ Connect to printers via 3G access

◆ View and print files on your local PC

◆ Print emails, contacts, and Web pages from your iPad

◆ Mount your iPad as an external drive

Print with AirPrint

If you are fortunate enough to have a printer that's compatible with the AirPrint system, then whenever your iPad is in the same network as such a printer, you can print directly to that printer.

Currently, there are 102 printers that will work with AirPrint, from five major printer manufacturers:

◆ Brother

◆ Canon

◆ EPSON

◆ Hewlett Packard

◆ Lexmark

Over one hundred printers is a lot to choose from, so you should be able to find a printer model that meets your needs and is AirPrint-compatible. If you have one of these printers and it is correctly set up on your network, then printing is very simple.

In most apps, you will find the Print function in the Share action menu—the idea being that users are "sharing" the screen content when they print it. There are exceptions, of course. In the iWorks apps (Pages, Numbers, and Keynote), the Print command is in the Tools action menu, so you may need to look around for the command.

Once you locate the Print command in your app, it's a simple matter to print.

To print:

1. Tap the Print command. The Printer Options action menu will open (see Figure 10.1).

Figure 10.1

The Printer Options action menu.

2. If a printer is not available, tap the Select Printer option. The Printer action menu will open, listing all compatible printers in that network (see Figure 10.2).
3. Tap the printer you want to use. The Printer Options action menu will reappear.
4. Tap Print. The page will be sent to the assigned printer.

Figure 10.2

Viewing available and compatible printers.

> **NOT EXACTLY SPEEDY**
>
> You may note that printing jobs sent from the iPad are a bit slower than the usual print job. That's because much of the work done to prepare the content for the printer is done on the printer, instead of the iPad. That means the printer has to do more work, and a lot more bandwidth is used to send content across the network to the printer.

If you have one of the few printers that doesn't have AirPrint capabilities, don't fret; with PrintCentral, you can print to nearly any printer on your network.

Set Up Printers with PrintCentral

After you install PrintCentral, you may be able to print directly to a printer immediately, if the printer is connected directly to the network.

"Connected directly to a network" is a concept that should be clearly defined. Many users assume that if they can access a printer not connected to their computer, it is therefore "on the network." This is actually a common mistake.

There are two ways of connecting a printer to a network. The first way is to share a local computer, which is a printer connected to someone's machine and their computer allows other users to use it remotely. The advantage of this method is that it enables users to get to older printers that can't be directly connected to the network. The disadvantage is the computer to which the shared printer is attached must be turned on for the printer to be used.

The other method is the direct network connection, where the printer has no connections to any computer, only the network, either through a network cable or WiFi. This method is preferred because the access to the printer is usually better.

PrintCentral enables you to make use of either type of connection, as you will see.

Network Printers

If your printer is directly connected to a network, and your iPad is connected wirelessly to that same network, you may discover PrintCentral has automatically done the configuration for you.

To connect PrintCentral to a networked printer:

1. Tap the PrintCentral app icon. PrintCentral will start with an initial notification dialog.

WHAT BROWSER?

Because few iPad apps, if any, provide options to print, PrintCentral's clever solution is to provide its own tools from which users can print. Need to print a Web page? Don't use Safari; use PrintCentral's browser.

---

2. Tap the option that appeals to you. PrintCentral will open to the Documents screen (see Figure 10.3).

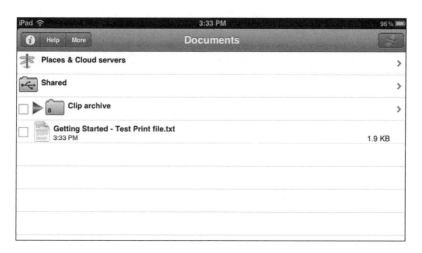

Figure 10.3

The Documents screen in PrintCentral.

3. To check to see if a networked printer has been configured, tap the Getting Started file. The contents of the file will appear in the preview window.

4. Tap the Printer icon. The Print dialog box will open, as seen in Figure 10.4.

Figure 10.4

The Print dialog box.

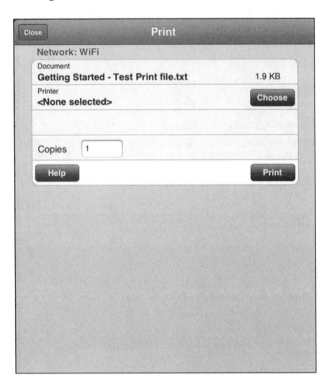

5. Tap Choose. The Printers dialog box will open (see Figure 10.5).

6. If you see the network printer you want to use, tap the printer option. The printer will be added to the Print dialog, and the Printer setup dialog box will appear immediately (see Figure 10.6).

7. Confirm that the printer is connected correctly and tap the Test buttons. A printer test page will print, and you will be asked to confirm the operation.

8. Tap Yes if the test page printed. The network printer is configured correctly.

If the network printer you want to use did not show up within the Printers dialog box, you can still add it.

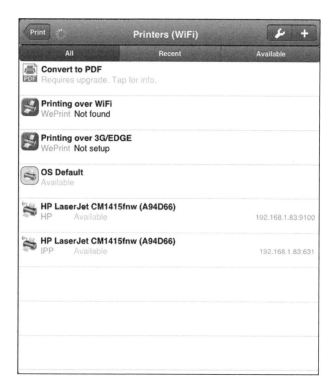

Figure 10.5
The Printers dialog box.

Figure 10.6
The Printer setup dialog box.

To add a network printer:

1. Following the previous steps to get to the Printers dialog box, tap the Add Printer button. The Add Printer dialog box will appear, and you will be reminded to use the WePrint application.

2. Tap Continue to close the reminder dialog and then tap the Printer tab to view the Printer page (see Figure 10.7).

Figure 10.7

The Add Printer dialog box.

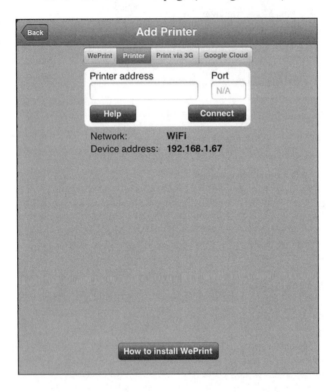

3. Enter the IP address of the printer to which you want to connect.

4. Enter a name for the printer in the Nickname field.

5. Tap Connect. The printer should be found and added to the Printers dialog box.

WePrint for Wi-Fi

Even if you have a networked printer, you can improve the quality of your print jobs by installing WePrint client software on your Mac or PC. WePrint acts as a printer server, routing the print jobs from your iPad to the printer connected to a computer on your network, either locally or via the network.

For users who do not have a network printer, WePrint is a required tool to use PrintCentral, because only through WePrint can your iPad reach the printer. But, if you already have your printer connected to the network, and have completed the steps in the previous section, you may be asking yourself why you would need to use WePrint. The short answer is quality.

When PrintCentral communicates directly with a networked printer, it uses software on your iPad to send a "generic" print job to that printer. This is done to save room on the iPad, because installing the printer software for every possible printer would eat up a lot of iPad storage. So your print jobs will be adequate, but not the best quality.

WePrint takes advantage of the fact that your computer already has the best software to use for your printer—it has to, otherwise you wouldn't be able to print from your PC or Mac. With WePrint, a print job is sent from the iPad to the WePrint software, which then hands off the job to your computer's printer software, which, in turn, sends it to the printer in the best format.

This may sound convoluted, but unless your network is under a very heavy traffic load, print jobs from the iPad via WePrint take very little extra time. Best of all, the WePrint software is free to download and install from http://mobile.eurosmartz.com/downloads/downloads_index.html.

Installing WePrint is no different than installing any other Windows or OS X application. You will be asked, during installation, if you want to allow WePrint to communicate outside of your computer's firewall. You will need to say yes; otherwise, your iPad will be blocked from handing off print jobs to WePrint.

After WePrint is installed and running on your computer, make a note of the Server Address and Port information shown on the Status page of the WePrint application (see Figure 10.8). You will need this information to configure the printer in PrintCentral.

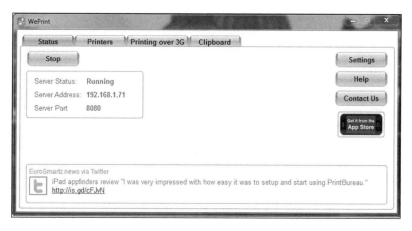

Figure 10.8

The WePrint application.

To use WePrint to connect to a printer:

1. In the Printers dialog box, tap the Printing over WiFi option. The Add Printer dialog box will appear, and you will be reminded to use the WePrint application.

2. Tap Continue to close the reminder dialog.

3. Enter the IP address of the WePrint Server to which you want to connect.

4. Enter a name for the server in the Nickname field.

5. Tap Connect. All printers on the WePrint computer should be found and added to the Printers dialog box.

WePrint for 3G/EDGE

Another great advantage of using PrintCentral is the capability to print documents from a cellular network to a printer that your WePrint computer can access.

The way this works is pretty ingenious. Since outside traffic into your home or school network is usually not a good idea due to security concerns, PrintCentral will email the print job to a specified email address. Every few minutes (you can specify how often), WePrint will check your email account for print job messages from your iPad. If it finds one, it will then send the job to your printer.

EuroSmartz recommends that you use a Gmail account, since PrintCentral and WePrint are each configured to handle that. However, you can use any other type of email account if you have the settings.

To connect to a printer via a cellular connection:

1. In WePrint, click the Printing over 3G tab. The Remote printing via proxy page will open.

2. Click the Settings button. The Preferences dialog will open to the Print via Proxy page (see Figure 10.9).

3. Click the Remote printing via Email/WebDAV server option. The configuration fields will appear.

4. Enter the information for the email account you want to use.

SEPARATE ADDRESS?

EuroSmartz recommends you obtain a separate account for receiving print jobs from PrintCentral. This is a choice point for you: If you don't plan on printing a lot of documents over the 3G connection, then just use an email account you already have.

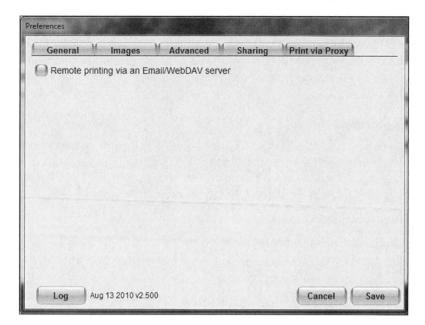

Figure 10.9

The Print via Proxy page.

5. Set the interval you want WePrint to check the email account for print jobs.

6. Click Test. If the login information is correct, you will see a success notice.

7. In the Printers dialog box, tap the Printing over 3G/EDGE option. The Add Printer dialog box will appear, and you will be reminded to use the WePrint application.

8. Tap Continue to close the reminder dialog.

9. Enter the account information for the email account you want to use.

10. Tap Connect. All printers on the WePrint computer should be found and added to the Printers dialog box.

Printing

Once you have the printer configuration set, you can now start printing. As mentioned earlier in this chapter, PrintCentral does not enable printing in existing iPad apps. Instead, it duplicates the functions of some of the more useful apps and lets you print content from PrintCentral.

Files

You have a lot of files in your work that may need printing at any given time. Some of them will be on your iPad, and some will be on your computer. With some easy configuration, you can use PrintCentral to handle them all.

Local Files

When you use PrintCentral to print a file, it will print documents to which PrintCentral has access. In the "File Sharing" section, we'll discuss the best way to give PrintCentral access to your files, but for now, let's walk through the basics of file printing in PrintCentral.

To print from PrintCentral:

1. In PrintCentral, tap the Files tab. The Documents screen will appear.
2. Tap the file you want to print. The contents of the file will appear in the preview window.
3. Tap the Printer icon. The Print dialog box will open.
4. Type the number of copies you want to print.
5. Tap Print. The document will be printed.

iWork Documents

If you have created a document in one of the iWork apps (Pages, Numbers, or Keynote), you may want to print the document. But there's no way to directly use PrintCentral to print from the iWorks apps. What to do? Get the file to a location from which Print Central can print it.

To set up iWork files to connect to a printer:

1. When ready to print a Pages document, tap the My Documents button (or the equivalent file manager in Numbers or Keynote). The My Documents screen will open.
2. Tap the Share icon. The Share action menu will appear.
3. Tap the Share via iWork option. An email message screen will appear.
4. Enter an email address of someone with whom you want to share the document, or your own email address, and tap Share. The announcement email will be sent, and the document will be sent to iWork.com.
5. In PrintCentral, tap the Web Pages tab. The browser will open.
6. Tap the Bookmarks icon. The Bookmarks page will open.
7. Tap the iWork.com bookmark. The browser will open to the iWork home page.
8. If needed, log into iWork.com using your Apple ID and password. The Shared Documents page will open (see Figure 10.10).

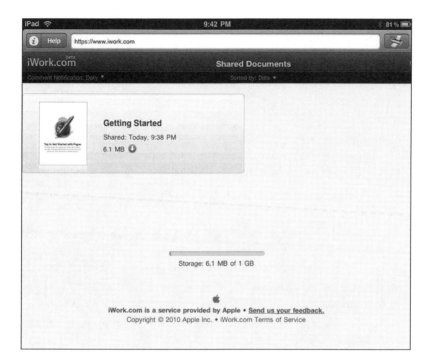

Figure 10.10

*Shared
Documents in
iWork.com.*

9. Tap the document you want to print. The document will open in the
   PrintCentral browser window (shown in Figure 10.11).

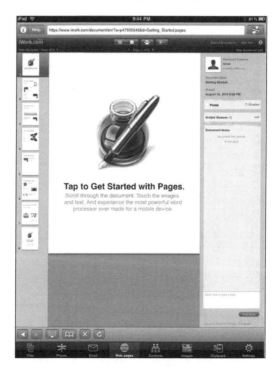

Figure 10.11

*Viewing an
iWork document
in PrintCentral's
browser.*

10. Tap the Printer icon on the iWork.com page. The Print dialog box will open.

11. Type the number of copies you want to print.

12. Tap Print. The document will be printed.

Email

Printing email messages and their attachments can also be done in PrintCentral. All you need to do is set up your account information, which PrintCentral can use to pick up copies of the messages in your Inbox.

1. In PrintCentral, tap the Email tab. The Email Accounts screen will appear.

2. Tap the Add a new account option. An accounts dialog box will appear.

3. Tap the account type you need. The Edit Account screen will open.

4. Type the settings for your email account and then tap Test. If the settings are correct, a green check mark will indicate your success.

5. Tap the Email Accounts navigation control to return to the Email Accounts screen.

6. Tap the email account from which to print. The account's mailbox page will open (see Figure 10.12).

Figure 10.12

An example of a multifoldered account.

7. Tap the mailbox folder that contains the message you want to print. The contents of the folder will be downloaded.

8. Tap the message you want to print. The contents of the message will appear in the preview window.

9. Tap the Printer icon. The Print dialog box will open.

10. Type the number of copies you want to print.

11. Tap Print. The message will be printed.

PRINTING ATTACHMENTS

If an email message has an attachment, click the attachment to open it within PrintCentral. Then click the Printer icon to start the printing process. You can use this method to mail yourself an iWork document as an attachment and print it in PrintCentral instead of sharing via iWork.com.

Web Pages

In the previous "iWork Documents" section, you already went through printing a Web page, but that was using iWork.com's print software to properly format the document for printing via PrintCentral. Most Web pages don't have such tools, and you should know how to handle different settings for Web pages in PrintCentral.

To print Web pages in PrintCentral:

1. In PrintCentral, tap the Web Pages tab. The browser will open.

2. Navigate to the Web page you want to print. The page will open in the PrintCentral browser window.

QUICK NAVIGATION

If you find a page to print while using Safari, select the Web address in the URL bar and use the Edit menu to copy the address. Paste it into the PrintCentral browser's URL bar to get to the same page fast.

---

3. Tap the PrintCentral Printer icon. The Print action menu will appear.

4. To print a screenshot of the page, tap Print from Screen option. To print the contents of the page, tap the Print from Address option. The Print dialog box will open.

5. Type the number of copies you want to print.

6. Tap Print. The Web page will be printed.

Contacts

Want to print out the information on one or your contacts? PrintCentral will connect you right to the Contacts data on your iPad and print them out as needed.

To print out information on your contacts:

1. In PrintCentral, tap the Contacts tab. The Contacts Groups screen will open.

2. Tap the group with the contact you want to print. The list of contacts will appear.

3. Tap the contact(s) to print. Each selected contact will be marked with a check mark.

4. Tap the Printer icon. The Print dialog box will open.

5. Type the number of copies you want to print.

6. Tap Print. The contact(s) will be printed.

Images

If you need to print a copy of the images on your iPad, here's how to do it

To print a copy of your images:

1. In PrintCentral, tap the Images tab. The Photos screen will open, as well as the Photo Albums action menu (see Figure 10.13).

2. Tap the album with the image you want to print. A gallery of images will appear in the action menu.

3. Tap the image to print. Each selected image will appear in the Photos screen.

4. Tap the images to print. The selected images will be marked by a box.

5. Tap the Printer icon. The Print dialog box will open.

6. Type the number of copies you want to print.

7. Tap Print. The image(s) will be printed.

Figure 10.13
Selecting images.

Clipboard

Sometimes you may need to print just a portion of a document, instead of the whole thing. You can use the iPad's editing tools to copy a selection to the iPad Clipboard and then print the selection from PrintCentral.

To print a Clipboard selection with PrintCentral:

1. In PrintCentral, tap the Clipboard tab. The Clip archive screen will open (see Figure 10.14).

Figure 10.14
The archived content of the clipboard.

2. Tap the clipboard items to select or deselect. Selected items will be denoted by a check mark.

3. Tap the Printer icon. The Print dialog box will open.

4. Type the number of copies you want to print.

5. Tap Print. The selected content will be printed.

File Sharing

Not only can PrintCentral do a good job printing, but it also features utilities to pull files to your iPad for viewing and editing without syncing with a computer.

Moving files to the iPad to view them is useful in and of itself, but once in PrintCentral, you can print them to whatever printer PrintCentral can access. One use-case scenario might occur when you need to print a document on your computer that's needed back at home while you're on a trip thousands of miles away.

Pretty handy.

You've already seen how PrintCentral uses its browser to connect to iWork.com. But there are even more direct connections available.

Network Sharing

With network sharing, you can turn your iPad into a remote drive that your computer can access over the network. Any files you drop into this drive will be available for viewing on the iPad, wherever you are.

To use network sharing:

1. In PrintCentral, tap the File tab. The Documents screen will open.

2. Tap the Network Sharing icon in the lower-left corner. The Network Sharing screen will appear (see Figure 10.15).

Figure 10.15
Starting the document server.

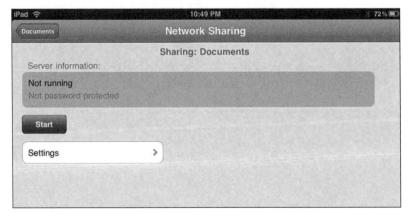

3. Tap Start. Connection addresses will appear.

4. In Windows or OS X, map a network drive to one of the addresses shown on the Network Sharing screen.

MAP A DRIVE?

In the OS X Finder, click the Go menu and select Connect to Server. Type the PrintCentral address. Click OK. A new icon to the mapped drive should appear on the desktop.

In Windows, right-click the Computer icon in Windows Explorer and select the Map Network Drive option. In the Map Network Drive dialog box, select a drive letter and type in the PrintCentral address. Click OK. A new folder to the drive should appear in Explorer.

KEEP THE CONNECTION GOING

In order to keep PrintCentral connected to your network drive, you must keep the Network Sharing screen open.

5. On your computer, copy or move the files you want on the iPad to the new network drive. They will appear in the Documents window of PrintCentral, even after the document server disconnects.

Google Docs

Not only can you connect to your computer's files with ease, but you can also access documents on the Internet to view and print. One popular Web collaboration site is Google Docs, to which PrintCentral can directly link.

To print a Google Doc with Print Central:

1. In PrintCentral, tap the Places tab. The Places screen will open.

2. Tap the Add Server icon. The Add Server Type dialog box will appear (see Figure 10.16).

3. Tap Google Docs. The Google Docs screen will appear.

4. Type in the login and password information and then tap Test. A green check mark will denote a successful connection.

5. Tap the Places navigation control. Google Docs will now appear in the Places screen.

6. Tap the Google Docs option. The contents of your Google Docs account will appear.

Figure 10.16

Add a server connection.

If you have Dropbox or other storage accounts on the Internet, use PrintCentral to connect similarly to those locations.

Conclusion

In this chapter, you discovered that printing from the iPad is not a myth, and it can be a valuable tool for your iPad in the workplace.

In Chapter 11, "In the iCloud," you'll find out how the iPad can be the portal to a new technology that lets you and your colleagues access, view, and edit your work anytime, anywhere.

Chapter 11

In the iCloud

Lately, there has been much debate about what it means to be successful in business computing. The introduction of netbooks, smartphones, and tablets like the iPad into the marketplace clearly puts business computing in a different space than that occupied by moribund desktop and laptop platforms.

Desktop computers (and later laptops) came about mostly because business users (and then home users) needed a way to duplicate the power of the client/server model with independent, number-crunching machines that would take the processing workload from the servers and on to the clients. Thus, the clients had to become more than just dumb terminals, and they had to have their own operating system and application framework to handle user data locally rather than remotely.

Today, the metaphor is shifting yet again. Servers have grown so powerful with virtualization and processing advances that you can run dozens of virtual server machines on one single piece of hardware. These virtual systems have started to take back the heavy workloads from the desktop/laptop clients. Some work is done locally, but more and more we are seeing really big workloads going back to the server environment, which, thanks to Internet connectivity, is euphemistically referred to as "the cloud."

Cloud computing is one of those terms that gets mangled a lot. When IT specialists refer to it, they should be talking about the automated ways in which all these powerful servers are managed and scaled. When consumers hear the term, they are taught to think that the cloud is any software run remotely. That's not really the cloud… the technical name for this is *software as a service* (SaaS). SaaS is very popular in the computing world, even if you've never heard the term. Facebook is a very large example of SaaS in action… so is YouTube. And so is Apple's newest SaaS offering: iCloud.

The iCloud service is Apple's successor to MobileMe, an Apple SaaS product for users of any Apple device, as well as Windows PCs. iCloud is a more streamlined iteration of that MobileMe service and a true replacement: MobileMe will be phased out of service in June 2012.

Since iCloud is available on the Web and through several OS X and iOS applications, it is seamlessly integrated with the tools you need to access your information from any machine. It is also perfect for business users who need to get to their work files no matter where they are. Better yet, the core services for iCloud, unlike those of MobileMe, are free of charge.

In this chapter, you will find out how to:

◆ Connect to Apple's iCloud service

◆ Sync information across multiple devices

◆ Back up your iPad to iCloud

◆ Safeguard your iPad device and data

Connecting to iCloud

iCloud is an online software service offered by Apple for users of any Apple device or any device that runs Windows.

iCloud's feature set is geared to consumers and businesspeople alike. Alongside features like photo and file sharing, iCloud provides 5GB of storage on the cloud to start and the option to purchase more storage if needed.

Other business-friendly tools include over-the-air email, a calendar, and contact synchronization across multiple devices. There's a feature that will let you find your iPad if you leave it behind somewhere and lock it down remotely to keep others from seeing your data.

You can even connect to your OS X computer remotely, through your iPad, so you can retrieve files or perform work that you accidentally may have left behind.

Signing up for iCloud can be done on any platform that can use the service.

Here's how to sign up for iCloud on the iPad:

1. Tap the Settings app icon. The Settings app will open.
2. Tap the iCloud option. The iCloud settings page will appear (see Figure 11.1).
3. Enter your Apple ID and Password in the appropriate fields. This is what you created when you first set up an iTunes account in Chapter 1, "First Step: Introducing the iPad."
4. Tap Sign In. The iCloud settings page will open, and a notification window will appear asking for permission to share your iPad's location (see Figure 11.2).
5. Tap OK. The settings page will be visible.

Figure 11.1

The iCloud settings page.

Figure 11.2

Do you want to share?

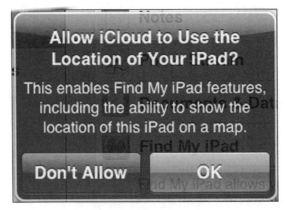

NO MATTER WHERE YOU GO, THERE YOU ARE

Apple is very cognizant of user privacy, so it will always ask you for permission when an application wants to share information, such as location, with Apple. In this case, the Find My iPad application is a very useful tool to have if your iPad walks away, and it's recommended that you allow this app to share the device's location with iCloud.

At this point, you will be able to pick and choose which of your iPad's core applications will be connected to iCloud. You might think, for instance, that all of your apps should be connected, but if you don't use the app in question, then there's really no need to waste bandwidth time having your iPad try to sync data that isn't even there.

Beyond the self-explanatory app settings, there are a few additional settings that can provide a lot of functionality should you choose to use them.

◆ **Photo Stream.** When activated, this tool will upload all new pictures from your iPad and will automatically synchronize them with any other iCloud-connected device you have.

◆ **Documents & Data.** This general setting enables any iCloud-enabled app not listed here in these settings to upload and save documents to iCloud's storage service.

◆ **Find My iPad.** Activates the Find My iPad locator service, discussed later in this chapter.

◆ **Storage & Backup.** Controls your backup settings for sending your iPad data to the iCloud service.

Synchronizing Across Multiple Devices

The beauty of using iCloud is having the capability to synchronize information such as contacts, Safari bookmarks, reminders, and calendar appointments. Not only will you be able to access the same information on any iCloud-enabled computer, but you can also log on to the iCloud site and see the same information from any computer or device with Internet capabilities, anywhere in the world.

The first thing to do is install iCloud on your computer. If you have an OS X machine with Lion (v10.7) or later, then iCloud is already available on your system. Windows users can install the iCloud client found at http://www.apple.com/icloud/.

Once the iCloud software is installed, don't look for it as a program in your Windows Start Menu or OS X Dock. The client application is actually installed directly within your system preferences.

For OS X users, click the icon and then the System Preferences menu option, followed by the iCloud option.

In Windows, click the Start Menu and then click the Control Panel option. In the Control Panel window, click the Network and Internet link; then click the iCloud link.

Either of these methods will start the iCloud Preferences client, shown in Figures 11.3 and 11.4.

Figure 11.3

*OS X iCloud
Preferences.*

Figure 11.4

*Windows iCloud
Preferences.*

To change the iCloud configuration settings on any device, open the settings window in either the Windows or OS X configuration clients or within the iPad's Settings app. Then simply click the checkbox or slide the switch to begin synchronization of that particular service.

YOUR FIRST TIME

The first time you sync from a device to iCloud, a warning dialog box will appear. Click Allow to make sure all your data is captured and no duplicates are created.

To access your information online from iCloud at any time, just start your favorite browser on any computer.

To access your information online from iCloud:

1. In your browser, navigate to www.icloud.com. The iCloud sign-in page will open (see Figure 11.5).

Figure 11.5
The iCloud sign-in page.

2. Enter your Apple ID and password information in the appropriate fields and click the Sign-In arrow icon. The iCloud home page will open (see Figure 11.6).

3. Click one of the options. That page will appear with the information from all of your iCloud devices. Figure 11.7 displays sample content when the iWork icon is selected.

Figure 11.6

The iCloud home page.

Figure 11.7

View iPad documents online at anytime.

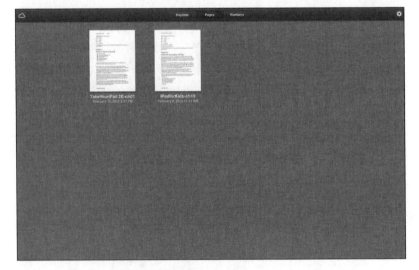

Back Up Your iPad to iCloud

One of the major changes brought to the iPad since it was first released was the capability to, if users chose, never to have to be connected to an iTunes-enabled computer again. The removal of this requirement opened up a lot of flexibility for business users, because now iPads did not need to be tethered to a particular machine.

One of the ways this is made possible is the feature that backs up the contents of the iPad directly over the air to iCloud. By default, Apple provides every iCloud user with 5GB of space within iCloud to store information from the iPad (or any other iOS device), with the option to buy more storage on an annual basis.

To back up your iPad to iCloud:

1. Tap the Settings app icon. The Settings app will open.

2. Tap the iCloud settings option. The iCloud settings pane will appear.

3. Tap the Storage & Backup option. The Storage & Backup pane will open (see Figure 11.8).

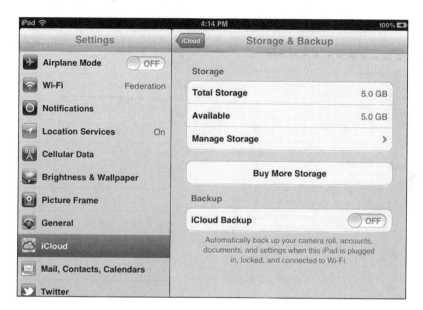

Figure 11.8

Configuring online backup options.

4. Slide the iCloud Backup setting to On. A Start iCloud Backup dialog will appear.

5. Tap OK. The dialog will close, and a new Back Up Now button will appear.

6. Tap the Back Up Now button. The backup process will start (see Figure 11.9).

It is quite possible, as time goes on, that the amount of data on your iPad will grow too large to be stored on 5GB of storage. If that happens, you can purchase more storage on an annual subscription basis.

First, you should see if you are even near the point where you have to buy more storage.

Figure 11.9

Backing up your iPad.

To manage storage use on iCloud:

1. In the Storage & Backup pane of the Settings app, tap the Manage Storage option. The Manage Storage pane will appear, shown in Figure 11.10.

2. If you want to see exactly what files are being stored by each iCloud-enabled app listed, tap the app in question. The list of files will be displayed.

3. To manage individual files, tap the Edit button. The Edit screen will appear, as shown in Figure 11.11.

4. Tap one of the file's Delete buttons to select the file for removal, or tap the Delete All button. A confirmation dialog will be displayed.

5. Tap the Delete button. The files will be removed.

6. Tap Done. The Edit pane will close.

Figure 11.10

Managing the iPad's storage.

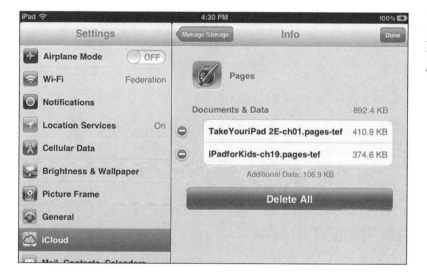

Figure 11.11

Pick and choose what files to keep.

To purchase more storage for backing up in iCloud:

1. On either the Manage Storage or Storage & Backup panes, tap the Buy More Storage buttons. The Buy More Storage action dialog will open, as seen in Figure 11.12.

Figure 11.12

*Getting more
iCloud storage.*

2. Tap one of the displayed Upgrade options. The option will be selected.

3. Tap the Buy button. The Apple ID verification dialog will appear.

4. Enter your Apple ID password and tap OK. The amount will be billed to your iTunes account, and the new storage will be made available to your iCloud account.

Securing Your iPad

Since the iPad is a mobile device, it makes sense that you would have it with you on the road, away from your place of business. It also makes sense that you may have left it somewhere and forgotten where it is. Or worse, someone may have walked off with it.

The good news is that you can track your iPad down using the Find My iPad tool included with iCloud. This handy tool will let you track down the location of your iPad based on cellular triangulation or known WiFi network locations, so you can get an idea of where the device might be.

To locate the iPad, log into the iCloud site and navigate to the Find My iPhone page. After you log in again, click the Find option. In a few moments, the location of your iPad will be displayed on a map (see Figure 11.13).

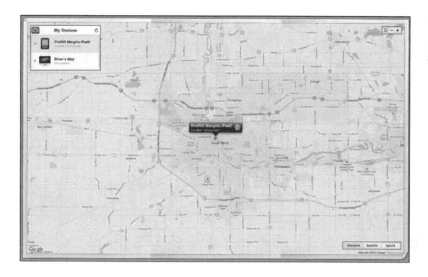

Figure 11.13
iPad missing? Not for long.

If you suspect the device was left in a public place, you can have the device start making noise and display a message to whomever might find it. You may be pleasantly surprised by the kindness of strangers.

Once the iPad is located, click the blue information icon on the location placard. The placard will expand to reveal more options (see Figure 11.14).

Figure 11.14
More options to deal with a lost iPad.

Click the Play Sound or Send Message button to open a message editor window. Enter a short message to whomever finds the iPad and click Send. The message will be sent (see Figure 11.15).

Figure 11.15

Broadcast for help.

> ## TALKING TO STRANGERS
>
> Humor aside, always be careful and don't send out too much contact information on the alert message. A phone number is usually enough. If someone calls back, arrange to meet them at a public place to retrieve your iPad device. And, of course, be sure to reward them for their kindness.

Alas, sometimes you may have lost the iPad to someone with nefarious intentions. You have two options when that happens. First, you can lock the iPad remotely with a numeric password that will render the iPad unusable until the password is entered. Just click the Remote Lock option and follow the onscreen instructions. Once you click Lock, the iPad will only unlock when the four-digit number is entered (see Figure 11.16).

If you have sensitive data on your iPad (and any personal contact information would qualify), you may want to take the more drastic measure of Remote Wipe, which will immediately reset the iPad to factory condition. You should only take this option if you are sure the device has been stolen or is otherwise irretrievable, because restoring the system's data if the device is ever recovered will take some time, and you will no longer be able to track the iPad.

Figure 11.16
*Lock the iPad
up.*

Conclusion

Using the iCloud service will afford you a lot of convenience with multidevice syncing and online storage, not to mention the peace of mind knowing that a lost iPad can be tracked with ease.

In Chapter 12, "Remote Desktop Connectivity," you'll explore another cool aspect of iCloud and Internet technology: the capability to log into and use your computer from your iPad.

Chapter 12

Remote Desktop Connectivity

- ◆ Exploring LogMeIn
- ◆ Setting Up LogMeIn
- ◆ Connecting with LogMeIn
- ◆ Working with LogMeIn
- ◆ Conclusion

For all of the talk about cloud computing, there is still the undeniable fact that most business computer users will make use of their PCs or Macs to get things done. Because of this bias, a lot of data will be situated on a desktop machine, as well as the specialized applications to handle that data.

There are many iPad apps that can duplicate some or all of desktop applications' capabilities, but there are still a lot of desktop applications that don't have an iPad equivalent yet.

Then there's the data. As you learned in Chapter 11, "In the iCloud," iCloud is a great tool to retrieve files that you've already made available to iCloud. But what happens when you need a file you didn't think to put into the iCloud service?

This is when remote desktop connectivity comes in handy. Remote desktop applications make use of the Internet to connect to your system from another location and use that computer as if you were sitting right in front of it. This is not just about getting to the folders and files remotely—you will actually be able to visually control and open any file and application on your PC or Mac.

There are drawbacks to this kind of connection. Even the fastest broadband connection won't be able to prevent slow control. It takes a lot of bandwidth to send a graphic image of your remote desktop to another computer, plus the instructions to manipulate the remote computer as the same time.

But, in a pinch, when you really need to get some business done by remote, being able to plug into your computer remotely can be a real convenience.

There are several iPad applications that can connect to remote PCs or Macs. In this chapter, you'll look at one of the best, LogMeIn, which will enable you to log into a PC or OS X machine. As you go, you will discover how to:

◆ Set up a remote desktop connection

◆ Connect to a remote PC or Mac

◆ Work with a remote desktop

Exploring LogMeIn

LogMeIn is a remote desktop solution that takes a two-pronged approach to providing connectivity.

LogMeIn uses what's known as open source software to deliver its functionality. Open source software is software that is freely created and contributed to by any developer who wants to improve upon it. LogMeIn has taken different open source software projects and added more bells and whistles to create a single application known as *LogMeIn Free*. Because of its open source origins, LogMeIn Free is free-of-cost, which makes it an attractive application to most businesses.

With LogMeIn Free, you can access a Mac or PC remotely and edit files on the remote desktop—but that's not all. If you want to transfer files to and from a remote desktop or print files remotely, you can use LogMeIn's commercial product, LogMeIn Pro, which is available for an annual subscription of $69.95 at the time this book went to press.

The best way to figure out if you want to use the Free or Pro version of LogMeIn is to sign up for the Free version and see if it meets your needs. If it does, you will be set. If you need the added functionality of the Pro version, then you can sign up for a free trial to determine if Pro is worth the annual cost.

FOR MORE LOGMEIN INFORMATION

A full product comparison chart for the LogMeIn software is available at https://secure.logmein.com/US/comparisonchart/comparisonFPP.aspx.

Regardless of what version of LogMeIn you use, here's how the iPad-to-computer connection is set up. On the remote desktop, you will install Free or Pro, and on your iPad you will install the LogMeIn app, which is available at the App Store free of charge.

At some point, LogMeIn will represent a significant investment for your business, relative to other iPad apps. You'll find that its ease-of-use and speed, however, still makes it an attractive option.

Setting Up LogMeIn

The most efficient way to configure LogMeIn is to visit the App Store to download and install LogMeIn on your iPad.

Once that operation is complete, you should then install LogMeIn on the desktop to which you want to connect remotely.

To install LogMeIn on a Windows machine:

1. In your desktop browser, visit https://secure.logmein.com/products/free/. The LogMeIn Free product page will open.

2. Click the Create an Account Link. The Create Account Web dialog will open (see Figure 12.1).

Figure 12.1

Create an account on LogMeIn.

3. Fill in the appropriate information in the fields on the page and click Continue. An activation email will be sent to the mail account you used to register, and the My Computers page will open (see Figure 12.2).

Figure 12.2

Add computers to your LogMeIn account.

ACTIVATE YOUR LOGMEIN ACCOUNT

Before you add computers to your LogMeIn account, open the activation email message and click or tap the verification link.

4. Click the Add Computer button. The Add Computer page will open.

5. Select the LogMeIn Free option and click the Continue button and follow the rest of the instructions on the page to install LogMeIn on your computer.

6. When the installation process is done, click Finish. The LogMeIn Pro client will be installed as a free trial.

7. On the Add Computer page in your browser, click the My Computers link. The computer should be added to your list.

Connecting with LogMeIn

Once a computer is added to your LogMeIn account, you can use the iPad LogMeIn app to connect to the machine.

To connect to a LogMeIn-enabled PC:

1. On the iPad, tap the LogMeIn app icon. The LogMeIn login page will appear (see Figure 12.3).

Figure 12.3
The LogMeIn login page.

2. Type the Email and Password information used to register for your LogMeIn account and tap Log Me In. A list of computers associated with your account will appear on the My Computers screen.

3. To connect to a computer remotely, tap the computer name in the list. If a login is set up for the remote machine, a login page will appear (see Figure 12.4).

Figure 12.4

Your remote desktop's login.

4. Enter the appropriate information and tap Log In. After a few moments, a picture of your desktop's screen will appear with a list of hints (see Figure 12.5).

Figure 12.5

Remote Control Hints.

5. Slide the Show hints control to Off if you don't want to see this list again and tap Continue to Computer. Your desktop will appear on the iPad screen.

GET A BETTER VIEW

For the best view of your desktop, rotate the iPad to the horizontal orientation (see Figure 12.6).

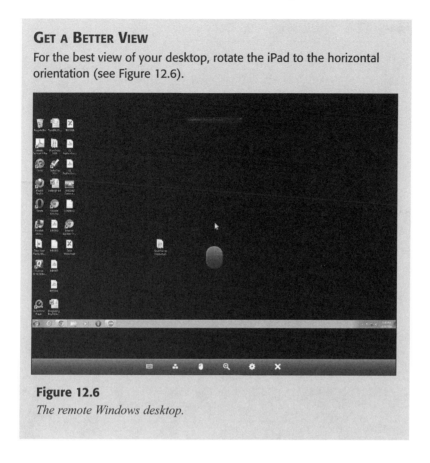

Figure 12.6
The remote Windows desktop.

6. To disconnect from the remote desktop, tap the X disconnect icon in the LogMeIn toolbar. A confirmation action menu will appear.

7. Tap the End Session option. You will be disconnected from your remote desktop.

Working with LogMeIn

LogMeIn provides almost seamless access to your remote desktop, allowing you to move the mouse around to open files and applications just as if you were sitting in front of the machine.

There are a few tricks involved in performing actions with the LogMeIn connection. For example, how do you perform a right-click option on the iPad screen? The list of hints displayed in Figure 12.5 was a pretty good guide to interfacing with the remote desktop, so we'll highlight those gestures in Table 12.1.

TABLE 12.1 Useful LogMeIn Gestures

Gesture	Action
Drag, single finger	Pan screen, move mouse
Drag, two finger	Scroll up/down
Drag, three finger, up/down	Show/hide keyboard
Drag, three finger, left/right	Switch monitors
Tap, single	Left-click
Tap, double	Double-click
Tap, double, with drag	Drag screen objects
Tap, two finger	Right-click
Pinch/Fan	Zoom out/in

These gestures allow you to duplicate the mouse actions you find on your PC or Mac computer.

There are other ways to control your remote desktop that don't involve a lot of finger gymnastics, if they're not your thing. Figure 12.7 highlights the LogMeIn toolbar located at the bottom of the LogMeIn screen.

Figure 12.7
The LogMeIn toolbar.

Keyboard   Combo keys   Left/Right click   Zoom   Settings   Disconnect

These controls duplicate and fine-tune the finger gestures found in Table 12.1.

◆ **Keyboard.** Displays the keyboard for LogMeIn.

◆ **Combo keys.** Displays an action menu for specialized key combinations, such as Alt-Tab and Ctrl-Alt-Delete on a remote Windows desktop.

◆ **Left/Right click.** Sets whether the next single tap on LogMeIn is a left- or right-click.

◆ **Zoom.** Zooms in to the last zoom setting. Tap again to view all of the desktop.

◆ **Monitors.** Switches between multiple monitors on a remote desktop, if installed.

◆ **Settings.** Activates the Settings action menu.

◆ **Disconnect.** Presents the End Session action menu.

The keyboard in LogMeIn is designed to provide all of the functionality of your remote desktop's keyboard. If you're connected to a Windows machine, as shown in Figure 12.8, you will see Windows-oriented functions.

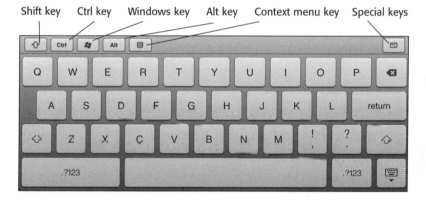

Figure 12.8
The LogMeIn keyboard.

You can use this keyboard just as you would on your Windows machine. If you tap the Special keys button, you will see additional keys displayed, such as function keys (see Figure 12.9).

Figure 12.9

The LogMeIn special keyboard.

> **FROM PRO TO FREE**
>
> When you first sign up for LogMeIn, the software on your desktop will be a fully functional version of LogMeIn Pro, which will be free for 14 days—after which, an annual subscription fee will be requested, or you can switch to LogMeIn Free.

If you want to switch to LogMeIn Free before the one-month trial ends, start the LogMeIn application on your desktop and click the About tab. Click the Switch Account or Subscription button and walk through the steps to convert your LogMeIn client to LogMeIn Free.

Conclusion

In a fast-paced business environment, having ready access to the tools you need to do your work is critical. The LogMeIn app enables your iPad to tie directly into your office desktop and get work done, no matter where you are.

In Chapter 13, "Ring Me Up: Point of Sale," we'll look at applications that will make your iPad become one of the most vital pieces of any retail business: a cash register.

Chapter 13

Ring Me Up:
Point of Sale

- ◆ Customizing Quick Sale
- ◆ Integrating Credit Card Transactions
- ◆ Making a Retail Sale
- ◆ Reporting Sales
- ◆ Managing Inventory
- ◆ Easy POS with Square
- ◆ Conclusion

If you own a retail business, you will likely be looking for as many ways to cut costs as possible. One area where cost-cutting measures can be implemented is in point-of-sale systems. Pricing on some of the point-of-sale (POS) systems can be in the tens of thousands of dollars, so this is clearly an area where money could be saved.

Retail and contractor businesses have come to recognize lately that mobile systems may be better suited to their needs than larger computers constrained to one location. The ability to invoice and receive payment from a customer at any location, be it in the store or out in the field, is a promise the iPad can deliver easily.

To accomplish this, you can use two of the best apps for retail and service businesses. The first is Quick Sale, a versatile and flexible POS app that enables you to ring up customers for retail items or contract services, accept full or partial payments, and deliver sales reports in a spreadsheet-friendly format. It even directly integrates with the Credit Card Terminal to accept credit card payments instantly. Quick Sale also has a robust inventory management system that will track items and let you know when it's time to order more.

And then there is Square, the incredibly easy-to-use POS app that enables credit card transactions to be accepted nearly instantly—and even includes a free credit card reader that plugs directly into your iPad.

In this chapter, you will learn about:

♦ Customizing your point-of-sale system
♦ Making a retail sale
♦ Accepting credit card payments
♦ Managing retail inventory
♦ Setting up and taking credit card transactions with Square in minutes

Customizing Quick Sale

Before you start using Quick Sale, it will be necessary to configure the app for your own business. The great thing about Quick Sale is that it's ready to go right out of the proverbial box, so it's really just a matter of customizing the placeholder information in Quick Sale to match your business name and other vital information.

DEMO MODE

When you begin to use Quick Sale, it starts in Demo Mode, which comes complete with dummy inventory items. For the purposes of this chapter, we will use the Demo Mode content to illustrate various activities, but it is important that you do not use Demo Mode in Quick Sale once you put it into production use. You cannot use Credit Card Terminal integration in Demo Mode, and any real data you input in Demo Mode will be erased once Production Mode is started.

The Quick Sale interfaces are fairly intuitive. The Sales screen is shown in Figure 13.1.

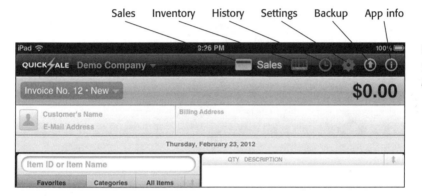

Figure 13.1
The Quick Sale Sales screen.

Much of this interface will be reviewed in the "Making a Retail Sale" section later in this chapter. For now, tap the Settings icon to open the Settings screen, seen in Figure 13.2.

To perform a basic configuration of Quick Sale, all you need to do is step through this screen and fill out the various fields to match your business information.

◆ **Quick Sale.** You can, if desired, upgrade the basic Quick Sale app to have more features, such as customized PDF invoices, inventory import and export, and signature capture.

◆ **Company.** Fill in your Business Name and Business Address information. Set your Default Tax Rate to your local requirements and adjust your Tax Label to match your local tax type (Tax, VAT, GST, PST, etc.).

◆ **Print/Email Invoices.** Change the Customer Message to something that reflects your business policy and information, as well as set the Theme Color for the Sales screen.

Figure 13.2

The Quick Sale Settings screen.

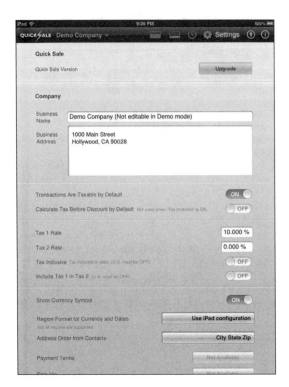

◆ **Reports.** Quick Sale will email invoices or invoice collections to a specified address. You can Pre-Fill the email address where reports should be sent and set the Report Format. If you plan to import the data directly into any kind of spreadsheet or database, be sure that either the HTML and CSV or CSV-only options are selected.

◆ **Printing.** Available only with the Quick Sale Pro upgrade, you can set how invoices will be printed.

◆ **Credit Card Processing.** If you plan to accept credit cards, you can set the Credit Card Processor to connect to the Credit Card Terminal (Inner Fence) or the iPay POS apps.

◆ **Devices.** Available only with the Quick Sale Premium upgrade, choose what type of barcode scanner you would like to use in conjunction with your iPad.

◆ **Advanced.** You can opt to Allow to Delete Invoices, set the Next Invoice No., and turn Demo Mode on or off.

◆ **Backup.** Set Dropbox support for Backup (available with Quick Sale Premium) and manage iTunes backups.

◆ **General.** Manage sounds and Demo Company settings.

After you make your changes to the Settings screen, tap any other screen icon to save the changes.

Integrating Credit Card Transactions

As noted in the previous section, you can connect the Credit Card Terminal (CC Terminal) or the iPay Mobile POS apps to Quick Sale in the Settings page. You can do this before or after you actually have the CC Terminal app installed on your iPad, but it's best to just go ahead and install the app before you connect.

CC Terminal enables you to accept credit card transactions on the iPad using a fast manual entry screen or using the new credit card reader the company will send you after you sign up. The app, which supports U.S., Canada, and UK businesses, accepts Visa, MasterCard, Discover, and American Express cards. Current pricing for U.S. merchants is $25/month, with an additional $0.24 plus 1.74% for each qualified transaction or plus 3.79% for a non-qualified transaction. ("Qualified" refers to a more secure transaction, where the customer's credit card information is gathered.)

CC Terminal uses Authorize.Net and Merchant Focus to process credit cards, and if you already have an Authorize.Net account or another Internet Merchant account, you can contact Inner Fence, the makers of the CC Terminal to see how to properly configure CC Terminal.

You can also use the PayPal service to accept credit card information, but it needs to be a PayPal Website Payments Pro account, not the standard PayPal account. Inner Fence recommends using the Authorize.Net service, but if you already have a PayPal Website Payments Pro account, you can quickly plug the PayPal information into CC Terminal and use it instead.

Like Square, the CC Terminal app will also send you a free credit card reader that you can plug directly into your iPad to scan credit cards.

WHEN 3G OR 4G MAY NOT BE A GOOD IDEA

If you work in a region where AT&T or Verizon coverage is problematic or nonexistent, you may need to reconsider the 3G or 4G options. One possible workaround, for instance, would be to use a mobile WiFi device from another cellular carrier and connect to the Internet via that device's WiFi network.

To configure CC Terminal:

1. Tap the CC Terminal app icon. The app will open to the home screen.

2. Tap the Settings icon. The Settings action menu will open.

3. If you don't have a merchant account, tap the Apply for Merchant Account option to open a sign-up page on the Inner Fence site. Follow the instructions there to sign up for an Authorize.Net account.

4. Type in your business name in the Merchant Name field.

5. Type in the email address where you want all emailed receipts to be carbon-copied in the PDF Receipt CC field.

6. If you have a merchant account already, tap the Account Type field and select one of the three options.

HAVE YOUR INFO READY

Before you are ready to sign up for an actual account, make sure that you have all your bank routing and account information first. This will save you a great deal of time and hassle.

---

7. Enter the Merchant Account information that will appear if you select one of the two real merchant account options.

8. Tap the Test Your Account option. The account settings will be used to send a test transaction to the merchant account service you are using. If successful, a notification window will inform you of that fact.

Once the merchant information is configured, you can use CC Terminal in conjunction with Quick Sale to make retail sales with a credit card.

Making a Retail Sale

Whether you're in your storefront or out in the field, Quick Sale will let you enter and complete transactions in a matter of seconds.

There are three primary types of transactions you can make with Quick Sale: cash, check, and credit card. Cash and check transactions are procedurally very similar.

To create a cash or check transaction:

1. In Quick Sale, tap the Sales icon. The Sales screen will appear (see Figure 13.3).

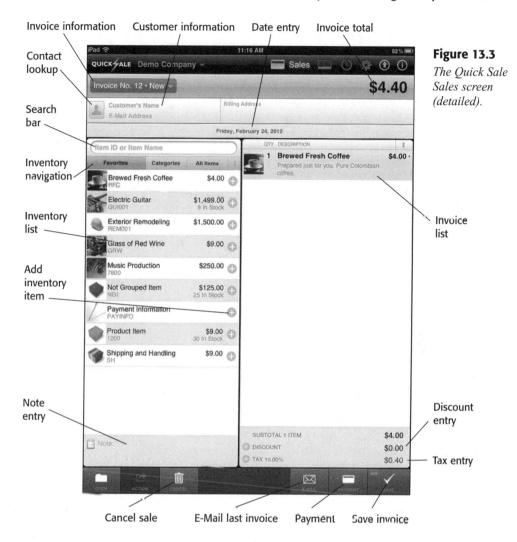

Invoice information   Customer information   Date entry   Invoice total

Contact lookup

Search bar

Inventory navigation

Inventory list

Add inventory item

Note entry

Invoice list

Discount entry

Tax entry

Cancel sale   E-Mail last invoice   Payment   Save invoice

Figure 13.3
The Quick Sale Sales screen (detailed).

2. To enter customer information, tap the Contact Lookup icon to select a contact from a list of existing customers from the Contacts app, or tap the Customer's Name and E-Mail Address fields to type the information in manually.

3. To find an inventory item, tap one of the Inventory navigation buttons to bring up the appropriate inventory list, or type the item's ID or name in the Search bar.

4. Once you find the item, tap the Add icon to add the item to the invoice list, as shown in Figure 13.4.

Figure 13.4

Add an item to the invoice list.

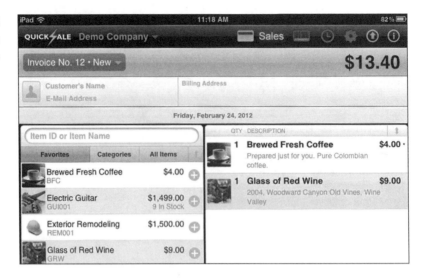

5. To add more than one of a particular item, continue to tap the Add icon. If you make an error, tap the Remove icon to adjust the amount.

6. Continue to add items until the customer's order is complete.

7. Tap Payment to begin the payment process. The Payment action menu will appear with the numeric keyboard (see Figure 13.5)

Figure 13.5

Entering a payment.

8. Tap the Method field to open the action menu of payment options (Cash or Check) and type in the amount the customer is paying you if it is different from the amount owed.

9. Tap Accept Payment. If change is required, the Quick Sale invoice will let you know the amount.

10. If needed, tap Overpayment Received. The next invoice screen will appear with a Change Due notice at the top.

TRY BEFORE YOU BUY

If you're just looking at CC Terminal as a potential tool for your business, select the Try It Out (No Account) option. This will enable you to submit dummy credit card numbers to simulate transactions.

When you need to conduct a credit card transaction, the procedure is almost the same, with some extra steps with CC Terminal.

To conduct a credit card transaction:

1. In Quick Sale, tap the Sales icon. The Sales screen will appear.

2. To enter customer information, tap the Contact lookup icon to select a contact from a list of existing customers from the Contacts app, or tap the Customer's Name and E-Mail Address fields to type the information in manually.

3. To find an inventory item, tap one of the Inventory navigation buttons to bring up the appropriate inventory list, or type the item's ID or name in the Search bar.

4. Once you find the item, tap the Add icon to add the item to the invoice list.

5. To add more than one of a particular item, continue to tap the Add icon. If you make an error, tap the Remove icon to adjust the amount.

6. Continue to add items until the customer's order is complete.

7. Tap Payment to begin the payment process. The Payment action menu will appear with the numeric keyboard.

8. Tap the Method field and select the Credit Card option; then type in the amount the customer is paying you.

9. Tap Accept Payment. The Credit Card Terminal action menu will appear (see Figure 13.6).

Figure 13.6

How will you enter the credit card?

10. Tap Go to Credit Card Terminal. The CC Terminal screen will open.

11. Type in the credit card information and tap Charge. An approval notification will appear.

12. Tap the screen, and the Quick Sale Sales screen will open with the sale completed.

If you accept partial payments in your business, such as when you are delivering big-ticket items or services, Quick Sale can accommodate those as well.

To accept partial payments:

1. In Quick Sale, tap the Sales icon. The Sales screen will appear.

2. To enter customer information, tap the Contact lookup icon to select a contact from a list of existing customers from the Contacts app, or tap the Customer's Name and E-Mail Address fields to type the information in manually.

3. To find an inventory item, tap one of the Inventory navigation buttons to bring up the appropriate inventory list, or type the item's ID or name in the Search bar.

4. Once you find the item, tap the Add icon to add the item to the invoice list.

5. To add more than one of a particular item, continue to tap the Add icon. If you make an error, tap the Remove icon to adjust the amount.

6. Continue to add items until the customer's order is complete.

7. Tap Payment to begin the payment process. The Payment action menu will appear with the numeric keyboard.

8. Tap the Method field; choose Cash, Check, or Credit Card; and type in the partial amount the customer is paying you.

9. Tap Accept Payment. The Partial Payment action menu will open (see Figure 13.7).

Figure 13.7

The Partial Payment action menu.

10. Tap Apply Partial Payment. The next invoice screen will appear with a Balance Due notice at the top.

Reporting Sales

After you have made a number of sales with Quick Sale, you will want to get the sales data from your iPad into whatever financial management application you use to manage your business.

Quick Sale enables you to email one or more invoices to a specified recipient, using either a nicely formatted HTML report or a comma-separated values (CSV) file, which strings out data as a series of values, separated by—you guessed it—commas.

CSV files are not fun to read for human beings, but they have one distinct advantage: They can be imported into spreadsheets, databases, and financial applications with relative ease. This means that Quick Sale reports won't have to be transcribed by hand into your accounting software, but should be directly importable.

To create a sales report:

1. In Quick Sale, tap the History icon. The History screen will appear (see Figure 13.8).

Figure 13.8

The Quick Sale History screen.

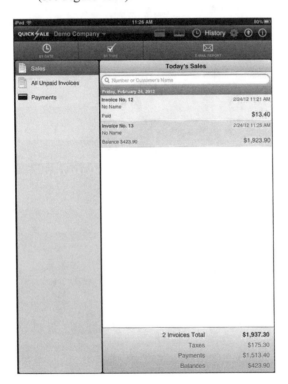

2. Tap the By Date or By Type buttons to view the group of invoices on which you want a report. A simple way is to tap By Date and then the Today option to gather all of this day's sales.

3. Tap all of the invoices to report.

4. Tap Send to E-Mail. The Send to E-Mail action menu will appear.

5. Tap the Detailed Report option. An email message window will open, complete with all the invoice information and an attached CSV file.

CSV Settings

Remember, you will want to be sure one of the CSV options is selected in Quick Sale's Settings screen to get the CSV attachment to appear.

6. Tap Send. The report will be sent to the intended recipient(s).

Managing Inventory

Quick Sale is not only a great point-of-sale tool, but it also does a pretty good job as an inventory management tool. It may not replace your existing inventory system, but Quick Sale can supplement how you manage your inventory.

The very first thing you will probably do when you start using Quick Sale is to enter inventory, so you can actually sell it later. Inventory is classified into four different types:

◆ **Service.** Any service, such as consulting or trade, conducted by your business.

◆ **Inventory Item.** An item sold that you track as part of your inventory.

◆ **Non-Inventory Item.** Sold goods that are not tracked (such as coffee that's a supplement to your business but not a specialty).

◆ **Charge.** The amount that you charge the customer. This can include late fees, shipping and handling, etc.

Getting items into the Quick Sale database can take some time, but it's well worth the effort. A nicely configured inventory set can even be used as a menu for customers to choose what they want.

To add an item to the inventory:

1. In Quick Sale, tap the Inventory icon. The Inventory screen will appear (see Figure 13.9).

2. Tap the New Item button. The New Item pane will activate.

3. Type in all of the relevant information for the item. If the item is an inventory item, be sure to enter the Quantity on Hand and the Reorder Quantity.

4. To add a photo of the item to the inventory, tap Add Photo. The Gallery action menu will appear (see Figure 13.10).

5. If you have your own picture saved on the iPad, tap Photo Library and navigate to the photo.

6. Tap the photo to select it. It will appear in the Choose Photo action menu.

Figure 13.9

The Quick Sale Inventory screen.

Figure 13.10

Add a picture of the item.

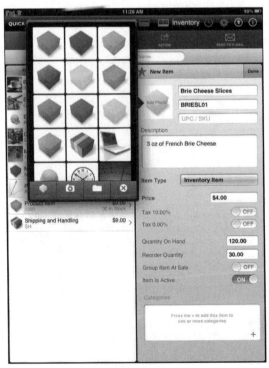

7. Tap and drag the photo, and pinch or fan it to have it fill the Move and Scale box.

8. When finished, tap Use. The photo will appear in the item listing.

9. If you want to make the item a Favorite, tap the star icon.

10. To place the item in a category, tap the plus icon in the Categories field and tap the category to which you want to assign the item.

11. Tap Done. The item will be added to the inventory.

To create more categories:

1. In the Inventory screen, tap the New Category button. The New Category pop-over will appear.

2. Type in the name of the new category and tap the Add Category button. You can now use the category for any of your items.

If you want to delete an item, tap it in the Inventory screen to select it and then tap Delete Item in the item pane. When the Confirmation action menu appears, tap Delete Item again to remove the item from the inventory.

Easy POS with Square

Square is very different from Quick Sale, because it's not a full-blown inventory and point-of-sale system. Rather, this popular app is built around the premise of getting businesses paid faster and making credit card payments easier for customers.

Like CC Terminal, Square handles credit card transactions from Visa, MasterCard, Discover, and American Express cards. But the cost structure is a little easier to manage for businesses— it's a flat 2.75% rate for all cards.

Signing up for the Square service is easy. You can visit the Squareup.com website and sign up there, or you can sign up using the Square app itself.

To set up a Square account:

1. When you first start the Square app, the splash screen will appear. Tap the Sign Up for Square button. The Create Account dialog will appear (see Figure 13.11).

2. Enter your name, email, and password information, and then tap Continue. The Accept Card Payments dialog will appear.

3. Tap Get Started. The Enter Information dialog will appear (see Figure 13.12).

4. Tap the Business button and enter your personal and business information.

Figure 13.11

Signing up for Square.

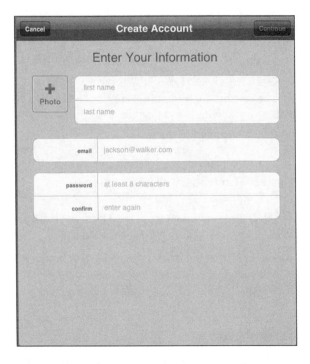

Figure 13.12

Enter your business information.

PRIVACY AND IDENTITY

As you enter your information, Square will ask you where you are located, which is a security feature to make sure that credit card transactions always take place in your business location. (You can change the location later if you need to do so.) Square will also ask you a number of personal questions about your history to confirm your identity as you complete the process, which can be rather startling. Don't worry, it's pulling the info from credit bureaus and extrapolating security questions from that information.

5. Once the personal and business information is verified, tap Next. The Bank Account Information dialog will appear, as shown in Figure 13.13.

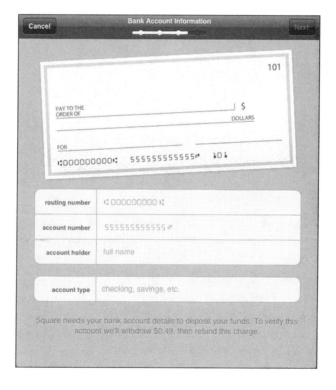

Figure 13.13

Enter your banking information.

6. Enter your bank routing and account information and tap Next. The Bank Account dialog will appear, informing you to check your account for test transactions in the next few days and confirming the success of the test at Square's website.

7. Tap Continue. The Free Reader dialog will appear.

8. If you would like to have a credit card reader mailed to you, tap the Mail My Free Card Reader button. The dialog will close, and the initial Square payment screen will appear (see Figure 13.14).

Figure 13.14

The Square home screen.

To enter a transaction in Square:

1. Using the numeric keyboard, enter the amount of the transaction. The amount will appear in the blue highlighted amount field.

2. Tap Add. A new Enter Amount line will appear.

3. When the transaction is complete, tap Charge. The payment screen will appear.

4. Swipe the card now. The card information will appear on-screen.

5. Tap Authorize Card. The signature screen will appear (see Figure 13.15).

6. Using a stylus, have the customer sign the screen and tap Continue.

7. Have the customer choose and provide the preferred information to get the receipt (see Figure 13.16).

8. Tap Send. The thank you screen will appear briefly, and the main payment screen will reappear.

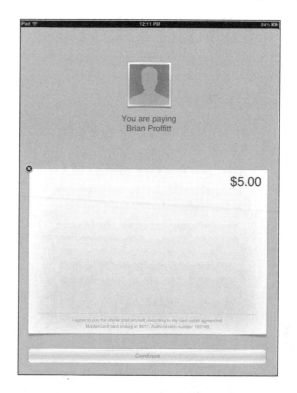

Figure 13.15
Signing off on the transaction.

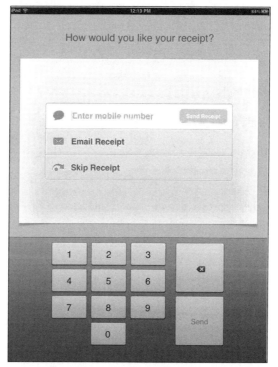

Figure 13.16
Choose the receipt method.

While Square is not a full-fledged POS app, you can enter item information within Square to make the system more robust. Simply tap the Account button to open the Account screen and add your items in the Item Library, shown in Figure 13.17.

Figure 13.17

Adding store items in Square.

Conclusion

Quick Sale and Square are versatile point-of-sale apps that let you manage the sales of your business. Having theses app will enable you to take the sales right to the customer, whether they're in the store or somewhere in the field.

In Chapter 14, "When the Work's Done: Invoicing," you'll take a look at other ways of invoicing sales and services on the go, using other powerful invoicing apps.

Chapter 14

When the Work's Done: Invoicing

- ◆ Creating an Invoice Template
- ◆ Creating an Invoice
- ◆ Sending Invoices to Customers
- ◆ Conclusion

If you have a business, then you know invoicing. No matter what services you provide, it does you little good if you don't have a way of informing your customers how much they owe for services rendered.

Chapter 13, "Ring Me Up: Point of Sale," focused on the apps needed to use your iPad effectively as a point-of-sale device. But some businesses—repair shops, contractors, technicians—don't always operate on a retail basis. In this instance, an invoice for services is often the only thing you need.

In some use-cases, you may need invoices that will combine services and sales, such as when a plumber or electrician completes a repair and needs to charge the customer for labor *and* parts.

You don't need heavy-hitter applications to generate these kinds of invoices. Something simple will do quite nicely. In this chapter, you will use the Invoice Studio app to accomplish these tasks:

◆ Customize your invoices
◆ Create a service invoice
◆ Send or print invoices to customers

Creating an Invoice Template

Invoice Studio is just what it says: a studio-like, form-based app that enables you to create invoices quickly in a mobile environment. When first started, Invoice Studio provides the blank template similar to the one shown in Figure 14.1.

The very first thing you will need to do for this application is to configure the template with your own business information. Before completing these steps, it's a good idea to have a graphic of your company logo ready on a computer within the same network.

PREPARING YOUR LOGO

Before you begin, you should make sure that your logo file is in your iPad's Photo library.

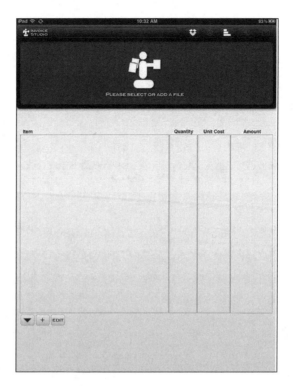

Figure 14.1

The Invoice Studio start page.

To create an invoice template:

1. Tap the Invoice Studio app icon. The base template screen will appear.

2. Tap the Invoice Studio button. The Invoice Studio action menu will be displayed.

3. Tap the Add (+) icon. A new invoice will be added to the action menu.

4. Tap the new invoice. The Invoice management screen will appear (see Figure 14.2).

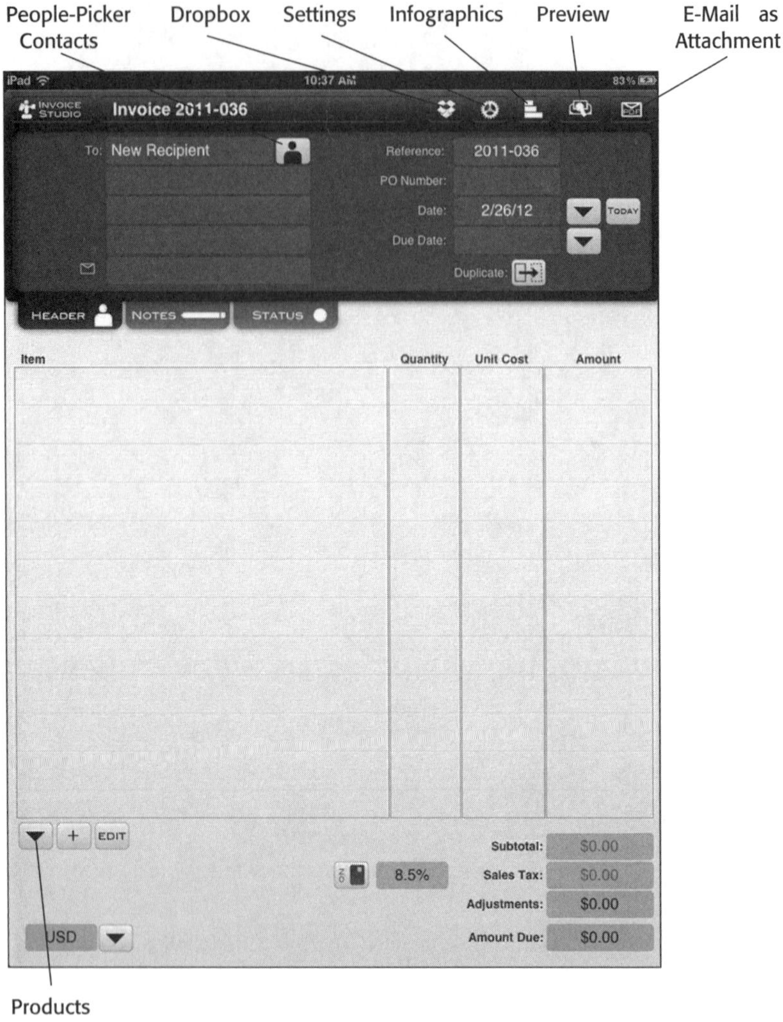

People-Picker   Dropbox   Settings   Infographics   Preview   E-Mail as
Contacts   Attachment

Figure 14.2

*The Invoice
management
screen.*

Products

5. Tap the Settings icon. The Settings and Information Options page will appear (see Figure 14.3).

6. Tap the Document tab. The Document page will appear (see Figure 14.4).

7. Click the Camera button in the Logo section. The Photos action menu will open.

8. Navigate to and select the logo graphic in your Photo library, tapping somewhere else on the screen to close the action menu. The logo field will be updated.

9. If you would like a Header for your invoice, tap the Off button in the Header section. The Header will be activated.

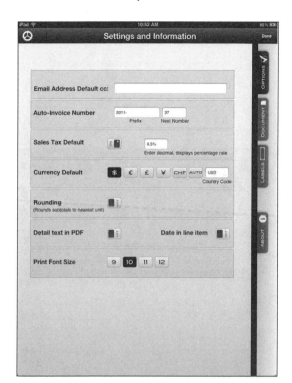

Figure 14.3

The Settings and Information Options page.

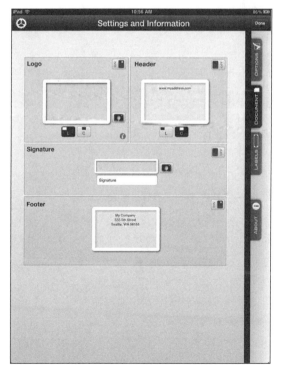

Figure 14.4

The Settings and Information Document page.

10. Tap the Header field and edit the contents of the header to your desires.

11. Tap the Footer field and edit it accordingly.

12. Tap Done. The blank invoice page will appear.

13. To see the template as it will be sent, tap the Preview button. A preview of the invoice will appear, as shown in Figure 14.5.

Figure 14.5

The new invoice.

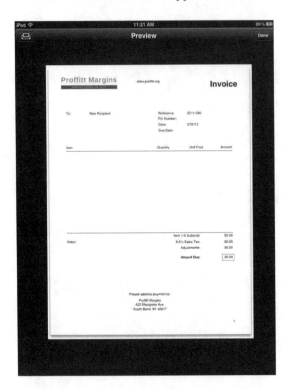

14. When finished, tap the Done button. The template preview will be closed.

Creating an Invoice

After the initial settings have been created for the invoice, the configuration will remain in place for each new invoice you create thereafter.

To create a new invoice:

1. In Invoice Studio, tap the Invoice Studio button. The Invoice Studio action menu will be displayed.

2. Tap the Add (+) icon. A new invoice will be added to the action menu.

3. Tap the new invoice. The Invoice management screen will appear (see Figure 14.2).

4. Tap the People-Picker Contacts icon. The All Contacts action menu will appear.

5. Tap the contact you want to invoice. The contact's information will populate the contact fields.

DO IT YOURSELF

If the person or company you want to invoice is not in your contacts, you can type in the information within the contact fields.

6. Add any PO and Due Date information in those respective fields.

7. Tap the Edit key at the bottom of the form. The invoice will be placed in Edit mode.

8. To add an existing product or service to the invoice, tap the Products icon. The Products screen will appear (see Figure 14.6).

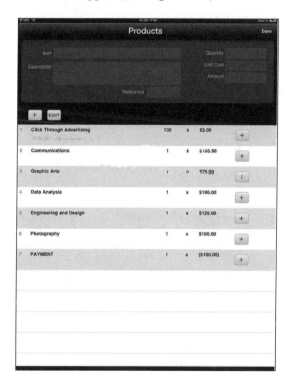

Figure 14.6

Choose products and services.

9. Tap an item in the list. The item's information will fill the fields at the top of the screen.

10. Adjust the Quantity, Description, or Unit Cost if needed and tap the Add (+) icon in the item line. The item will be added to the invoice.

11. To add a new item, tap the main Add (+) icon and fill in the information in the appropriate fields.

12. When finished, tap the Done key. The Items will be added to the template, and the total will be calculated (see Figure 14.7).

Figure 14.7

A completed invoice.

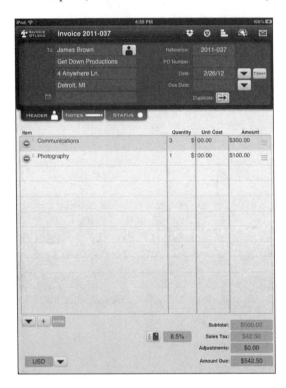

13. Tap the Done button. The invoice will be completed.

14. When finished, tap the highlighted Save key. The invoice will be saved.

Sending Invoices to Customers

While you can't print an invoice directly from Invoice Studio, you can email an invoice directly to the customer and to your own business address for later accounting procedures.

1. To send an invoice by email, tap the Invoice Studio button and tap the invoice you want to send.

2. Tap the E-Mail as Attachment button. A message window will open with the invoice attached.

3. Edit the To and Subject fields and tap Send. The invoice will be sent to the customer and any other address specified.

But what if your customer doesn't have an email address? In that case, send the message to the email account attached to the PrintCentral app (see Chapter 10, "From iPad to Paper: Printing") and use PrintCentral to print a copy of the invoice.

Conclusion

Invoice Studio performs one task and one task well: It enables you to configure clear and concise invoices no matter what kind of business model you use.

No matter how you conduct your business, it's always a challenge to find more customers. Advertising is the old standby way of getting the word out, and while it can work, tapping into the power of social media may give your business the boost it needs for a lot less money. In Chapter 15, "Shout to the World: Social Media," you'll find out how to broadcast your business to the world, using the iPad's social media tools.

Chapter 15

Shout to the World:
Social Media

- ◆ Making a Business Facebook Page
- ◆ Getting Friendly with Facebook
- ◆ Setting Up a Twitter Account
- ◆ Managing Tweets with Twitterrific
- ◆ Conclusion

Conference calls have expanded the dimensions of business conversation, and mailing lists added to the collaborative discussions that could happen online. But it wasn't until the ascension of sites like Facebook, YouTube, Flickr, and Twitter that we experienced true social media: a huge always-on conversation using text and multimedia that anyone could watch and join.

All of these social media sites, and others, are more than just fun ways to share your life with friends and family (though they're good at that, too); social media can provide an incredible outlet for your business to reach your customers. Just as communication between a business and its customers used to be one-way and one-dimensional—you placed ads, you talked to customers individually—businesses now have the capability to connect to as many customers as they'd like, using tailor-made messaging.

More importantly, the conversation is now two-way. You can talk to your customers, and they can talk to you. Sometimes that conversation isn't always fun, but it's an honest part of your business, and with the right tools and attention, even the most disgruntled customers can be allies if they know you're listening.

In this chapter, you'll look at two apps that will help manage the conversation on two of the most popular social media sites today: Facebook and Twitter. Specifically, you'll learn how to:

◆ Create a Facebook fan page for your organization

◆ Work with the Facebook iPad app

◆ Set up a Twitter account

◆ Use the Twitter app to manage your tweets

WHAT ABOUT LINKEDIN?

LinkedIn is a fantastic social networking site for professionals, one that is highly recommended for business owners and professionals in any industry. Sadly, the official LinkedIn app is only optimized for the iPhone, not the iPad, at press time. No third-party apps for the iPad have been released, either.

Making a Business Facebook Page

It's pretty hard not to have heard of Facebook, the social media site that enables friends, associates, and colleagues to connect with each other through personal, business, or affiliate connections.

Facebook is not the first social media site, but through tight management of undesirable content and general protection of its users' privacy, it has grown to be the largest. It is not without its flaws. Those self-same privacy rules have become weaker as Facebook explores ways to generate revenue for itself and its partner vendors. Time will tell how this issue will resolve itself, but for now, Facebook is definitely a place where your customers are located.

To highlight your business, you will want to create an Official fan page on Facebook (as opposed to a Community fan page, which is more appropriate for general topics or causes). There are any number of ways you can set up a fan page, and there are several excellent references on the Internet to help you make your page look great. For the purposes of this book, let's walk through the basic steps to set up an Official fan page.

To set up an Official fan page:

1. In your favorite browser, navigate to www.facebook.com/pages/create.php. The Create a Page page will open, as shown in Figure 15.1.

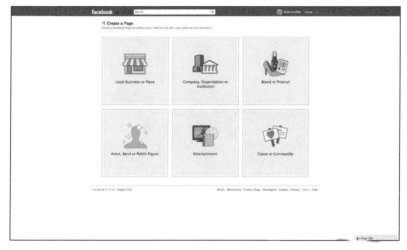

Figure 15.1

Create a Facebook page.

2. Click the Local Business or Place button. The business page fields will appear within the box.

3. In the Choose a Category field, select the business type that best applies to your organization. If one does not match, select the Local Business option.

4. Enter the name of your business in the Business or Place field.

5. Fill in the remainder of the fields.

6. Check the agreement check box and then click Get Started. A Set Up page for your business will appear (see Figure 15.2).

Figure 15.2

A Set Up page for your business.

7. Follow the steps recommended on the Set Up pages to build your business page. After the basic information is entered, the basic template page will appear, although you can continue to edit your page as you wish.

> **GREAT TIPS FOR FACEBOOK**
>
> Mashable.com, a premier social media news and information website, has excellent tips and how-tos for building great Facebook fan pages for business.

Getting Friendly with Facebook

When the iPad first launched, Facebook was one of those apps that was available on the iPhone, but not on the iPad. Fortunately, the developers at Facebook have put together an excellent native app that fully supports the Facebook platform.

Facebook's basic structure works something like this: You, as a Facebook user, can connect to friends (which can include family and professional colleagues) who, in turn, will connect back to you, while also connecting to their circle of friends, thus expanding the network to a very large, interconnected set of relationships.

Facebook users participate on various levels, updating their status at various intervals, promoting events, sending messages, sharing photos, or engaging in live chats with friends who are online at the same time. Not all of the activities on Facebook are geared toward socializing; there are games, polls, and other diverting activities that can keep you engaged, should you want to participate.

The Facebook app acts as a direct gateway to many of the social activities on Facebook, though not the entertainment aspects. As a businessperson, this is good, because much of what you will want to use Facebook for will be connecting to people—specifically, your customers.

Once you have logged into your Facebook account with the Facebook app, you will see an interface similar to that found on the actual Facebook site. The News Feed on the Home screen is shown in Figure 15.3.

Figure 15.3

The News Feed shows what's happening with friends and colleagues right now.

At the top left of the app, you will see a small menu switch. Tap that switch, and the other pages you can access will be displayed.

Tap the Events option to view the latest events your colleagues have sent out. If you want to view older events, tap events in the Past Events section (see Figure 15.4).

The Nearby option will enable you to check in and broadcast your current location and view your friends' locations if they've opted to share that information. You may want to be careful with this sort of information, because location privacy is something you want to strongly manage for personal safety reasons.

Figure 15.4

Viewing events,
upcoming and
past.

If you tap your displayed button, you will see the Profile screen, which displays the Wall, Info, Photos, and Friends pages. The Wall page, shown in Figure 15.5, shows your status updates and any public messages anyone has written to you.

The Info page will show your personal information that you have opted to share with your friends and colleagues, the Photos page will display any images you have uploaded to Facebook, or images you're in that your friends have tagged with your name, and the Friends page will display a pictorial directory of your friends.

PHOTO MANAGEMENT

At this time, the Facebook app can view, tag, and save photos in a Facebook account.

Of course, you are interested in seeing that business page you just created. Facebook organizes all of the fan pages of which you are a part—either as a fan or an administrator—in the Friends section.

Tap on the business page you created in this list, and the official fan page will open, as seen in Figure 15.6.

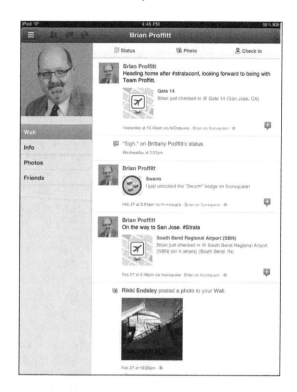

Figure 15.5
A look at your Wall.

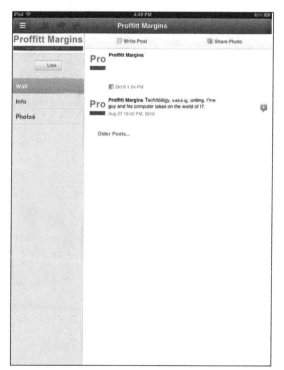

Figure 15.6
Your business page.

There's not a lot to see in your new business page, but there's a lot you can do as news about your business grows among your customers. Once they find you on Facebook (which you can help along by vigorously mentioning it to them when you do business with them), they will be able to write messages to you on your business wall.

To respond to a comment:

1. To respond to a comment from a customer on the business wall, tap the Comment icon underneath the message. The Write a comment sidebar will appear.

2. Type a reply to the comment and tap Send. Your reply will appear next to the original post by the customer, and Facebook will notify them of your reply.

Another way to communicate with your customers is using Facebook chat. This only works if the customer has actually "friended" your business page (or you personally). If they have, you can chat with them if you are online at the same time as they are.

To use Facebook chat:

1. Tap the Messages icon in the top toolbar of the Facebook app. The Messages action menu will open (see Figure 15.7).

Figure 15.7

Chatting with customers.

2. To start a conversation, tap a friend in the list, which displays anyone who is online. A chat window will display in the action menu (see Figure 15.8).

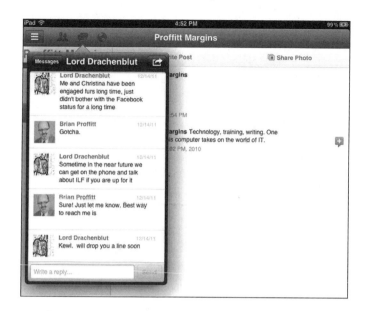

Figure 15.8

Starting a chat.

3. Tap the chat field and enter the start of a conversation, tapping Send when your comment is complete.

4. Continue the conversation with the customer until its conclusion. Tap anywhere on the screen, when finished, to close the action menu.

Setting Up a Twitter Account

Facebook is an excellent way to connect to your customers on a personal level, but even with the Facebook app, communication can be a little time-consuming. If you want to get the word out quickly, you might want to use Twitter to disseminate information.

Twitter is a social media service that lets users broadcast information to anyone who actively follows them… in 140 characters or less.

Why a 140-character limit? It goes back to Twitter's original use: the ability to aggregate text messages from phones to more than one recipient at a time. Since text messaging from phones is limited to 140 characters, so are Twitter messages—even if you use the Internet or an iPad client to send a message.

You might think that such a short limit on messages would be very constraining, but with a little practice, they can be quite informative. The brief quality of "tweets" also tends to lend itself to a more humorous style of writing, as wit and creativity are needed to get your messages to stand out in a cacophony of tweets.

To start using Twitter, you will need to set up an account. You may already have one, but for business use, it's strongly recommended you establish a separate account, to make sure your business and personal lives are kept separate.

To set up a Twitter account:

1. Using your preferred browser, visit http://twitter.com. The Twitter home page will open.

2. Fill in the fields in the New to Twitter section and click the Sign up for Twitter button. A human confirmation dialog box will appear.

3. Type the confirmation words and click Finish. The Find sources page will appear.

4. Click a topic related to your business to view a list of popular Twitter users in that category.

5. Click Follow to start building your network.

6. Click the Next Step: friends button. The Find Friends page will open.

7. Use the various online services to find colleagues and customers.

8. Once you have tracked down colleagues using the established networking services, click the Next Step: search button.

9. Search for individuals you know are on Twitter. When you find them, click the Follow button for each one.

10. Click the Next Step: You're done! button. Your new Twitter account's page will be displayed.

Managing Tweets with Twitterrific

After you have a Twitter account set up for your business and have confirmed your account via email, you can use the iPad to manage the account.

There are a lot of apps for the iPad that can manage Twitter effectively, and in August 2010, Twitter released an official app for the iPad. Of the apps in this category, the native Twitter app is the most responsive.

When you start Twitter, the first thing you need to do is sign into your Twitter account.

To sign in to your Twitter account:

1. Tap the Twitter app icon to start the Twitter app. The app will open to the splash screen.

2. Tap Add Account. The Add Account dialog box will appear (see Figure 15.9).

Figure 15.9

The Add Account dialog box.

3. Type the Username and Password information for the Twitter account you want to add and tap Save. The account will be added to the Accounts action menu.

4. Tap the account. The account settings menu will appear, and the selected tweets will appear in the main display (see Figure 15.10).

5. Tap the tweet category you want to view. The tweets you want to see will be shown.

Twitter has four classes of tweets:

◆ **Timeline.** Any tweet message sent out by someone you follow.

◆ **Mentions.** Any tweet that mentions your user name.

◆ **Messages.** Direct, private messages to your Twitter account.

◆ **Favorites.** Any tweet that you have bookmarked to view later.

The most common task you will perform with Twitter is sending out your own tweets. These can be notices of sales, special events, or maybe just something interesting you found on the Internet you'd like to share with your clients.

To send a tweet:

1. Tap the Compose icon in the lower-left corner of Twitter. The New Tweet dialog will open (see Figure 15.11).

Figure 15.10

The main Twitter app page.

Figure 15.11

The New Tweet dialog.

2. Type in a message. Note the character status icon will decrease in value as you enter characters and spaces.

SHORTENING URLs

If you copy and paste a long URL into your tweet message, you may find it will take up most or even more than your 140 characters. To fix this, type or paste the URL into your message in the New Tweet window. The URL in the tweet will be auto-replaced with a shorter substitute URL that will take users to the same location as the original URL.

---

3. When your tweet is finished, tap Send.

Another common activity on Twitter is retweeting someone else's message. It's important to understand the difference between a retweet and a reply. A retweet sends the original message out to all of the users who follow you, with the Twitter ID of the original user. A reply is a public tweet addressed to the original sender that lets you follow up on something the initial person wrote.

To retweet a Twitter message:

1. Tap the message to which you want to reply

2. Tap the Retweet icon in the message you want to retweet. An action menu will open (see Figure 15.12).

Figure 15.12

How to respond to a tweet.

3. Tap Retweet. The post will be retweeted to all of your followers.

ADDING YOUR TWO CENTS

If you want to retweet a tweet and add a comment, such as why you are sharing the message, tap the Retweet with Comment option. This will display the original tweet in the New Tweet window, enabling you to add a comment with however many characters you have left.

TWITTERQUETTE

It is considered very bad form to retweet someone's message without the user name of the original sender in the retweet. It's better to shorten the words in their tweet a little bit rather than remove the credit.

Replying to a message sends a public reply to something they wrote. The key word there is *public*: be sure the content of your reply is not something that shouldn't be shared.

To reply to a tweet:

1. Tap the Reply icon in the message to which you want to reply. A New Tweet dialog will appear.
2. Type in a message. Note the character status icon will decrease in value as you enter characters and spaces.
3. When your reply is finished, tap Send. The reply will be posted.

DON'T FORGET THE @

Anytime you mention, reply, or direct message a Twitter user, you need to precede their user name with the @ symbol. Otherwise, Twitter will not view it as a mention, reply, or direct message.

Conclusion

The power of social media is very useful in a business climate where you need to get the message about what you do out to new and existing customers fast. Facebook and Twitter are two excellent mediums to generate these messages, and the iPad has great apps to manage the messages.

In Chapter 16, "Box It Up: Shipping," we'll see how the iPad can go old-school and help you track messages of a different sort—the kind of messages where you send shipments and packages to your waiting customers.

Chapter 16

Box It Up: Shipping

◆ Tracking Shipments

◆ Tracking Vendor Shipments

◆ Notifying Customers of Shipping Status

◆ Conclusion

Being connected to the Internet as a business means that your customers are more likely not to be face-to-face, but potentially scattered around the world. So while communication is handled easily, you may find yourself shipping and receiving packages on a regular basis.

While there aren't apps for the iPad available (yet) to start a delivery process, there is an excellent application called *Delivery Status Touch* that will enable you to track outbound and inbound shipments from a very large variety of shipping carriers.

In this chapter, you'll learn how to:

◆ Track a shipment through the carrier

◆ Track a shipment from a popular ecommerce vendor

◆ Notify customers of the status of their shipment

Tracking Shipments

When you send packages out to customers these days, virtually every shipping company you use, whether the U.S. Postal Service, Canada Post, UPS, or DHL, assigns a tracking number to each package and gives it to you, the shipper, so you can mark its progress as it travels across town or across the world.

DST enables you to enter those tracking numbers and determine the location of the shipment so you can have piece of mind knowing the delivery will arrive on schedule—and act when something goes awry.

To track your shipment:

1. Tap the Deliveries app icon. The DST app will open.
2. To track a new delivery, tap the Add icon. The Add Delivery dialog box will appear (see Figure 16.1).
3. Tap the From field to choose a new carrier, if needed. The From list will appear (see Figure 16.2).
4. Flick through the list and tap the carrier option you need. The Add Delivery dialog box will reappear.
5. Tap the Tracking No. field and type the tracking number for the package.
6. If you want to track the item in DST by a proper name, tap the Item Name field and type in a label for the shipment.
7. Tap Save. The carrier will be contacted, and if the tracking number was correct, the status of the delivery will be displayed (see Figure 16.3).

Figure 16.1
Add a new delivery.

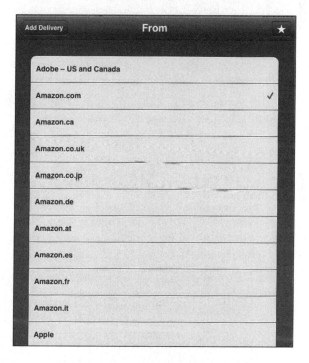

Figure 16.2
DST can track shipments with a huge variety of carriers.

Figure 16.3

Tracking a shipment.

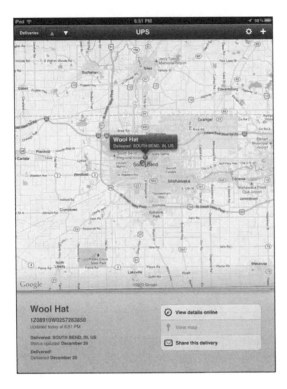

8. To view the location of the package, tap the map.

9. To view more information from the carrier's site, tap the View details online button. The map will replaced by a browser view of the carrier's tracking page.

Tracking Vendor Shipments

Not only can DST track shipments by carrier, but it can also track packages sent out by select vendors: Amazon, Google, and Apple. If you have a shipment coming in from one of these vendors, you can track the package no matter what carrier they are using.

To track shipments sent out by specific vendors:

1. Tap the Deliveries app icon. The DST app will open.

2. To track a new delivery, tap the Add icon. The Add Delivery dialog box will appear.

3. Tap the From field. The From list will appear.

4. Flick through the list and tap the vendor option you need. The Add Delivery dialog box will reappear.

5. Tap the Order No. field and type the order number for the shipment.

6. Tap the Email field and enter your email ID that you use to log into the vendor.

7. Tap Password and type in the password for your vendor account.

8. If you want to track the item in DST by a proper name, tap the Item Name field and type in a label for the shipment.

9. Tap Save. The vendor will be contacted, and the status of the delivery will be displayed.

Notifying Customers of Shipping Status

It's all well and good to track your shipments for your own sake, but let's face it—the real reason you want to know about the shipment is because the customer just called wondering where it is.

If the customer is tech-savvy, you could just send the tracking number, but often you will want to do it just to see for yourself. If you have the customer's email on file, you can send the up-to-date status to them right from DST.

To send a status report to a customer:

1. In DST, tap the Up or Down buttons until you reach the shipment you want to share with the customer.

2. Tap Share this delivery. An email message window will appear

3. Type the recipient information in the To field.

4. Tap Send. The notification message will be sent.

Once the recipient receives the email message, she can click the link to view the details of the shipment herself. If the recipient is a vendor who uses Delivery Status on her PC, she can add the shipping information directly to Delivery Status.

Conclusion

Delivery of goods and vital information is an expected part of every business. With DST on the iPad, you can track shipments easily as they're coming or going around the world.

Another aspect of working in an online environment is the need to meet with clients and vendors who could be scattered around the country or the planet. Meetings, no matter how much we don't like them, have to be done. But with travel so cost prohibitive, some meetings can get expensive. It's better then to conduct meetings online, which is what will be covered in Chapter 17, "Face-to-Face, Face-to-Web: Meetings."

Chapter 17

Face-to-Face, Face-to-Web: Meetings

- ◆ Connecting with WebEx
- ◆ Participating in a WebEx Meeting
- ◆ Using FaceTime
- ◆ Setting Up FaceTime
- ◆ Making a FaceTime Call
- ◆ Video Mirroring with FaceTime
- ◆ Whiteboarding with Air Sketch
- ◆ Conclusion

Imagine the cost and logistics to attend a business meeting in Los Angeles when you are based in New York City.

Just in terms of time, you would spend at least two hours getting to one of the airports and actually boarding a plane, then another five hours flying across the country, followed by two hours (if you're lucky) to get to the meeting itself. You will absolutely need to stay at least one night and then reverse the whole procedure again to return the next day.

So, to attend a two-hour meeting in LA, you have used up 24–36 hours of time, and that's if everything goes smoothly. And while some of that time is productive (especially if you have an iPad), it is very likely that you're not going to get as much work done as if you were in the office. And your personal schedule is shot.

These arguments for using online meetings instead of travel are well known and make a lot of sense. The Internet affords all of us the opportunity to connect with customers and co-workers via phone, PC, and now the iPad to get things talked over.

There are many iPad clients for online meetings, some better than others. One of the most complete clients is Cisco's WebEx for iPad client, which will let you view any shared document and participate in the meeting via audio.

WebEx for iPad is not the only meeting app in town, either. iPad2 users will have access to FaceTime, which also delivers the promise of affordable, portable, and decent quality videoconferencing to individual users.

Another fantastic use of the iPad is as a whiteboard. Imagine the capability of drawing a sketch on the iPad and having it appear on any browser on your network.

In this chapter, you'll learn how to:

◆ Connect to an online meeting with WebEx for iPad

◆ Communicate in an online meeting with the iPad

◆ Initiate a private chat in WebEx for iPad

◆ Use Air Sketch to present real-time graphics

Connecting with WebEx

When a WebEx meeting is first organized, invitations are sent out via email to all of the attendees to let them know the day and time the meeting is being held and to deliver connection information for the meeting.

WebEx for iPad primarily uses the Internet for attendees to connect, enabling them to view presentations and video and if they have the right equipment, initiate a two-way audio conversation. The requisite equipment is a microphone, which surprisingly is lacking on many computers even today.

OBTAINING THE RIGHT APP

There are two versions of the WebEx app out there: the older WebEx client and the newer universal WebEx for iPad. This is the app you should get, as it flows better on the larger iPad screen.

Not so with the iPad. With its built-in microphone and speakers, you can verbally communicate with other meeting participants immediately.

GETTING BETTER SOUND

Although they are not required to use WebEx (or any other voice-over Internet app), a good pair of headphones with a microphone is very useful for better sound quality.

There are three ways to connect to a WebEx meeting. First, within the Mail app, you can tap the meeting link. This will immediately connect to the meeting. If the WebEx meeting is scheduled in your Calendar, you can tap the meeting link there to also join the meeting. If you have the nine-digit meeting number, you can enter the information in the WebEx app to connect as well.

To connect to a WebEx meeting:

1. Tap the WebEx app icon. The WebEx app will open (see Figure 17.1).
2. Tap the Join by Meeting Number button. The Join by Meeting Number dialog will appear.
3. Tap the Meeting Number field and type in the meeting number.
4. Edit your name, if necessary.
5. Tap Join Meeting. WebEx will begin the connection process (see Figure 17.2).

Figure 17.1
*The initial
WebEx screen.*

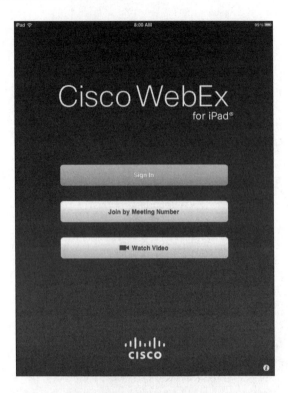

Figure 17.2
*Connecting to a
meeting.*

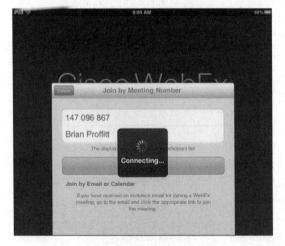

Participating in a WebEx Meeting

When you initially connect to a meeting, what you see will depend on
how long the meeting has been in progress. If, for instance, the meeting
hasn't started, or the meeting presenter has not shared a presentation yet,
you may see the default information screen, which will look something
like the one shown in Figure 17.3.

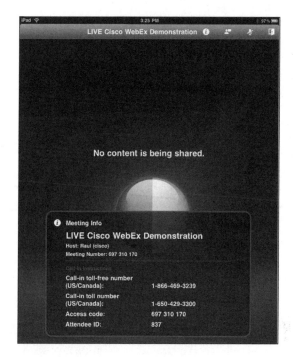

Figure 17.3
A meeting information screen.

If you ever want to view this information while the meeting is in progress, just tap the Info icon to view the Meeting Info action menu (shown in Figure 17.4).

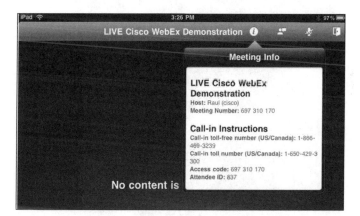

Figure 17.4
The Meeting Info action menu.

If the meeting is in progress, the presenter may have begun to share a presentation. This will be displayed in the Document Sharing screen, shown in Figure 17.5.

Figure 17.5

Viewing a presentation.

As the meeting progresses, the identity of whomever is speaking will be displayed in real time within a pop-up notification box (see Figure 17.6).

Figure 17.6

Know who is speaking instantly.

At any time during the meeting, you can start a text chat session with one or all of the participants.

To start a chat session:

1. Tap the Participants icon. The Participants action menu will appear (see Figure 17.7).

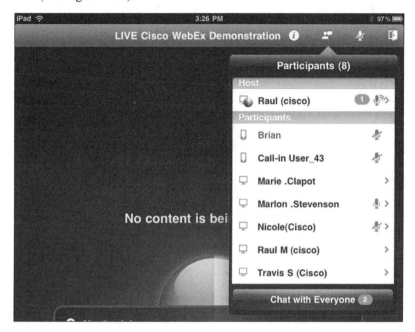

Figure 17.7

Chat with any or all of the other attendees.

2. Tap the participant with whom you want to chat. The participant's action menu will appear.
3. Tap the Chat option. The Chat screen will open.
4. Tap the conversation field and type in a comment to the chat recipient.
5. Tap Send to send the message.
6. Tap Close when the chat session is over. The meeting screen will reappear.

When you need to mute your microphone (which is always polite, to reduce general background noise), tap the Mute icon and tap Mute Conversation in the action menu. If you want to join the audio conversation again, tap the Mute icon again and tap the Unmute Call option (see Figure 17.8).

Figure 17.8

Mute yourself as needed.

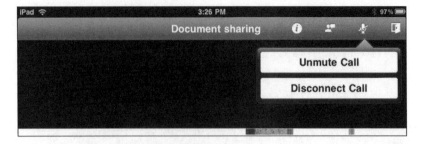

Once the meeting is over, or you need to leave, tap the Exit icon. The Exit notification box will appear (see Figure 17.9).

Figure 17.9

Leave the meeting.

Using FaceTime

FaceTime is not something new to the iPad 2, though the iPad 2 is the first model that can actually use it, thanks to the new on-board front- and rear-facing cameras. This is something that, with the improved new cameras in the 2012 iPad, will have even better performance.

FaceTime was actually created for the iPhone 4 in the summer of 2010, the first device from Apple to feature a dual-camera setup.

It's this double-camera configuration that makes FaceTime work so well. Until recently, most mobile devices, when they had a camera, used a photo/video capture lens that was located on the back of the device—in other words, the side of the device that was on the opposite side of the device's video screen. Think about a two-video call, and you can quickly imagine such a situation becoming very awkward very quickly.

With the iPhone 4, and now the iPad 2 and 2012 iPad, FaceTime can enable you to engage easily in video calls with any FaceTime-enabled device in the world.

But in that statement alone, there are hidden limitations. Note that connectivity is limited to other FaceTime-equipped devices. Right now, that includes all iPad 2 and 2012 iPad devices, any iPhone 4 (and beyond), fourth-generation iPod Touch devices, and any desktop or laptop with Mac OS X 10.6.6 or higher, so we're not exactly talking to a small user base.

Still, Windows and Linux users are not able to use FaceTime, and don't look for FaceTime on the Android mobile platform anytime soon, either, given the animosity between Apple and Google over their respective mobile platforms.

This means that as you seek out possible connections for your meetings, you will need to deliberately search for other colleagues who have the correct devices.

Another, perhaps more well-known, limitation is the inability for FaceTime devices to send their signals over any cellular network. This is due to the sheer amount of data each video call creates: upwards of 3 MB per minute. That number may seem a bit abstract, but think about your own cellular data plan and any financial caps that might exist with it, and you will quickly see why pushing a FaceTime call of any significant length could be a very expensive proposition.

That expense is mainly incurred by the cellular carriers. Increasingly, data carriers in North America, Asia, and Europe are learning that unlimited data plans will quickly jam their networks with traffic, and they have taken great pains to limit data traffic to keep their networks clear. This is why, to date, Apple has been unable to negotiate a plan with any cellular carrier to have video calls.

The result of this behind-the-scenes technical discussion means that anyone who is using FaceTime must connect over a wireless network (or, for Mac users, a wired Ethernet connection will also work). This WiFi-only limitation has gotten quite a bit of knocking in the media, but to be honest, even 3G and 4G iPad owners can typically find a wireless network somewhere.

The good news is, once you find such a network, it is very simple to set up a FaceTime connection. But first, you need to configure FaceTime to be ready to receive and send calls.

Setting Up FaceTime

When you first use your iPad, FaceTime will likely be disabled by default. That's because you must register your contact information with the FaceTime app so callers can reach you. This contact information is in the form of an email address, one of which must be added to FaceTime.

To configure FaceTime:

1. Tap the Settings icon on the home screen. The Settings app will open.

2. Tap the FaceTime setting. The FaceTime sign-in pane will open, as seen in Figure 17.10.

Figure 17.10

The FaceTime sign-in pane.

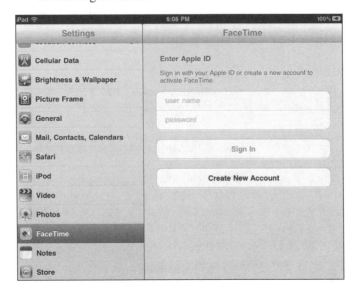

3. Type the email address or user name for your Apple ID into the user name field.
4. Type your Apple ID password into the password field.
5. Tap the Sign In button. The address confirmation screen will appear (see Figure 17.11).

Figure 17.11

Confirm the address you want to use for FaceTime.

6. Tap the Next button. The address will be accepted, and the FaceTime settings pane will appear (see Figure 17.12).

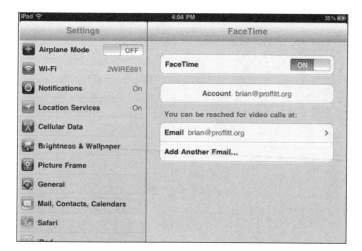

Figure 17.12

The FaceTime settings pane.

If you ever decide to disable your FaceTime app, you can use the Settings app to manage this.

To disable FaceTime:

1. Tap the Settings icon on the Home screen. The Settings app will open.
2. Tap the FaceTime setting. The FaceTime settings pane will open.
3. Slide the FaceTime control to Off. FaceTime will be disabled on your iPad.

After FaceTime is initially configured, you can give the email address you entered to associates to use to contact your iPad with their FaceTime devices.

Making a FaceTime Call

Very likely the hardest part of making a FaceTime call is finding someone with whom to connect. If your circle of friends and colleagues are dedicated Apple users, this problem is a bit easier to manage.

To date, there is no app or online directory that enables you to find out which of your contacts has FaceTime capabilities. You will need to find them using the old-fashioned way: ask them.

Once you identify someone with whom you can connect, making a FaceTime call is a breeze.

To make a FaceTime call:

1. Tap the FaceTime app icon. The FaceTime Home screen will appear (see Figure 17.13).

Figure 17.13

The FaceTime Home screen.

2. Tap a contact with whom you want to connect. The call will start immediately.

3. When the recipient answers, their image will appear in the large screen, and your image will appear in the smaller picture-in-picture.

4. When the call is complete, tap the End Call button. The call will end, and the Home screen will appear.

That's pretty much it; nothing fancy is needed. The quality settings are all automatic, although it's always good to have plenty of light available when making any video call.

When a call comes into FaceTime, a trilling tone will sound, and you will be given the choice to Accept or Decline the incoming call. Tap Accept, and the call will begin.

Another feature of FaceTime makes use of the rear-facing camera, so you can show the caller something else while still being able to view him on the iPad screen. For instance, an employee wishing to share a project demo could use the rear camera to show off his work, while still watching his caller on-screen.

To use this feature, simply tap the camera switch button during a call. To reactivate the front-facing camera, tap the camera switch button again.

Video Mirroring with FaceTime

Another new hardware feature of the iPad 2 and 2012 iPad, which hasn't gotten a lot of attention yet, is the capability to send the screen content from the device to another screen, such as a monitor or television screen.

Known as *video mirroring*, this is very useful if you ever want to run a demonstration of an iPad app for a larger group of people (such as a corporate meeting), and it's ideal for broadcasting FaceTime calls to a lot of people at once. The iPad could do this, but only to Apple-compatible devices. The newer iPads enable video mirroring to a much larger set of monitors.

To use video mirroring, all you need to do is purchase the correct video adapter for your iPad 2 or 2012 iPad. If you want to connect to a computer monitor or TV with a VGA input, you should get the VGA Adapter. To connect to an HDTV, purchase the Digital AV Connector. Both of these connectors are available for purchase online at the Apple website or at any Apple retail outlet.

To set the iPad 2 or 2012 iPad to feed to a widescreen monitor:

1. Tap the Settings icon on the Home screen. The Settings app will open.
2. Tap the Video setting. The Video settings pane will open, as seen in Figure 17.14.

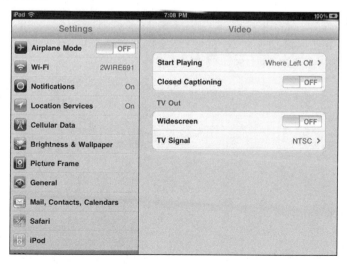

Figure 17.14

The Video settings pane.

> **VIDEO ON THE ROAD**
>
> If you are connecting to a TV from somewhere other than North America, you may want to switch the video output to PAL in the Video settings pane.

3. Slide the Widescreen control to On.

Whiteboarding with Air Sketch

A ubiquitous feature of many conference rooms is the whiteboard, complete with smelly markers and dry eraser. When someone gets an idea, she jumps up, snaps the cap off, and starts free sketching to her heart's content.

With the Air Sketch app, you can accomplish all of this with the iPad itself. Air Sketch enables users to draw a sketch free-hand that is transmitted in real time to any browser on your network.

The interface for Air Sketch is very simple, as shown in Figure 17.15.

Figure 17.15

The Air Sketch interface.

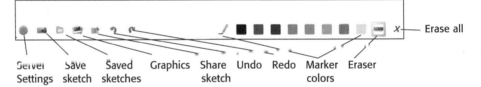

Server Settings | Save sketch | Saved sketches | Graphics | Share sketch | Undo | Redo | Marker colors | Eraser

Erase all

To begin drawing on Air Sketch, all you need to do is tap one of the eight marker colors and start drawing with your finger or an iPad stylus. You can choose colors from the bottom right corner of the screen, as seen in Figure 17.16.

If you want to save any sketch, tap the Save sketch icon. To retrieve it, tap the Saved sketches icon to open an action menu that lists all the saved sketches to date (see Figure 17.17).

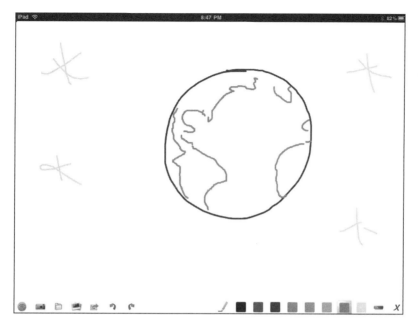

Figure 17.16
The author is not quitting his day job.

Figure 17.17
Retrieving saved sketches.

To insert graphics from your iPad into any sketch:

1. Tap the Graphics icon. The Photo Albums action menu will appear.
2. Navigate to the image you want to insert and tap it. The image will be inserted within the sketch (see Figure 17.18).

279

Figure 17.18

The image tools in Air Sketch.

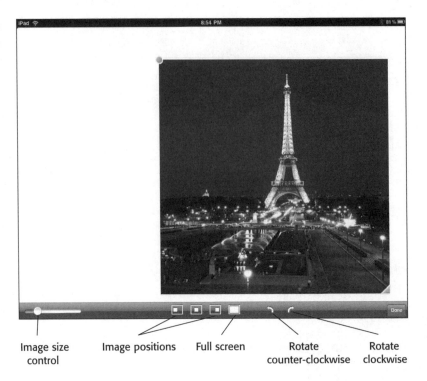

Image size control   Image positions   Full screen   Rotate counter-clockwise   Rotate clockwise

3. Tap and drag the round graphic handle to move the image window on the sketch.

4. Tap and drag the corner graphic handle to resize the image window.

5. Slide the image size control to reduce or enlarge the size of the image.

6. Tap and drag the image to move it within the image window.

7. Tap Done when finished editing the image.

As fun as Air Sketch is as a simple drawing tool, the real magic happens when you set Air Sketch to broadcast what's being drawn on the screen in real time.

To set Air Sketch to broadcast what's being drawn on the screen in real time:

1. Tap the Server Settings icon. The Server Settings action menu will appear (see Figure 17.19).

2. If you want to have added security for your sketch session, slide the Require Login control to On. Type a user name and password that will be required for any user to join the session.

3. Tap the Mail icon. A message window will open with the link to the Air Sketch session.

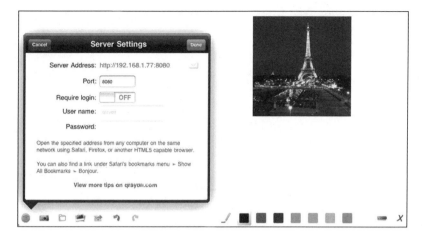

Figure 17.19

The Server Settings action menu.

4. Address the message and tap Send. The invitation will be sent.

5. As a recipient, click the link within the invitation window to open it in the default browser. As the session continues, the exact contents of the Air Sketch interface will be duplicated on the browser.

Conclusion

The ability to communicate important ideas through presentations and collaborative discussions is key to any successful business. With tools like WebEx, FaceTime, and Air Sketch, you can quickly view and even share your ideas in any meeting.

Content on the Internet is also a vital part of business communication. The iPad is a great tool for receiving Web content, and as you'll learn in Chapter 18, "Write Online: Web Content Creation," it can be a good platform for creating Web content, too.

Chapter 18

Write Online:
Web Content Creation

- ◆ Connecting to a Blog
- ◆ Posting a Blog Entry
- ◆ Editing a Blog Entry
- ◆ Conclusion

It has been argued that the advent of the Internet, particularly the capability for anyone to produce content and publish it for everyone to see, has been as much of a shift to the workplace as the printing press was to the education of cultures. It's still too early to see the long-term cultural impact of content creation via blogs, but already it's rocked the traditional media industry. Why read a newspaper when the expert across town has reported an event on his blog?

Businesses have been a little slower than individuals to see the benefits of blogging. But many savvy businesspeople are beginning to see that by sharing stories, you can connect to potential partners and customers in ways that no sales pitch ever could.

In this chapter, you'll learn how to use the BlogPress app to:

◆ Connect to an existing blog

◆ Post blog entries to your blog

◆ Add images to your blog

◆ Edit blog entries

Connecting to a Blog

Most blogging websites use a content management system (CMS) to enable users to post and edit blog entries. These systems will manage blogs quite well, and some are sophisticated enough to manage the content of entire websites, not just a blog page.

BlogPress is a useful app because it enables you to connect to 11 different content management systems. Each has its own strengths and weaknesses, but typically the system you will work with will be determined by your company's IT department, or if you're a business owner, the blog system used by your preferred provider.

The blog systems to which BlogPress can connect are the following:

◆ **Blogger.** Owned and operated by Google, this flexible blog system enables user to post content of many types free of charge.

◆ **MSN Live Spaces.** A component of Microsoft's Windows Live system, Live Spaces features basic blogging tools free of charge.

◆ **WordPress.** This very popular blogging CMS has become robust enough to manage entire websites. The WordPress software is free, and can be hosted on a stand-alone site or as part of WordPress.com.

◆ **Movable Type.** Another popular blogging platform, Movable Type is considered to be the top of the line for blogging. MT is free, but must be hosted on a stand-alone site.

◆ **TypePad.** A blog network like Blogger or Live Spaces, TypePad charges a monthly fee to host and manage blogs. But it doesn't impose ads on your visitors like the free blog services do.

◆ **LiveJournal.** One of the first blogging networks, LiveJournal is no longer on the cutting edge of technology and is very ad-heavy; however, its simple interface is still attractive to beginning users.

◆ **Drupal.** This free and robust CMS actually is designed to handle entire websites. BlogPress works with Drupal's Blog module. Drupal must be hosted on a stand-alone site.

◆ **Joomla!.** The author's personal favorite CMS, Joomla!, is another free whole-site CMS. BlogPress connects through the MetaWeblog plug-in for Joomla!. Joomla! must be hosted on a stand-alone site.

◆ **Tumblr.** A relative newcomer on the blog scene, Tumblr features small blogs that users create to voice ideas quickly or link to items. Think Twitter, just with more text.

◆ **Squarespace.** A hosted blog system like TypePad, the new Squarespace service offers innovative design for customers and a variety of pricing plans.

◆ **My Opera.** A blogging network geared specifically for users of the Opera browser.

That's a lot of options, but that's what makes BlogPress so attractive: the capability to connect to many different systems. Not only that, but BlogPress will connect to multiple accounts, so if you have a work blog on one system and a personal blog on another system, you can switch between these content systems with just a few taps.

MINIMUM REQUIREMENTS

BlogPress will enable users to connect seamlessly to these content management systems, but some of the systems will need prior configuration. Visit http://blogpressapp.com/?p=feedback to learn more about preparing Joomla!, WordPress, and MSN Live Spaces for connecting with Blogpress.

ALL-IN-ONE

BlogPress is great for connecting to a variety of blog platforms. If you have a specific CMS that you're using, you might want to search for that CMS's corresponding app in the App Store. Drupal, Joomla!, and WordPress, for instance, each have excellent apps that not only control content for blogs, but content for entire websites as well.

To connect with a blog system:

1. Tap the BlogPress app icon. The BlogPress app will open with an initial notification dialog (see Figure 18.1).

Figure 18.1

You need to set up at least one blog before using BlogPress.

2. Tap OK. The Select Provider screen will appear (see Figure 18.2).

Figure 18.2

The available providers.

3. Tap the provider option to which you want to connect. The Add Blog screen will appear, as shown in Figure 18.3.

4. Type the appropriate information within the Account Information section.

5. Tap Save. BlogPress will try to connect, and if successful, the Settings screen for the blog will appear (see Figure 18.4).

Figure 18.3
Enter your blog account info.

Figure 18.4
The blog is ready to be configured.

6. To add another blog to BlogPress, tap Add another blog. The Add Blog screen will appear, and you can repeat steps 3–5 to complete the activity.

Posting a Blog Entry

The hard part of creating a blog entry should just be the creative process—not the tools that you use to post the entry.

To post a blog:

1. Tap the Manage button. The Manage action menu will appear (see Figure 18.5).

Figure 18.5

The Manage action menu.

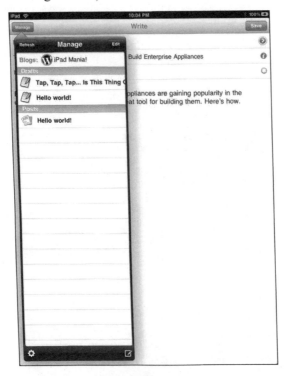

> ### MULTIPLE BLOGS
>
> If you want to change the blog on which you're going to post, tap the Blogs option at the top of the Manage action menu and tap the blog you want to use. You can also tap the blue options icon in the Write screen to change the blog.

2. Tap the Write icon. The Write screen will appear (see Figure 18.6).

3. Type a title for the blog and tap the Options icon. The Options dialog box will open (see Figure 18.7).

4. Tap the fields in the Categories and tags section and apply any tags or categories to the blog entry. These are set up in your blog system.

5. If you just want to save blog entries to your site and not have them be live right away, slide the Publish control to Off.

6. Tap Publish Date. The Publish Date dialog box will appear, where you can change the date and time of the blog entry.

Figure 18.6
The Write screen.

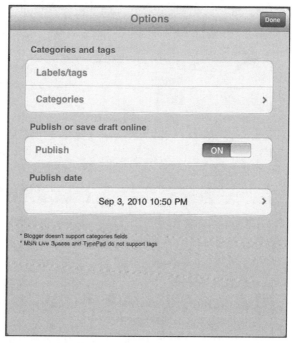

Figure 18.7
The Options dialog box.

7. Tap the Options button. The Options dialog box will reappear.

8. Tap Done. The Options dialog box will close.

9. If you want, tap the Location icon to assign a location tag to your blog.

10. Tap the body area of the screen and type in a blog entry.

11. When Finished, tap Save. The Saving Blog pop-over will open, where you can publish the blog entry immediately or save as a draft.

12. For now, tap Save Draft Only. The entry will be saved as a draft.

Editing a Blog Entry

Whether a blog entry is posted and live on your site, or saved as a draft, you can immediately access it to make changes.

To edit a blog entry:

1. Tap the Manage button. The Manage action menu will appear.

2. Tap the entry you want to edit. The Write screen will appear with the entry.

3. To format text, double-tap text to select it and drag the selection handles to encompass all of the text you want to format.

4. Tap the HTML button. The Insert HTML action menu will appear.

5. Tap the formatting option you want to apply. HTML tags will be applied to the selected text, as shown in Figure 18.8.

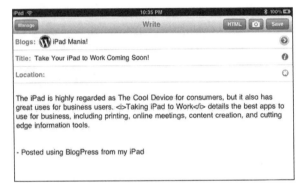

Figure 18.8

Using HTML to format.

6. To add a hyperlink, double-tap text to select it and drag the selection handles to encompass all of the text you want to link.

7. Tap the HTML button. The Insert HTML action menu will appear.

8. Tap the A option. The A action menu will appear.

9. Type the full URL in the Link field and tap Done. The selected text will be tagged with hyperlink information.

10. To insert a graphic, place the cursor where you want to insert the figure and tap the Image icon. The Photo Albums action menu will open.

11. Navigate to the artwork you want to insert and tap it. The image will be inserted in the blog entry (see Figure 18.9).

12. To post the entry, tap Save. The Saving Blog pop-over will open.

13. Tap Publish Now! The blog entry will be saved to the website to which BlogPress is connected (see Figure 18.10).

Figure 18.9
Graphics are easy.

Figure 18.10
The posted blog entry.

Conclusion

With the power of blogging, you can communicate any aspect of your business quickly and accurately, reaching exactly the people you want to reach in as much time as it takes to draft your message.

Of course, reaching that audience can be a very tricky business. Sure, you've posted on your website everything from banners to business cards, but is anyone visiting your website? And if they are, who are they, and where are they coming from? The answers may surprise you, and in Chapter 19, "Track Online: Website Management," you'll learn how to track your site's visitors so you can see for yourself who's coming to visit.

Chapter 19

Track Online: Website Management

- ◆ Connecting to Your Google Analytics Account
- ◆ Interpreting the Analytics Data
- ◆ Viewing Analytics Reports
- ◆ Conclusion

Those of us who surf the Internet a lot (sometimes even professionally) see them sometimes—dusty, creaky reminders of the World Wide Web. They're like seeing an abandoned gas station at the side of a desert road. You know that once there was enough traffic and customers to make that gas station a vibrant business, but something changed and took all the traffic away, leaving nothing behind but wood and antique pumps sitting on cracked concrete, fading in the sun.

That's what Web page counters look like to Internet visitors. A few Web hosting services still offer them as tools, and if you ever find one making that offer, walk away quickly. They're either overhyping the supposed value of Web counters, or they genuinely believe Web counters are useful—in which case, they are woefully lacking in real hosting skills.

The main reason why Web counters are so *not* useful is the advent of a new technology known as *Web analytics*. With Web analytics, an analytics service will monitor the traffic on your website and not just count visitors. It will track where the visitors came from, how long they stayed, and what they looked at while they were there. Perhaps most importantly, analytics will provide metrics on what brought them to your site.

There are two kinds of analytics services: commercial services for larger websites that can start at $200/month, but offer detailed, customized reports about the traffic coming and going on your site; and Google Analytics, which is free of charge and offers detailed, customized reports about the traffic coming and going on your site.

FREE? MUST BE CHEAP

If you're one of those people who thinks that something that is free is automatically chintzy, nothing could be further from the truth with Google Analytics. So how can they not charge a penny for this wonderful service?

The answer lies in Google's real moneymaker: Web advertising. By helping websites improve their traffic, any website that deploys Google ads will also have higher traffic (think all boats rising in the same tide). More traffic for sites with Google's ads means more revenue for Google.

Knowing more about the details of your website's traffic enables you to focus on the areas of your site that are getting more attention. If you're running a cheese store and nearly everyone coming into your site is coming in to view the page with your great aunt's Apple-Cheddar Cobbler recipe that you just tossed out there on a whim, maybe you should put similar recipes in that section of the site. And be sure there's a button that links to your online catalog so they can buy the exact cheese they need for these recipes. And maybe put packages together of each of the recipe's ingredients so they can buy those as gift baskets or convenience items, which you can sell at a higher profit margin.

You can see how analytics can be useful.

The iPad features a very useful app, Analytics HD, that logs into your Google Analytics account and brings back all of the useful information you would find on the Google Analytics site, nicely formatted to the iPad interface. In this chapter, you'll discover how to use the Analytics HD app to:

◆ Connect to a Google Analytics account

◆ Interpret the analytics data

◆ View specific analytics reports

Connecting to Your Google Analytics Account

Before you can begin to use Analytics HD, you will need to set up a Google Analytics account, if you don't have one already.

To do this, visit www.google.com/analytics/ in your browser and either sign in or sign up for a Google Analytics account, using a Google ID. The Google Analytics site is pretty straightforward—just follow the guided pages to enter all of your site and contact information.

At the end of the process, you will be given what's known as a *code snippet* to insert in the basic HTML code of your website. Once you or your IT administrator (depending on your level of technical skill) insert this code into your site, Google Analytics will be able to "talk" to your site and begin the tracking.

WHERE'S MY SITE?

If you are wondering why your site isn't showing up on the Google Analytics site right away, be patient. It can take anywhere from 30 minutes to 24 hours for Google Analytics to begin tracking, and usually another 24 hours to have enough time to get enough data to generate a report.

Once the account is created and running smoothly, you can connect to your analytics account via Analytics HD.

To connect to your analytics account via Analytics HD:

1. Tap the Analytics HD app icon. The Analytics HD app will open with an initial login dialog (see Figure 19.1).

Figure 19.1

You need to connect to your Google Analytics account.

2. Enter your Google Analytics login and password information and tap Go. The Analytics screen will appear with the Settings action menu open (see Figure 19.2).

Figure 19.2

Choose the site to monitor.

3. Tap the site you want to view. The Dashboard screen will appear, as shown in Figure 19.3.

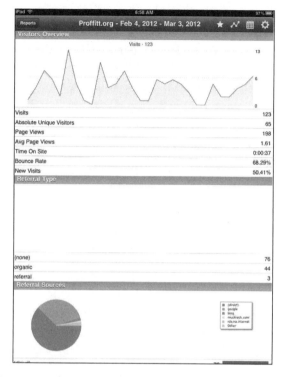

Figure 19.3

The Dashboard screen.

Interpreting the Analytics Data

Entire books have been written on how to effectively utilize analytics data from any source, so we won't spend a lot of time getting deep into the numbers that you see in Analytics HD. The key thing to remember as you view all these numbers and fancy graphs is that you need to figure out what's bringing people to your site and what's keeping them there.

It makes a difference, for instance, if your site is being found on Google or Yahoo! versus getting traffic referrals from another site related to your business. Or, heaven forbid, traffic from a disgruntled customer's blog who has made it his life mission to make you miserable.

If your traffic is visiting one page or section of your site more than others, it makes sense to focus your content and development efforts on improving that part of the site before any other.

In the Dashboard screen of Analytics HD, you can see a lot of useful information. Each section is a summary of information you can find in the Reports action menu, so use the Dashboard as a first glance at your site's metrics, from which you can figure out what report to drill down and read.

The Visitors Overview contains very useful information:

◆ **Visits.** The number of visits your site has received.

◆ **Absolute Unique Visitors.** The number of unique visitors your site has received.

◆ **Page Views.** How many pages were read by each visitor?

◆ **Avg Page Views.** The average number of pages each visitor read.

◆ **Time On Site.** How much time each visitor spent on the site.

◆ **Bounce Rate.** The more visitors stay and read once they arrive on your site, the lower your bounce rate will be.

◆ **New Visits.** The percentage of visitors who are new to your site.

The Referral Type (Visits) section lays out the numbers and percentages of incoming traffic's origins:

◆ **CPC.** (Cost per Click). Visits referred from an ad campaign for your site.

◆ **Organic.** Visits from users just typing in the URL of your site.

◆ **None.** Visits Google Analytics was unable to determine.

◆ **Referral.** Visits referred from other sites.

The Referral Sources (Visits) section breaks down the data for just the referrals, letting you know from where visitors were sent to your site.

Country (Visits) lists the nations from where visitors arrived, while the City (Visits) section lists individual metropolitan areas.

Keywords (Visits) displays the specific keywords people entered on Google and other search sites that brought them to your site.

Content (Page Views) lists the pages on your site that get the most visits.

All data in Analytics HD is displayed from a certain period of time. The default period is one month.

To change the date range for reports:

1. Tap the Date button. The Date Range action menu will appear (see Figure 19.4).

2. To change the start date for a reporting period, tap Start and then use the spin controls to change the date.

3. To change the end date for a reporting period, tap End and then use the spin controls to change the date.

4. Tap Save. The new reporting period will be saved and applied to the Dashboard.

Figure 19.4

The Date Range action menu.

Viewing Analytics Reports

The Dashboard reveals great overview information, but the real gems are to be found in the Reports available on Analytics HD.

For instance, the Keywords report is often invaluable because it shows you what terms are bringing visitors to your site. If you were to notice that the highest search term is cheese recipes, then the more you can legitimately integrate that term into the content of your site, the more weight search engines will give to your site and hopefully more prominence in future results.

But take care: You can't just throw "cheese recipes" willy-nilly all over your site. It has to make sense and be a natural part of your site. Otherwise, search engine algorithms and the humans that run them will penalize your site for trying to game their system.

To examine your site's most popular keywords:

1. Tap the Reports button. The Reports action menu will appear.

2. Tap the Keywords option. The Keywords screen will appear.

3. To view the data as percentages, tap the % Visits button.

Conclusion

Analytics can deliver a lot of powerful information about your business website. By paying attention to your visitors, you can improve your bottom line with a few well-thought out strategies.

Running a business is a challenging prospect on a good day. Tracking inventory, revenue, and managing customers is more than a full-time job. In Chapter 20, "Make a List: Task Management," you'll learn how to organize your tasks to make your business life (and maybe your personal life) a lot easier.

Chapter 20

Make a List:
Task Management

- ◆ Creating Tasks in Things
- ◆ Creating Projects
- ◆ Organizing Tasks
- ◆ Conclusion

The iPad is perfect for task management, since you can pretty much take it anywhere you go, but there are different ways to approach task management apps. You can make all of the lists you want, using the simple lists in the Reminders app, but if your lists aren't well organized or easy to use, then all the to-dos in the world won't help you. In fact, they may make your stress level higher.

One popular way to approach task management is the Getting Things Done (GTD) methodology, invented by management consultant David Allen. GTD essentially advocates applying a "do it, delegate it, defer it, drop it" rule to get your inbox empty, and explains how to apply your attention the best way to each task so there's never a sense of being overwhelmed.

There are other ways to approach task management, of course, and you may already have a personal system you're using. In any case, it's important to use an iPad app flexible enough to adapt to any task system you have. Getting Things Done for iPad is an independent app that fits well with the GTD methodology, but also is light enough to work a number of different approaches.

In this chapter, you'll discover how to use the Things for iPad app to:

◆ Create a task

◆ Organize your tasks efficiently

◆ Schedule tasks

◆ Group tasks into larger projects

Creating Tasks in Things

Things for iPad is what's known as a *list manager*. You enter your tasks within the app, and they are immediately assigned to a list. Which list you use depends on the timing of the task, or whether it's a stand-alone task or part of a larger project.

To create a task in Things:

1. Tap the Things app icon. The Things for iPad app will open on the Next screen with a helpful initial message.

2. Tap the Add icon. The New To Do action menu will open (see Figure 20.1).

3. Type the title for the task in the Title field.

4. To add a tag to the task, tap the Tags field. The Tags action menu will appear (see Figure 20.2).

Due Date   Notes   Tags   Title

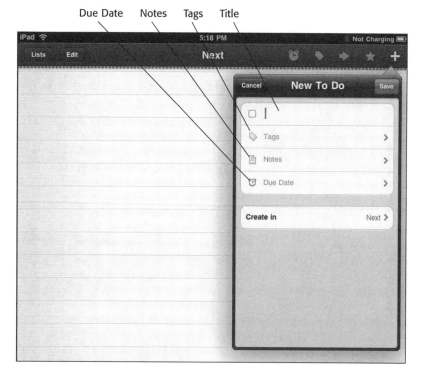

Figure 20.1

The New To Do action menu.

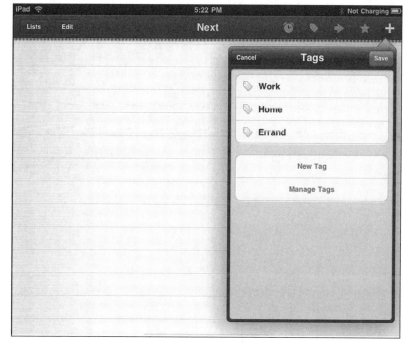

Figure 20.2

The Tags action menu.

5. If you want to create a new tag, tap the New Tag control. The New Tag action menu will appear.

6. Type a new tag name and tap Save. The new tag will appear as a selected tag on the Tags action menu.

7. Select additional tags, if necessary, and tap Save. The New To Do action menu will reappear.

8. To add any comments to the task, tap the Notes field. The Edit Notes action menu will appear.

9. Type any comments for the task and tap Save. The New To Do action menu will reappear.

10. To add a deadline for the task, tap the Due Date field. The Edit Due Date action menu will appear (see Figure 20.3).

Figure 20.3

The Edit Due Date action menu.

11. Enter a new due date for the task.

12. To change the date when the task will appear in the Today list, tap Show in Today and adjust the length of time the task will appear in the Today list before the due date.

13. Tap Save. The New To Do action menu will reappear.

14. Tap Create In and select the list in which you want to place the task. The list will be selected, and the New To Do action menu will reappear.

15. Tap Save. The task will appear in the desired list (see Figure 20.4).

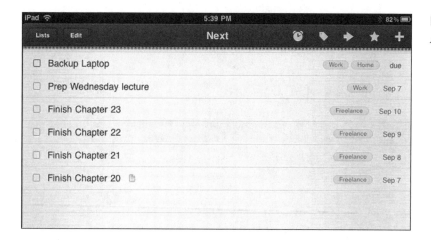

Figure 20.4
An entered task.

If you have a task coming up that you will need to start later, you will need to put it in the Scheduled list. The scheduled task setup is similar to that of creating a regular task.

To create a scheduled task:

1. Tap the Add icon. The New To Do action menu will open.
2. Type the title for the task in the Title field.
3. Add tags, notes, and a due date for the task.
4. Tap Create In and select the Scheduled list. The list will be selected, and the New To Do action menu will reappear.
5. Tap Save. The Schedule action menu will appear (see Figure 20.5).

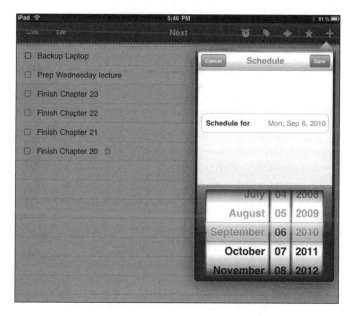

Figure 20.5
Scheduling a task.

6. Enter a start date for the task and tap Save. The task will appear in the Scheduled list, and it will not appear in the Next list until the start date you specified.

To navigate between lists, tap the Lists button. This will open the Lists action menu shown in Figure 20.6.

Figure 20.6

The Lists action menu.

Tap one of the list options to view that list.

If you want to view your tasks in chronological order, tap the Due Date icon to view tasks sorted by the due date.

To revert to a normal view, tap the Close icon on the sort message indicator. To view tasks with a certain tag, tap the Tags icon. The Filter by Tag action menu will appear, as shown in Figure 20.7.

Figure 20.7

Filter for tagged items.

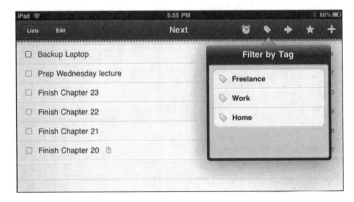

Tap the tag for which you want to filter, and just those tagged tasks will appear.

To mark a task as finished, tap the checkbox next to the task. The task will be dimmed and at the end of the day will appear in the Logbook list, where you can keep track of things you have done.

Creating Projects

Not only can you set up individual tasks in Things, but you can also create larger, multistep projects, which will enable you to better organize your bigger to-dos into smaller, discrete steps.

To create a project in Things:

1. Tap the Lists button and tap the Projects list. The Projects screen will appear with a helpful initial message (see Figure 20.8).

Figure 20.8

Adding new projects in Things.

2. Tap the Add icon. The New Project action menu will open (see Figure 20.9).

Figure 20.9

The New Project action menu.

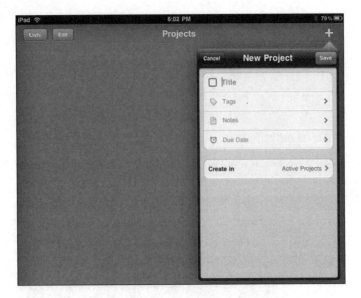

3. Type the title for the project in the Title field.

4. To add a tag to the project, tap the Tags field. The Tags action menu will appear.

5. Tap a tag and tap Save. The New Project action menu will reappear.

6. To add any comments to the task, tap the Notes field. The Edit Notes action menu will appear.

7. Type any comments for the task and tap Save. The New Project action menu will reappear.

8. To add a deadline for the task, tap the Due Date field. The Edit Due Date action menu will appear.

9. Enter a new due date for the task.

10. To change the date when the task will appear in the Today list, tap Show in Today and adjust the length of time the task will appear in the Today list before the due date.

11. Tap Save. The New Project action menu will reappear.

12. Tap Create In and select the list in which you want to place the task. The list will be selected, and the New Project action menu will reappear.

13. Tap Save. The project will appear in the desired list (see Figure 20.10).

To add a task to a project, tap the project in the Projects list. The project will open, and you can add tags as well as filter tasks within the project just as you would a list.

Figure 20.10

An entered project.

Organizing Tasks

Tasks in Things are organized into lists. At any point, you can move a task into another list. This includes active projects, which can be considered lists in Things.

To move a task:

1. In the list with the tasks you want to move, tap the Move icon. A notification message will appear (see Figure 20.11).

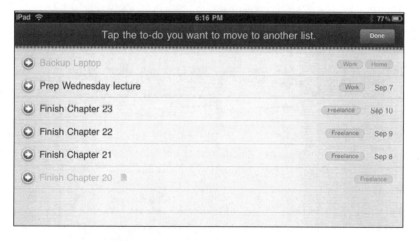

Figure 20.11

Selecting the task to move.

2. Tap the Task to move. The Move to List action menu will appear (see Figure 20.12).

Figure 20.12

The Move to List action menu.

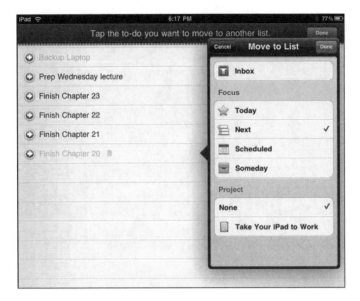

3. Tap the list where you want to move the task and tap Done. The Move to List action menu will close, and the task will be listed in its destination list or project.

4. Repeat steps 2–3 until all tasks are reassigned to their new lists.

5. When all of the tasks have been moved, tap Done. The move operation will be complete.

To edit any task within a list of projects, simply tap the task. The Info action menu will appear, which will enable you to edit any parameter of the task (see Figure 20.13).

Figure 20.13

Editing a task.

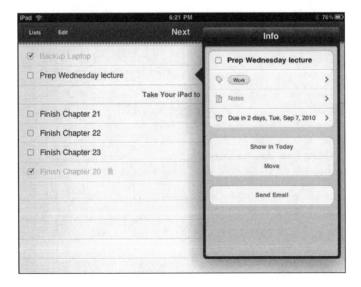

If you get ahead of schedule and find you want to tackle a future task or one of your Someday tasks today, tap the starred Today icon in Things. A notification message will appear (see Figure 20.14)

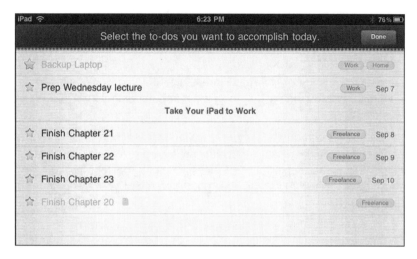

Figure 20.14

Selecting the task to do today.

Tap the tasks to do today and then tap Done. The tasks will be moved to the Today list. Finally, you can change the order of tasks and delete them outright.

To change the order of tasks or delete them:

1. In the list with the tasks you want to remove or realign, tap the Edit button. The Edit controls will appear (see Figure 20.15).

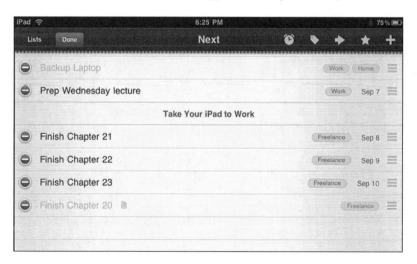

Figure 20.15

Editing a task list.

2. Tap and drag the task by the Move icon on the far right of the list to relocate its position in the list.

3. Tap the Delete icon to remove a task. The Delete button will appear.

4. Tap Delete. The task will be completely removed from Things.

Conclusion

No matter which approach to task management you prefer, Things for iPad is a fast, flexible task management app that can conform to your business needs.

Depending on your business, you may find that you need a more robust project management solution to handle multiple projects with tightly integrated phases. In Chapter 21, "See the Big Picture: Project Management," you'll discover how to use the iPad to keep on top of your business from the highest level.

Chapter 21

See the Big Picture: Project Management

- ◆ Creating Projects in SG Projects
- ◆ Building New Tasks
- ◆ Viewing Projects
- ◆ Editing Projects
- ◆ Editing Tasks
- ◆ Conclusion

As you read in Chapter 20, "Make a List: Task Management," there are numerous ways to approach project management. In the business world, the "Getting Things Done" approach can work, but for more complex projects and tasks, a more traditional project management approach might work better.

Traditional project management has a more project-centric point of view than task management tools like Things for iPad, which was featured in Chapter 20. Task management tools enable you to create tasks and perhaps group those tasks into larger projects (if they enable grouping at all).

Project management tools start with the assumption that you are going to build a project first and then add the tasks necessary to get the project completed. The nice thing about this approach is that by creating a series of sequential and parallel tasks, you can more accurately determine the total length of time it should take to complete the project, if everything goes on schedule.

STILL LIKE GETTING THINGS DONE?

If you still prefer the "Getting Thing Done" method, you will definitely want to try Omnifocus for iPad. Omnifocus is a task-centric approach to project management, similar to Things, but has a number of extra features (such as context for tasks and projects) that enable you to manage fairly robust projects. Like Things, Omnifocus can work with its Mac OS X desktop counterpart.

An excellent project-centric project management app for the iPad is SG Project, formerly known as *Project Pad*. This app works in much the same way as larger applications like Microsoft Project, although it is much more streamlined and mobile friendly. In this chapter, you'll use the SG Project app to:

◆ Create a project

◆ Build normal, milestone, and child tasks

◆ View projects using Gantt view

◆ Edit tasks and projects

Creating Projects in SG Projects

The old adage goes something like this: how do you eat an elephant?

One bite at a time.

And that's the real trick behind project management: looking at a really big goal (opening a new store across town, or exceeding last year's sales numbers by 40 percent) and parsing it into smaller, finite steps. If you break huge insurmountable projects into these smaller tasks, not only is the end result perceived as achievable, but you also have a path in place for the project.

Before you can build that path, you first have to create the project in SG Project.

To create a project in SG Project:

1. Tap the SG Project app icon. The first time you open the SG Project app, it will open to the Welcome screen.
2. Tap the Project button. The Select Project action menu will appear.
3. Tap the New Project button. The Create New Project action menu will appear (see Figure 21.1).

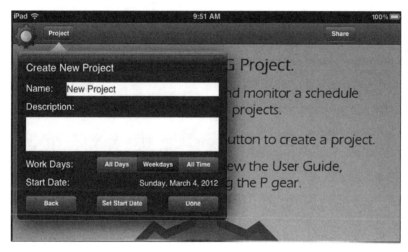

Figure 21.1

The Create New Project action menu.

4. Type a name and a description for the new project.
5. To change the start date, tap the Set Start Date button. The date controls will appear.
6. Enter the date to start the project.
7. Tap Done. The Project screen will appear as an empty task list (see Figure 21.2).

When you want to create a new project after the initial start of SG Project, tap the Project button and tap New Project in the Select Project action menu.

If you have a similar project to start (such as the 2012 version of a project you completed in 2011), you can duplicate it and all of the tasks within very quickly.

Figure 21.2

A new project.

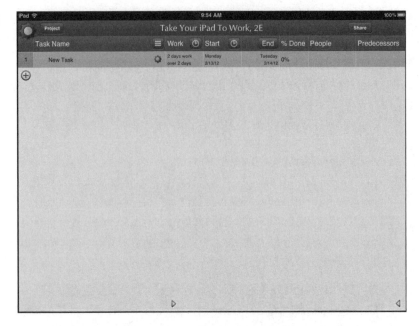

To duplicate a project or other tasks:

1. Tap the Project button. The Select Project action menu will appear (see Figure 21.3).

Figure 21.3

The Select Project action menu.

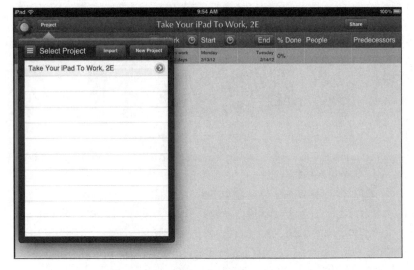

2. Tap the blue info icon next to the project you want to duplicate. The Edit Project action menu will appear.

3. Tap the Duplicate Project button. The name of the project will have "(copy)" added to the end of the title.

4. Type a new name and a description for the duplicate project.

5. To change the start date, tap the Set Start Date button. The date controls will appear.

6. Enter the date to start the project.

7. Tap Done. The new Project screen will appear with an empty task list.

Building New Tasks

Within SG Project, there are three kinds of tasks that can be created:

◆ **Normal Tasks.** A normal task is a task with a non-zero duration (meaning that the task start and end dates are different) and no child tasks.

◆ **Milestone Tasks.** A milestone task is a normal task with no duration (the start date and end date are the same).

◆ **Parent Tasks.** A parent task is any task that has children, which are component tasks that make up the larger parent task.

To create a normal or milestone task (virtually identical steps):

1. In a project screen, tap the Add Task icon. A New Task item will appear (see Figure 21.4).

Figure 21.4

A New Task item.

2. Long-press the Task Name and type in a new name for the task.

3. Long-press the Work field. The Work slide control will appear (see Figure 21.5).

4. Slide the circular control to indicate the number of days anticipated to complete the task. The interval between the Start and End dates will automatically change to match the specified duration. If you decrease the duration to zero, the task will become a milestone task.

5. Tap the Start date. The Date control will appear.

6. Enter the date to start the task.

7. If any part of the task is completed already, tap the % Done field and slide the control to the percentage of the task that is completed thus far. Setting the % Done value to 100% indicates a completed task.

8. If you want to add color coding to the task, tap the task number field. The color selection pop-over menu will appear (see Figure 21.6).

Figure 21.5

The Work slide control.

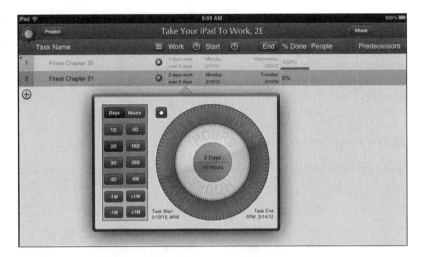

Figure 21.6

The color selection pop-over menu.

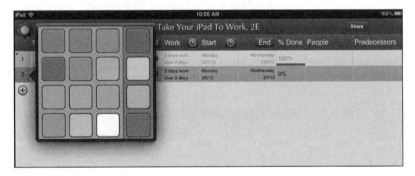

9. In Landscape mode, more fields are available. Tap the People field. The Assign People action menu will appear.

10. Tap the New Person button. The Enter New Person action menu will appear.

11. Type the name and email of the task's owner in the menu and tap Done. The Assign People action menu will reappear.

12. Tap the Owner checkbox. The task will be assigned to that person.

13. Tap anywhere on the screen. The Assign People action menu will close.

14. To link the task to prerequisite tasks, long-press the Predecessors field. The Predecessors action menu will appear (see Figure 21.7).

15. Tap the Predecessor checkbox for the task that must be done before this one can be completed. The linked task icon will appear.

16. Tap outside the Predecessors action menu. It will close, and the task number for the linked task will appear in this task's Predecessors field.

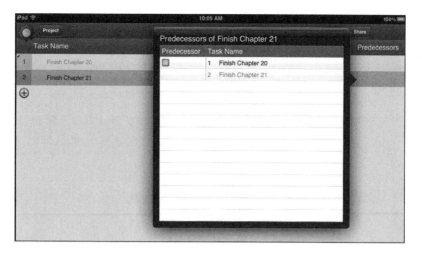

Figure 21.7

The Predecessors action menu.

Creating a parent/child task is similar in these steps, but you will use the SG Project's indenting and outdenting controls to determine the "level" of the task. When the indentation level of a task becomes deeper than the task immediately above, the indented task becomes the child of the task above, and the task above becomes its parent.

To create a child task:

1. In a project screen, tap the Add Task icon. A New Task item will appear.

2. Long-press the Task Name and type in a new name for the task.

3. Long-press the Work field. The Work slide control will appear.

4. Slide the control to indicate the number of days and hours anticipated to complete the task. The interval between the Start and End dates will automatically change to match the specified duration. If you decrease the duration to zero, the task will become a milestone task.

5. Tap the Start date. The Date control will appear.

6. Enter the date to start the task.

7. If any part of the task is completed already, tap the % Done field and slide the control to the percentage of the task that is completed thus far. Setting the % Done value to 100% indicates a completed task.

8. If you want to add color coding to the task, tap the task number field. The color selection pop-over menu will appear.

9. Tap the People field. The Assign People action menu will appear.

10. Tap the name of the task owner in the menu and tap elsewhere on the screen to close the Assign People menu.

11. To link the task to prerequisite tasks, long-tap the Predecessors field. The Predecessors action menu will appear.

12. Tap the checkbox for the task that must be done before this one can be completed. The linked task icon will appear.

13. Tap outside the Predecessors action menu. It will close, and the task number for the linked task will appear in this task's Predecessors field.

14. Tap the Gear icon. The Task Edit menu will appear (see Figure 21.8).

Figure 21.8
The Task Edit menu.

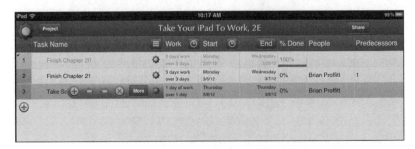

15. Tap the Indent icon. The task will be indented one level, and the task above will be set in boldface to indicate its parent status (see Figure 21.9).

Figure 21.9
Parent and child tasks.

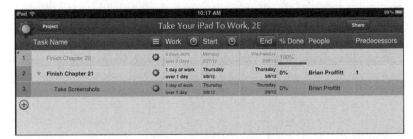

THE PARENT/CHILD RELATIONSHIP

As you build child tasks within parent tasks, note that if you increase the duration of a child task beyond that of a parent task, the duration of the parent task will increase to the duration of the child task. If multiple child tasks are added and their total duration is more than the parent's duration, the parent duration will also be increased.

Viewing Projects

If you are like most businesspeople, you will probably be managing more than one project at a time. SG Project only displays one project at a time, but you can switch to another project in two taps. Just tap the Project button to display the Select Projects action menu and then tap the project you want to see. That project's screen will be displayed.

The default view you will see in SG Project is the table view, but it is not the only way to view a project. If you are familiar with the Gantt view of project management, you can view your project through that lens.

Double-tap the small triangle icon in the lower-right corner, and SG Project will switch to a split view, which has the table listing on the left and the corresponding Gantt view on the right, as shown in Figure 21.10.

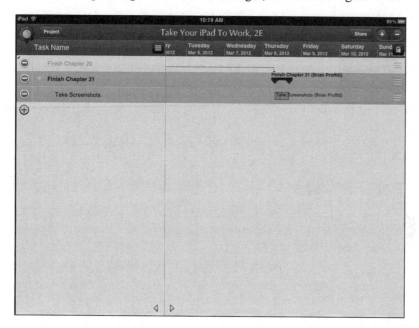

Figure 21.10

The Split view in Landscape mode.

You can use the plus (+) and minus (-) icons over the Gantt view to decrease or increase the duration units of the Gantt view. Tap the (+) icon once, and the Gantt view in Figure 21.10 will display the units in days instead of weeks.

To view just the Gantt view, double-tap the triangular control in the Table pane to minimize the pane and show the Gantt view.

Editing Projects

If you need to edit anything about a project, such as its name or start date, just follow these simple steps.

To edit a project:

1. Tap the Project button. The Select Project action menu will appear.

2. Tap the blue info icon next to the project you want to edit. The Edit Project action menu will appear.

3. Edit the Name, Description, or Start Date of the project.

4. Tap Done. The changes to the project will be applied.

Projects within SG Project can be removed completely, using the standard iPad editing tools.

To remove projects within SG Project:

1. Tap the Project button. The Select Project action menu will appear.

2. Tap the Edit button. The Edit controls will appear.

3. Tap the Delete icon to remove a project. The Delete button will appear.

4. Tap Delete. A notification dialog box will appear.

5. Tap Delete. The project will be completely removed from SG Project.

6. Tap the Edit button again. The edit controls will disappear.

Editing Tasks

Editing a task in SG Project is pretty easy. In Table view, tap the field within the task listing that you want to change. You will immediately be able to change the value for the field.

Sometimes as you build a project, you may realize that one task should not actually happen before another. In this case, you should move the task within the project list.

Using the edit controls, you can reorder and delete any task you want.

To reorder and delete tasks:

1. In the Task list, tap the Edit button. The Edit controls will appear.

2. Tap and drag the task by the Move icon on the far right of the item to relocate its position in the list. As you move the task, any parent/child relationships and linked tasks will immediately shift their durations and dates to correspond with the new order.

3. To remove a task, tap its Delete icon. The Delete button will appear.

4. Tap Delete. The task will be completely removed from the project.

5. Tap the Edit button again. The edit controls will disappear.

Conclusion

SG Project offers iPad users a traditional and flexible project management tool that is well suited for most enterprise tasks. With its intuitive task linking and relationship building, it can help you manage the daunting task of completing those really big projects.

Of course, no project in the world is worth doing if your business has a poor relationship with customers. Even as enterprise businesses grow more refined, the old adage that the "customer is always right" has never been truer. In Chapter 22, "Manage the Customer: CRM," you will learn how to keep track of all of your customers so you can make sure all their needs are met—before they find a business that might treat them better.

Chapter 22

Manage the Customer: CRM

- ◆ Adding Contacts
- ◆ Editing Contacts
- ◆ Working with Contacts
- ◆ Exporting Data
- ◆ Conclusion

Customer resource management is one of those business terms that seems to apply a complicated meaning to a fairly simple concept: Take care of your customers, and they'll take care of you.

In an ever-complicated world where communication with anyone around the world is instantaneous, taking care of your customers can be a challenge. You have to balance their needs with your time and keep track of multiple customers all at once. This is the challenge that customer resource management (CRM) was designed to meet—keeping in contact with your customers and partners, and also managing the tasks and conversations you have with them.

There are several enterprise-level CRM applications that corporations use: SAS, Siebel CRM, and SugarCRM are three popular options. As of press time, the latter two, Siebel CRM and SugarCRM, had dedicated iPad app clients. If your organization uses these platforms, it's worth your time to download and try these apps for yourself.

If you want a general purpose CRM app for the iPad, you will want to try Contacts Journal, which builds on the iPad's existing Contacts app by adding the capability to task any to-do event or conversation associated with a contact. This is a very basic, yet essential, component of any good CRM client. In this chapter, you'll learn how the Contacts Journal app:

◆ Creates new contact

◆ Edits existing contacts

◆ Adds to-dos and conversations for a contact

◆ Exports data to use in other applications

Adding Contacts

If you already have a number of business contacts in your iPad Contacts app, you can import your entire Contacts list and then select only the business contacts to create a pure business list.

To import the contacts list:

1. Tap the CJournal app icon. The Contacts Journal app will open.

2. Tap the Add button. The Add Contact action menu will appear.

3. Tap Import from Contacts. The Contacts list will be imported to Contacts Journal (see Figure 22.1).

4. Tap each name on the Import screen to import it. To select all of the names, tap the double-check button.

5. Tap Add. The selected contacts will appear in the Contacts Journal's Contacts screen (see Figure 22.2).

Figure 22.1

The to-be-selected contacts on the Import screen.

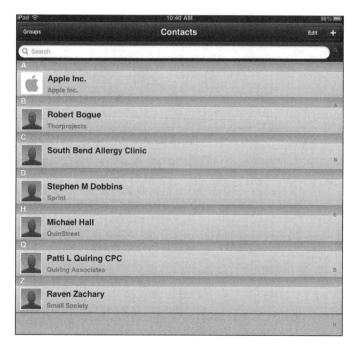

Figure 22.2

Imported contacts.

When you want to add a new contact directly to Contacts Journal, it's much the same as adding a contact in any other iPad contacts manager, just with more information.

To add a new contact directly to Contacts Journal:

1. Tap the Add button. The Add Contact action menu will appear.

2. Tap Create Contact. The New Contact screen will appear (see Figure 22.3).

Figure 22.3

The New Contact screen.

3. Type the relevant information into all of the fields you can.

4. If a field does not match your needs (such as the Home email field, where you only have the person's business address), tap the field name. A Label screen will appear.

5. Tap an appropriate label. The label will be selected and added to the New Contact screen, where you can add the data for that field.

MAKE NEW LABELS

If you want to create a new label for a field, tap the Add Custom Label option in the Label screen to open the Custom Label screen. There, you can enter a new label for the field.

---

6. If you have an image for the contact, tap the Add Photo field. The Photo Albums screen will open.

7. Navigate to and tap the image you want to use for the contact.

8. When you are finished adding the contact data, tap Done. The new contact will appear on the Contacts screen.

Editing Contacts

Editing individual contacts is not difficult, and with the flexibility of all the field configurations in Contacts Journal, the amount of different information you can apply to a contact is quite significant.

To edit an existing contact:

1. Tap the contact to edit. The contact's screen will open.

2. Tap the Info icon. The contact Info screen will appear.

3. Tap the Edit button. The Info screen will expand to reveal more fields (see Figure 22.4).

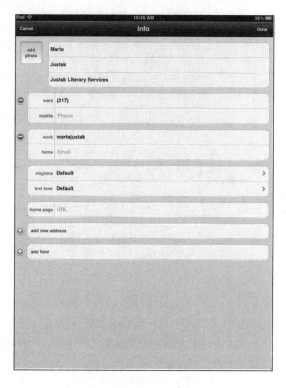

Figure 22.4

The contact Info screen.

4. Edit the fields you need, adding or customizing fields as needed.

5. When you are finished editing the contact data, tap Done. The edited contact will appear on the Info screen.

6. Tap the Contacts icon to return to the Contacts screen.

If you need to remove a contact, merely swipe the contact listing on the Contacts screen to the right. The Delete button will appear. Tap Delete and when the confirmation dialog box appears, tap Yes to remove the contact.

Working with Contacts

Reaching out to contacts is essential when you work with them, and Contacts Journal enables users to make direct contact with customers and partners right from the iPad. This can be done with email, or if your iPad has Skype installed, through voice calls.

Skype for Voice Calls

The Skype iPad app is very useful to have, and not just because Contacts Journal integrates with it. Skype uses voice-over IP technology to enable users to connect free-of-charge to other Skype users and get significant savings for domestic and international calls. The Skype app is still configured for the iPhone and hasn't been enhanced for the iPad platform as of press time. Still, for a basic voice application, it does a great job and its integration with Contacts Journal alone is enough to give it a look.

To connect to a contact by email:

1. Tap the contact to email. The contact's screen will open.

2. Tap the email icon. A pop-over menu will appear giving you a choice of email addresses to use.

3. Tap the appropriate email address. The New Message screen will open, preaddressed to the contact.

4. Type the message and tap Send. The email will be sent.

A similar procedure is used to make a voice call if Skype is installed.

To make a voice call using Skype:

1. Tap the contact to call. The contact's screen will open.

2. Tap the phone icon. A pop-over menu will appear giving you a choice of phone numbers to use.

3. Tap the appropriate phone number. The Skype app will start, and the phone call will be initiated.

If you have to perform a general task related to the contact, you can attach a to-do list to the contact listing.

To attach a to-do list to your contact:

1. Tap the contact to associate a to-do. The contact's screen will open.
2. Tap the To-Do button. All to-dos for the contact will be listed.
3. Tap either the Add button or the Add To-Do button. The Add To-Do dialog box will open (see Figure 22.5).

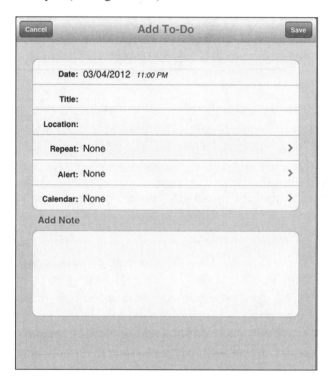

Figure 22.5

The Add To-Do dialog box.

4. Tap the Date field. The Date pop-over menu will appear.
5. Select a due date for the to-do and tap Done.
6. Tap the Title field. The Title pop-over menu will appear.
7. Select a title for the to-do and tap Done.

NEED MORE TITLES?

If you want to add a custom title to the Title field for to-dos and logs in Contacts Journal, tap the Add Other option. A keyboard will appear enabling you to enter a custom title.

8. Add all of the remaining information for the to-do and tap Save. The to-do will appear in the contact's To-Do list (see Figure 22.6).

Figure 22.6

The contact To-Do list.

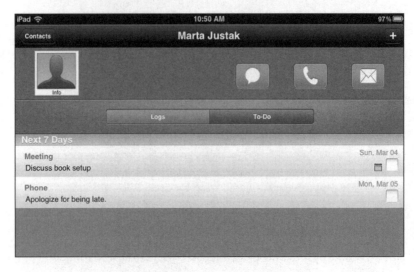

You can also track conversations you've had with a contact, which is useful for tracking ongoing projects and keeping a record of your business dealings.

To track conversations:

1. Tap the contact to add a conversation log. The contact's screen will open.
2. Tap the Logs button. All conversation logs for the contact will be listed.
3. Tap either the Add button or the Add Log button. The Add Log dialog box will open (see Figure 22.7).
4. Tap the Date field. The Date pop-over menu will appear.
5. Select a due date for the log and tap Done.
6. Tap the Title field. The Title pop-over menu will appear.
7. Select a title for the log and tap Done.
8. Add all of the remaining information for the conversation log and tap Save. The conversation log will appear in the contact's Logs list.

To view all to-dos and logs within Contacts Journal, tap their respective view buttons on the CJ toolbar. This will display the complete lists of all to-dos and logs.

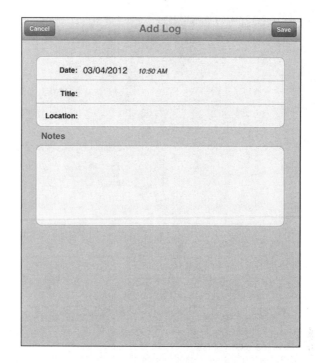

Figure 22.7
*The Add Log
dialog box.*

Exporting Data

When you want to move a copy of the Contacts Journal data to another CRM application, you can export the data as a basic comma-separated value file that can be imported to any spreadsheet and most database-enabled CRM platforms.

To export data:

1. Tap the More button in the toolbar. The More screen will open.

2. Tap Export. The Export screen will open, as shown in Figure 22.8.

3. Tap the appropriate options you want for the export file, making sure to tap the CSV option in the Format field.

4. Tap Generate. A message window will appear with the CSV file attached.

5. Address the email message and add any text.

6. Tap Send. The message will be sent to its intended recipient.

Figure 22.8

The Export screen.

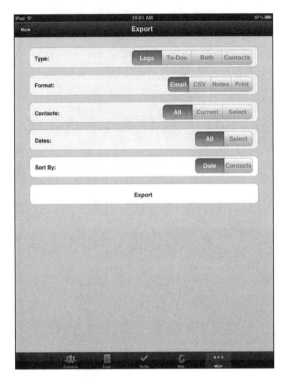

Conclusion

Contacts Journal may not have all of the bells and whistles of a big-time enterprise CRM platform, but it has what counts—the ability to associate to-dos and conversations with clients and customers on the go, which is the core for any CRM app.

Relationships with customers aren't the only thing that's tricky to manage in a geographically distributed business. Getting work done in such an environment is also challenging when team members are scattered around the building or around the planet. In Chapter 23, "From the Home Office: Enterprise Collaboration," you'll find how to connect to the popular SharePoint enterprise collaboration platform so you can work with documents no matter where you find yourself.

Chapter 23

From the Home Office:
Enterprise Collaboration

What does the word "collaboration" mean to you? The term is often used yet rarely understood. Most people think it means "working together," which is odd because collaboration tools often allow you to work together while being apart.

Such a collaboration tool is Microsoft SharePoint, a collaborative document-sharing server platform that enables users to share documents they need.

Fully understanding what SharePoint is can be challenging, but there are many things that are easy to understand about how SharePoint can be a part of your business. At the most basic level, SharePoint is a Web-based system. That means all you need is a Web browser to access SharePoint. On the iPad, an even better way is to use the SharePlus app to connect directly to a SharePoint site. Once connected, SharePlus lets you take advantage of many SharePoint features, including:

◆ Managing events on a SharePoint calendar

◆ Viewing and editing SharePoint items

◆ Opening documents from a SharePoint site in the iPad

Connecting to a SharePoint Site

SharePlus is designed with SharePoint in mind, so as long as you have the appropriate privileges on the SharePoint site, you can log in and navigate the site just as you would from a browser.

To get connected to a SharePoint site:

1. Tap the SharePlus app icon. The SharePlus app will open.

2. Tap the Navigator button. The Home action menu will open, as seen in Figure 23.1.

3. Tap the Add Site button. The Add Site dialog box will open (see Figure 23.2).

4. Enter a Name and full URL for the SharePoint site to which you want to connect.

5. Type in your Username and Password for that site.

6. Tap Done. The site will be added to the Home action menu (see Figure 23.3).

7. Tap the site listing. After a brief connection process, the site's action menu will open (see Figure 23.4).

Figure 23.1

The Home action menu.

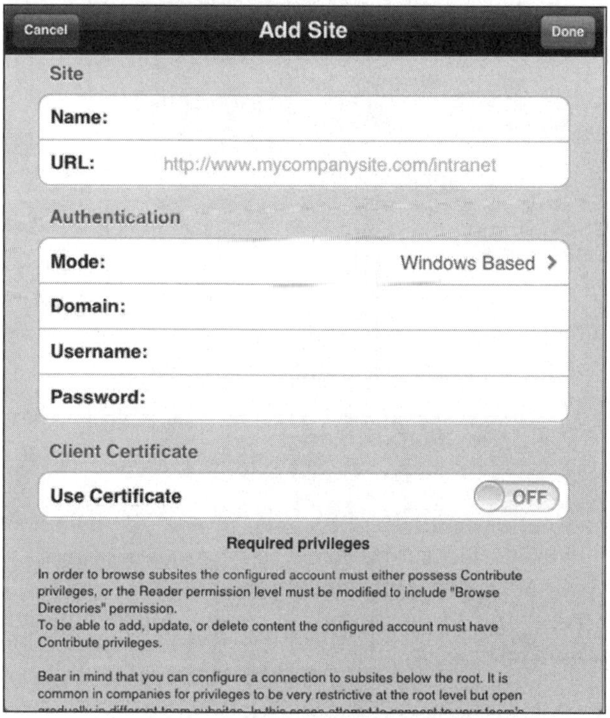

Figure 23.2

The Add Site dialog box.

Figure 23.3

The new site.

Figure 23.4

The contents of the new site.

Navigating around the SharePoint site is a matter of drilling down through the menus in the site's action menu. Tap any menu option to open the content of the list you selected. As you can see in Figure 23.5, a SharePoint list or library can contain SharePoint items, folders, and stand-alone documents.

Figure 23.5

The contents of a SharePoint list.

To navigate back, just tap the back-arrow icon to move back up the folders in the SharePoint site. Once you get to the top level of the site, tap the Navigator button to access the top-level libraries and lists again.

Managing Events

Collaboration comes in many forms. In the digital age, many people are encouraged to try online chats, shared document sessions, or email conversations to exchange ideas. Sometimes, though, a good old-fashioned face-to-face meeting is what's needed. SharePoint can create an online home for meetings, allowing attendees to be invited, agendas to be set, and tasks to be assigned.

Before all of this can happen, a new event must be created in the SharePoint calendar. As the event is created, you can designate the creation of a meeting workspace—a special area on your team site where users can get the latest information about the meeting before and after it happens.

To add a new event to a SharePoint calendar:

1. Navigate to the Calendar list in your SharePoint site. It will be visible on the Calendar screen.

2. Tap the Add icon. The New Event screen will appear (see Figure 23.6).

Figure 23.6

The New Event screen.

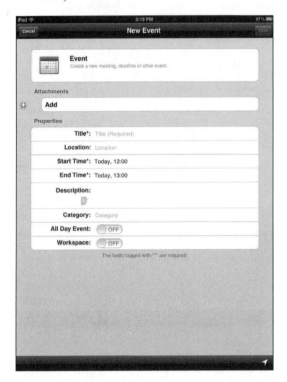

3. Fill in the appropriate fields. Take care to enter data in the required fields, which may vary from calendar to calendar.

4. Tap Save. The new item will appear on the Calendar.

Managing Items

SharePoint lists and libraries use *items* to manage content. Everything in SharePoint is an item, which acts as a container for many different types of documents within. In a document library, for instance, the items each contain a document—perhaps a Word document or an Excel spreadsheet. In a calendar (which is just a specialized list), the event itself is an item.

Even though the item acts as a container for the content within, it can still be edited. This is useful when you're tracking issues about the item's document or the item itself.

To edit an item's properties in SharePoint:

1. Navigate to the item to edit in your SharePoint site.

2. Tap the Edit button. The edit action menu will open.

3. Tap Edit Item. The editing controls will appear (see Figure 23.7).

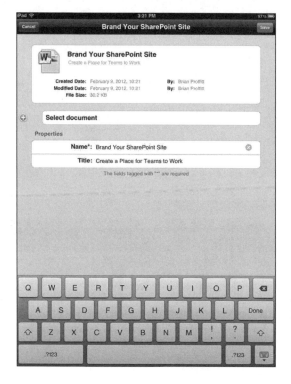

Figure 23.7
Editing a SharePoint item.

4. Edit the appropriate fields. Take care to make sure that data is in the required fields, which may vary between lists and between libraries.

5. Tap Save. The item will be edited.

Opening Documents

Perhaps the coolest feature of SharePlus is its capability to open documents directly from the SharePoint site. This is very useful for iPad users, since no importing is needed to get documents onto your device. Just tap and go.

To open a document for editing:

1. Navigate to the document to edit in your SharePoint site.

2. Tap the document's icon. The document will immediately open in the SharePlus viewer window (see Figure 23.8).

3. To edit the document, tap the Edit button. The Open In action menu will appear (see Figure 23.9).

4. Tap the editing app you want to use. The document will be opened in that app, ready for editing.

Figure 23.8

Viewing a SharePoint document.

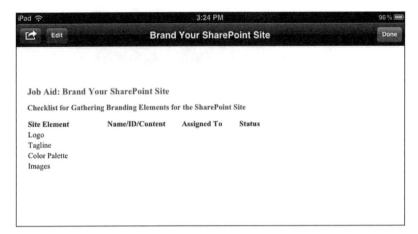

Figure 23.9

The Open In action menu.

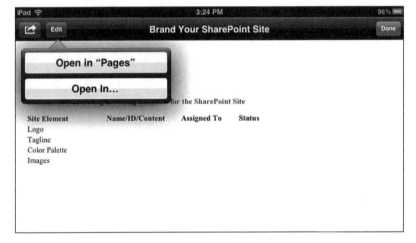

Conclusion

If your organization uses SharePoint for document collaboration and content management, SharePlus is the perfect app for iPad users to use to connect to the SharePoint site and access many of the features that SharePoint offers while on the go.

However, as much as we may prefer to stay in the office to work, the fact is that travel is a part of many business plans. Even with the Internet and instant collaboration, there will be times that you will need to pack that suitcase and take your show on the road. Never fear, because as you'll begin to learn in Chapter 24, "Get Ready to Go: Travel Arrangements," on the road is perhaps the place where the iPad truly shines as a business platform.

Chapter 24

Get Ready to Go:
Travel Arrangements

If the Internet has made the world a smaller place, then it has also served to increase our desire to meet each other face-to-face. Our daily contact with coworkers brings a need to share business experiences from their points of view and collaborate in real time. For that reason, and many more, don't look for business travel to be going away anytime soon.

The iPad is an almost perfect travel companion for business. Besides all of the business apps outlined in this book (and more), the lightweight form factor makes it ideal for planes and trains—especially when the person in front of us leans her seat back.

The travel benefits of the iPad start even before you leave on your trip. Two great apps can help you plan and track your trip in real time: Kayak and FlightTrack Pro. In this chapter, you'll learn how to:

◆ Search for the best travel deals using Kayak

◆ Make reservations for air, hotel, and rental cars

◆ Track any flight in the world live with FlightTrack Pro

Now Boarding: Kayak

Perhaps the industry that benefited the most from perfected ecommerce has been the travel industry, although we might have a hard time selling travel agents on that. There are dozens of travel websites providing the self-service capability to book travel and accommodations. In the U.S. alone, Expedia, Hotwire, and Priceline are just a few of the big travel sites providing this service.

With such diversity, a valid question becomes, which one gives you the better rates?

Kayak is an app that makes the answer to such a question moot. Kayak searches several travel sites at once and reports back all of the fares and rates it finds—letting you find and book a flight, hotel stay, or rental car from one easy interface.

Searching for a Flight

Kayak features a very comprehensive interface for flight searching that lets you see most of your trip options on a single screen. This lets you change these options at a glance, which makes searching for possible flights a lot easier than backing up to another screen on your browser to make changes.

To find a flight on Kayak:

1. Tap the KAYAK app icon. Kayak will open to the Explore screen, with Boston as the default city (see Figure 24.1).

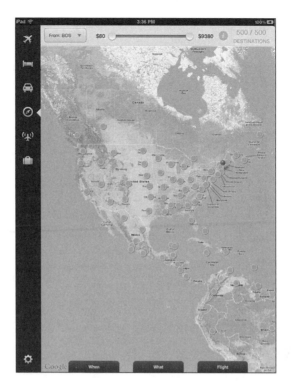

Figure 24.1

The initial Kayak Explore screen.

2. Tap the Flights button. The Flights screen will appear, as seen in Figure 24.2.

Figure 24.2

The Flights screen.

3. To start the flight search, tap the From field. The Choose Origin Airport pane will appear (see Figure 24.3).

Figure 24.3

The Choose Origin Airport pane.

4. Tap the Current location option or type the name of a city in the From Airport search box and tap the corresponding airport option. The airport will appear in the From field.

AIRPORT CODES

Savvy travelers know the airport code for their home airport, having seen it on their baggage claim tags so many times. You can enter that three-letter code in any field and Kayak can use it.

5. Tap the To field. The Choose Destination Airport pane will appear.

6. Tap the Current location option or type the name of a city in the To Airport search box and tap the corresponding airport option. The airport will appear in the To field.

7. Tap the Depart field. The Depart action menu will appear.

8. Tap the date of departure. The departure date will appear in the Depart field.

9. Tap the Return field. The Return action menu will appear.

10. Tap the date of return. The return date will appear in the Return field.

11. Tap the + or – icons in the Travelers field to set the number of passengers on the trip, if needed.

12. To change the class, tap the Cabin button. The Select Class pop-over will appear.

13. Tap the desired class option.

14. Tap the Search button. Kayak will search for the flights that match your criteria, from lowest to highest fare (see Figure 24.4).

Figure 24.4

Found flights.

After the initial search, you may want to start looking for options beyond price, such as when the flight leaves and arrives, or how many stops the flight makes. Depending on the frequent flyer mile program you might belong to, you may want to prefer certain airlines over others.

When Kayak displays results, it uses filters to parse out which results are shown to you. By default, all filters are selected when results are initially displayed, so the most results are shown. You can navigate through the Filter pane and tap different options to fine-tune the reported results.

For instance, tapping on the Airports tab in the Filter pane will show the airports involved in the trip. By tapping options, you can eliminate options, particularly in the Layover Airports category.

The Times option lets you set preferred times for take-off and departure on each leg of the trip. As you change any of the Filter pane options, you may see dramatic changes for the results of your search.

Booking a Flight

Once you get the times, airlines, and other flight parameters set, hopefully at a price your company can handle, you can reserve the flight. Kayak doesn't actually reserve the flights but instead seamlessly connects to the travel site on which it found the rate so you can complete the reservation there.

To reserve a flight through Kayak:

1. Tap the flight you want to book. The Flight Details action menu will appear, as seen in Figure 24.5.

Figure 24.5

Information about your flight.

2. Tap Book Now. Kayak will refer you to the site that provided that flight. If successful, Kayak will pass along all of the data it gathered about the flight to the third-party site, which should open to a booking page with the information already filled in (see Figure 24.6).

Figure 24.6

The travel site with your booking information.

3. Continue with the booking process on the travel site to complete the reservation.

Finding a Hotel

If you want to reserve a room at a hotel, you can still do that. Kayak handles hotel search and reservation operations with ease.

To search for a hotel and set up a reservation:

1. Tap the Hotel icon. The Search Hotels action menu will appear, as seen in Figure 24.7.

2. Enter the information for your stay in the appropriate fields and tap Search. After a few moments, the results of the search will be displayed.

3. When you find a hotel you want to reserve, tap the hotel's listing. A selection of booking options will appear in a pop-over (see Figure 24.8).

4. Tap the Book Online button for the site you want to use for reserving the room. The travel site will open and your pre-entered information will appear.

Figure 24.7

Searching for hotels.

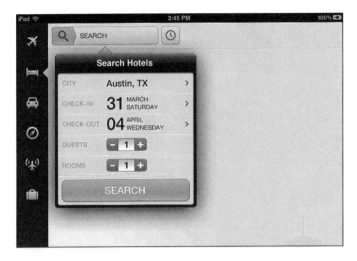

Figure 24.8

Choose a booking site.

5. Continue with the booking process on the travel site to complete the reservation.

Get a Rental Car

As with reserving a hotel room or flights, Kayak can be used to complete the rental car reservation process.

To rent a car:

1. Tap the Rental Car icon. The Search Cars action menu will appear.

2. Enter the information for the car in the appropriate fields and tap Search. After a few moments, the results of the search will be displayed.

3. When you find a car you want to reserve, tap the Select button. The Choose a site pop-over will appear.

4. Tap the Book Now button for the travel site you want to use for reserving the car. The travel site will open and your pre-entered information will appear.

5. Continue with the booking process on the travel site to complete the reservation.

READY TO EXPLORE?

If you're feeling adventurous, tap the Explore screen in Kayak and find out just how far you can go on a given fare. Just configure your location, dates, what you'd like to do, and how many stops you're willing to make, and Kayak will display all the possible destinations on the global map, shown in Figure 24.9. Tap on any orange dot to see details about the location and flights.

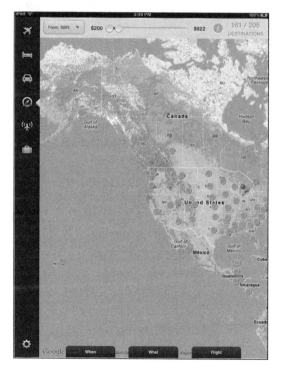

Figure 24.9

Hawai'i, here I come.

In-Flight: Tracking Your Flight

When you're facing security lines, luggage check-in, and other airport headaches, the last thing you want to find out is that your flight has been delayed. The smallest delay can create a ripple effect on your entire travel plans, and if you're going to miss a connection or your ride from the airport will be delayed, the faster you know, the faster you can react.

FlightTrack Pro is the app that will help you track any flight you need, whether it's next week's business trip or your mother-in-law's incoming flight. Every flight is important in its own way.

Setting up FlightTrack Pro is simple—all you need is the flight number for the flight you're tracking and the dates of departure.

To search for and save flights:

1. Tap the FlightTrack app icon. FlightTrackPro will open (see Figure 24.10).

Figure 24.10

The initial FlightTrack Pro screen.

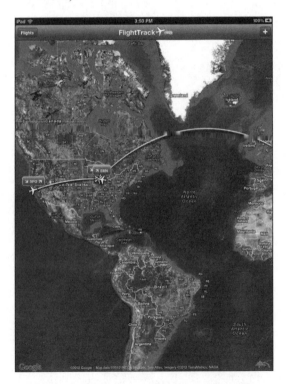

2. Tap the Add icon. The Add Flight action menu will appear (see Figure 24.11).

Figure 24.11
*The Search
action menu.*

3. Tap the Airline field. The Airline action menu will appear.

4. Type the airline name. Matching airline options will appear in the menu.

5. Tap the appropriate airline. The Search action menu will reappear.

6. Type the flight number in the Flight # field.

7. Tap the Departs field. The Departure Date action menu will appear.

8. Enter the date of departure and tap Search. The Search action menu will reappear.

9. Tap Search in the Search action menu. Possible matches will appear in the Flights action menu (see Figure 24.12).

10. Tap the flight you want. The flight's action menu will appear (see Figure 24.13).

11. Tap Save. A map of the plane's route and its position in flight will be displayed.

FLIGHT UPDATES

As schedule changes to the flight are made, the changes will be updated with notification messages. Tap OK to close or View to view the flight's information in a pop-over menu.

Figure 24.12

The Flights action menu.

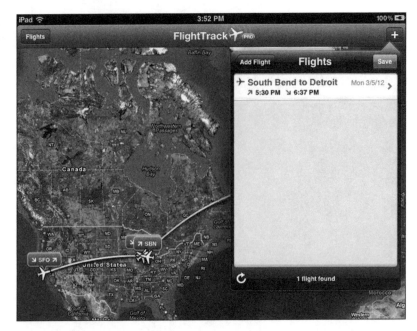

Figure 24.13

The flight's information.

12. To view the status of the flight at any time, tap the plane on the map to see the flight's information.

FlightTrack Pro also enables users to connect to TripIt, a social network for travelers, so they can see who's traveling near them as they're on the go. For more information, or to connect to an existing TripIt account, tap the Flights button and then the Info icon.

Conclusion

Traveling isn't always the best part of working in a job, but it doesn't have to be unpleasant. With some planning and tracking apps on your iPad, you can keep on top of your plans and be prepared for changes along the way.

Once you're in the plane, or on the train, or riding in a taxi, it doesn't have to be all work. The iPad can be a great source of entertainment to make your trip go that much faster. In Chapter 25, "On the Plane: Multimedia," we'll take a look at one of the most central iPad apps, iTunes, and find out how to listen to music and watch movies to your heart's content.

Chapter 25

On the Plane: Multimedia

- ◆ Getting Multimedia: iTunes
- ◆ Multimedia Playback: Music and Videos
- ◆ Internet Video: YouTube
- ◆ Conclusion

In Chapter 1, "First Step: Introducing the iPad," you learned about the origins of the iPad, and its relationship with earlier Apple devices, such as the iPod, iPhone, and iPod Touch.

When it first appeared, the iPad was derisively referred to as a giant iPod Touch, and in some ways that description had some truth to it. The interfaces are similar, and there's quite a bit of shared functionality. If that's the case, then like the iPod Touch, the iPad should be able to display multimedia files with relative ease.

And that is indeed within the iPad's capabilities. Since the screen is much larger than its iPod and iPhone cousins, the iPad does a superior job of showing the latest movies and television shows with the Videos app. There is also the YouTube app, which taps into the vast community of video content on the YouTube website. It is also a great music player, thanks to the Music app.

From a business perspective, you might not think such apps are worth much, beyond welcome diversions from a long business trip. While it's important not to underestimate the value of such diversions, being able to listen to audio books on business topics or watch training videos on the YouTube or Videos app is of great value to your business.

In this chapter, you'll learn how to:

◆ Purchase multimedia content in the iTunes store

◆ Acquire an audio podcast

◆ Play back multimedia content on the iPad

◆ Find and view YouTube content

Getting Multimedia: iTunes

As you learned in Chapter 4, "Fourth Step: Using the iPad Apps," the content of iTunes on your desktop machine is identical to its iPad counterpart in terms of apps. This is also the case with music and movies in the iTunes store.

Finding and installing multimedia content with the iPad is just as easy as using the iTunes application. To get an idea of how you can purchase content for the iPad, here's how to find and purchase a music album with the iTunes app.

To find and purchase music using iTunes:

1. Tap the iTunes icon to start the iTunes app (see Figure 25.1).

Figure 25.1

The iTunes app.

2. Tap the Music button on the iTunes toolbar if it's not on the Music page already.

3. Tap the Search bar and type in the artist or album name you're looking for. Suggested options will be displayed in the Suggestions menu as you type.

4. Tap the artist or album name that matches your search. The results will be displayed on the Search screen, as shown in Figure 25.2.

5. Tap the album or song you want to view. The album's pop over window will open (see Figure 25.3).

6. To find out how other users liked the music, read the Customer Reviews section.

7. When satisfied you want to buy this album, tap the price button at the top of the window. The button will change to a green Buy Album button.

8. Tap the Buy Album button. A login dialog box will appear.

9. Enter your iTunes Password information for the iTunes Store and tap OK. The album will be downloaded, as shown on the Downloads page (see Figure 25.4).

Figure 25.2

Tracking down music.

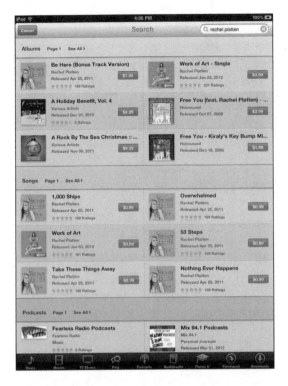

Figure 25.3

The album's window.

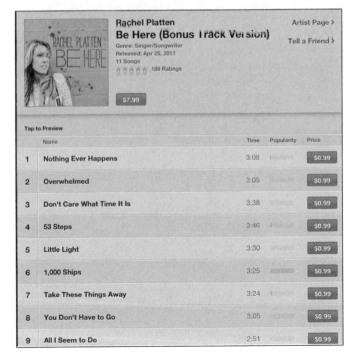

Figure 25.4

Downloading music.

The procedure for buying video content, be it movies or TV shows, is identical to acquiring music. With music, you can buy whole albums or individual songs (though getting the whole album is typically less expensive per song). If you buy TV shows, you can get one episode at a time or entire seasons' worth of content.

Getting audio books also uses a similar process, although usually you can only buy the entire book. Many audio books have a Preview feature that allows you to hear some of the content before you purchase it.

iTunes also enables you to download audio or video podcasts, which are free programs, usually episodic, that cover a huge variety of topics: business, technology, news, music... if you can think of a topic, someone's likely done an episode or an entire series of podcasts about it.

To get podcasts for your iPad:

1. Tap the Podcasts button on the iTunes toolbar. The Podcasts page will open (see Figure 25.5).

Figure 25.5

Tracking down a podcast.

2. Tap the Search bar and type in the topic or program name you're looking for. Suggested options will be displayed in the Suggestions menu as you type.

3. Tap the podcast that matches your search. The results will be displayed on the Search screen.

4. Tap the podcast you want to view. The podcast's pop-over window will open (see Figure 25.6).

5. To find out how other users liked the podcast, read the Customer Reviews section.

6. When satisfied you want to listen to one of the podcast's episodes, tap the episode's Free button. The button will change to a green Get Episode button.

7. Tap the Get Episode button. A login dialog box will appear.

8. Enter your iTunes Password information for the iTunes Store and tap OK. The podcast will be downloaded.

Figure 25.6

The podcast window.

Multimedia Playback: Music and Videos

One major difference between the iPad version of iTunes and the desktop version is that the desktop version allows you to play back videos and music right from within the iTunes application.

On the iPad, this functionality is not within the iTunes app, but instead is handled by other specialized apps. Any audio files (music, audio podcasts, and audio books) can be listened to via the Music app, and video content (movies, TV shows, and video podcasts) can be viewed by the Videos app.

To listen to audio content in the Music app:

1. Tap the Music app icon. The Music app will open as seen in Figure 25.7.
2. To view the music content by album, tap the Albums button. The Albums page will appear, as seen in Figure 25.8.
3. Tap the album to play. The album's pop-over window will appear.
4. Tap any song in the album. The album will begin to play from that point.
5. To stop or otherwise control the playback, tap the album cover. The playback controls will appear, enabling you to fast forward, reverse, control volume, etc.

Figure 25.7

The Music app.

Figure 25.8

The Albums page.

6. To return to the Music screen, tap the Back arrow in the lower-left corner of the screen.

Listening to an audio book or podcast is similar, although these categories are not as organized as the Music section of the Music Library, since typically you will have a lot more songs to organize than podcasts and audio books. Simply find the book or podcast to listen to and tap it to start playback.

To watch videos:

1. Tap the Videos app icon. Videos will open, as seen in Figure 25.9.

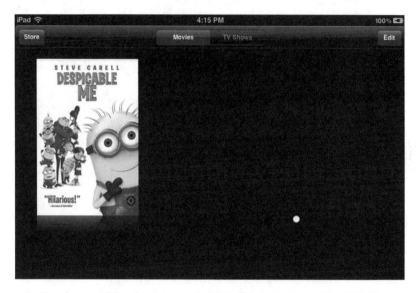

Figure 25.9

The Videos app.

2. To view a TV episode, tap the TV Shows button. The TV Shows page will appear.
3. Tap the video to play. The video's playback information screen will appear (see Figure 25.10).
4. Tap the episode to watch and then the Play control. The video will begin to play.
5. To stop or otherwise control the playback, tap the video. The playback controls will appear, enabling you to fast forward, reverse, control volume, etc.
6. To return to the playback information screen, tap the Done button.
7. To return to the main Videos screen, tap the Videos button.

Figure 25.10

The video's playback information screen.

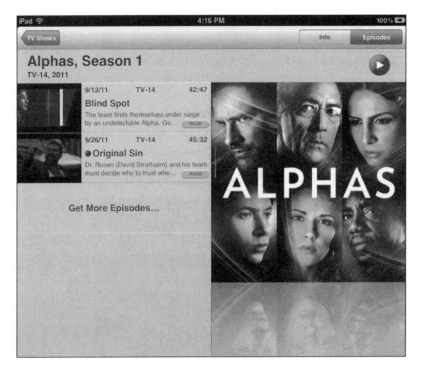

Internet Video: YouTube

When YouTube first started, it was a site where people with perhaps too much time on their hands would upload home videos to share with friends and family. Some of these videos were interesting to more than the intended audience, and quite soon a community started developing to produce videos of higher quality and substance than creative wedding videos.

Today, YouTube is an Internet powerhouse, and businesses are fast realizing its potential as a platform for corporate information. For the cost of making a decent video, businesses can share marketing content with customers and on private YouTube channels, training videos with employees. There's no need to worry about distributing these videos because the distribution platform is already there.

To view YouTube videos on the iPad, you need to use the YouTube app because they won't appear within the Safari browser. If you click on a YouTube link in a Web page, however, the YouTube app will immediately open and begin playback, so the functionality is, while slower, still seamless.

INTERNET REQUIRED

YouTube videos require an active Internet connection to work, so plan your viewing time accordingly.

To look for and view videos from within the YouTube app:

1. Tap the YouTube app icon. The YouTube app will open (see Figure 25.11).

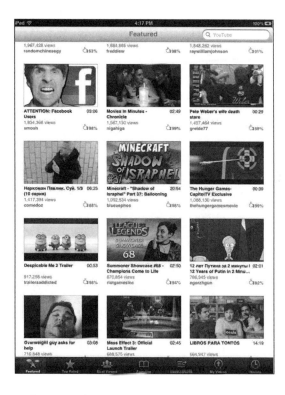

Figure 25.11

The YouTube app.

2. Tap the Search bar and type in the topic you're looking for.
3. Tap the Search key. The results will be displayed on the Search screen.
4. Tap the video you want to view. The video's information screen will open.
5. Tap the Play control to start the video, or wait a few moments and the video should start automatically.

> **FOR BEST VIEWING**
>
> For the best viewing of any video content, whether with the YouTube or Videos app, turn the iPad to the landscape position.

Conclusion

As video and audio content become easier for businesses to create, having a mobile platform to view or listen to such content is a big advantage. The iPad will connect you to a myriad of useful content, as well as more entertaining content to keep you relaxed while on the road.

In Chapter 26, "Continuing Education: iBooks," you'll find out how the iPad performs as an electronic book reader, which will let you read whole libraries of business topics wherever you go.

Chapter 26

Continuing Education:
iBooks

- ◆ Finding Your Reading Material
- ◆ Reading in iBooks
- ◆ Conclusion

Since the invention of the personal computer, industry observers have constantly predicted the death of books.

The written works of humankind, they argue, would no longer be found in the bound-paper format that collects dust on the bookshelves of the world, but rather in the form of electrons displaying information on a screen.

And yet it hasn't come to pass. Books, newspapers, and magazines are still printed by the millions, with only small signs of slowing down.

Part of the resistance to electronic books has been social inertia: There's something more "real" about being on paper. Why else are most legal agreements written down? If it's something we can hold and feel, the words carry more social weight, it seems.

Another part of this resistance has been the delivery method of electronic books. Devices were either too big or bulky, or it was hard to purchase an ebook and transfer it to a device. Or reading the book onscreen was simply too painful (sometimes literally).

Consumer acceptance of electronic books changed sharply when Amazon.com introduced the Kindle portable reading device in 2007. Here was a device with easy-to-read text and a delivery method superior to any other device at the time—free cellular data access. This meant that you could buy a book anywhere with cell coverage and have it delivered to you for just the cost of the book.

The iPad's form factor makes it an ideal device for reading electronic books, too. Although access to buying books is limited to WiFi or a paid 3G plan, it's still very easy to get a copy of the latest business guide, computer manual, or personal work on the iPad in seconds.

In this chapter, you'll learn how to use the iBooks app to:

◆ Find electronic books in the iBooks Store

◆ Purchase books for the iPad

◆ Read your purchased books

Finding Your Reading Material

iBooks is the free app from Apple that, while not included with the iPad, is strongly suggested as your first downloaded app when you first connect to the iTunes Store with the iPad. If you didn't download it then, you should go ahead and download it to start your iPad reading experience.

To buy a book for iBooks:

1. Tap the iBooks icon to start the iBooks app. The first time it starts, you will be asked to sync your reading progress and bookmarks (see Figure 26.1).

Figure 26.1

Syncing iBooks.

SYNCING EXPLAINED

As you read your books, iBooks will keep track of your progress, as well as any bookmarks you might have inserted in your books. If you plan to read your book on another iBooks-equipped device, such as an iPhone, synchronization will enable the other device to pick up right where you left off on the iPad and copy your bookmarks. If you don't have other iBooks devices, tap Don't Sync.

2. Tap the Sync option you want. The primary iBooks screen (an empty bookshelf) will appear.

3. Tap the Store button. The Store screen will appear (see Figure 26.2).

4. Tap the Search button bar and type the title or author name you're looking for. Suggested options will be displayed in the Suggestions menu as you type.

5. Tap the book or author name that matches your search. The results will be displayed on the Search screen, as shown in Figure 26.3.

6. Tap the book you want to view. The book's page will open (see Figure 26.4).

7. To read more about the book, tap the More link below the Description paragraph.

8. To find out how other users liked the book, read the Customer Reviews section.

9. When satisfied you want to buy this book, tap the price button at the top of the window. The button will change to a green Buy Book button.

10. Tap the Buy Book button. A login dialog box will appear.

Figure 26.2

The iBooks Store.

Figure 26.3

Finding the book you want.

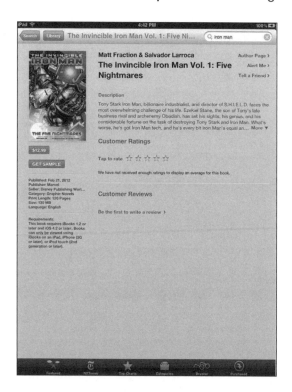

Figure 26.4

The book's information page.

11. Enter your iTunes Password information for the iTunes Store and tap OK. The book will be downloaded, with the progress shown on the main iBooks screen (see Figure 26.5).

Figure 26.5

Downloading a book.

Reading in iBooks

After you have a book downloaded, reading it is simply a matter of tapping the book on the iBooks shelf to open it (see Figure 26.6).

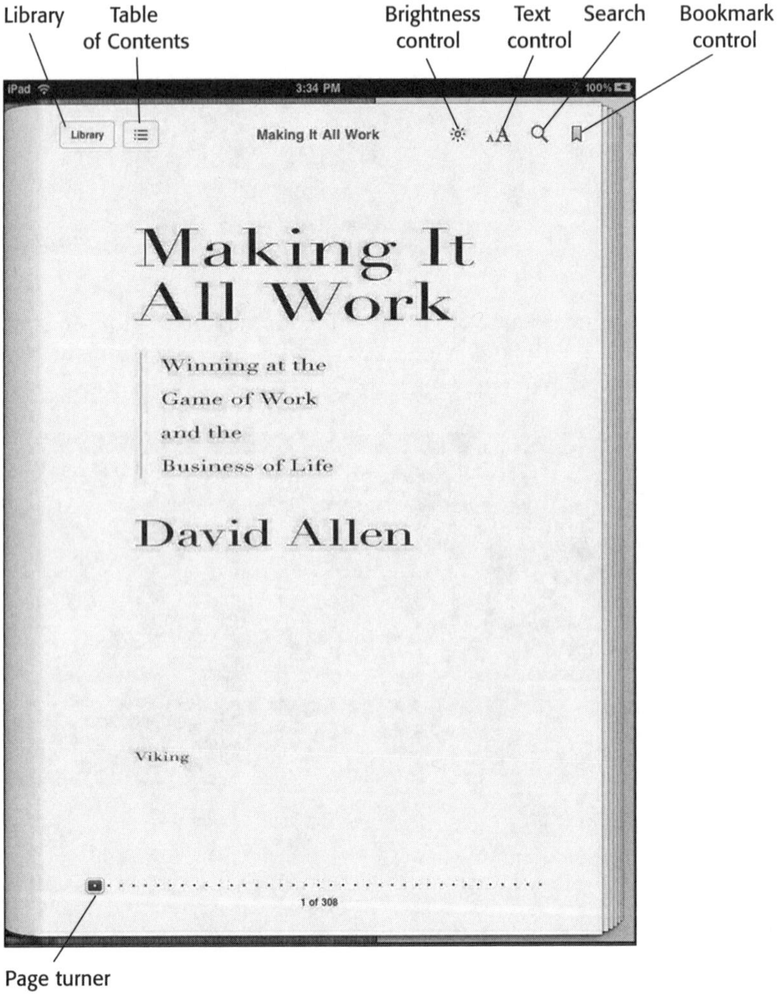

Figure 26.6

Reading a book.

Page turner

To turn the page of a book forward, flick your finger to the left (as if you were flipping a paper page). You can also tap the right edge of the page.

To flip back a page, flick your finger to the right or tap the left edge of the page.

Navigating beyond one page at a time can be done a couple of ways. Tap anywhere on the page to bring up the page controls seen in Figure 26.6. Then tap the Table of Contents button to view the Table of Contents page.

To move to another location in the book, tap any of the chapter or section headers that are visible. The book will be opened to that spot.

If you have any bookmarks inserted in the book, you can use the Bookmarks page to navigate to that bookmark. Tap the Table of Contents button and in the Table of Contents page, tap the Bookmarks button. Any bookmarks in the book will be listed, as shown in Figure 26.7. Tap the bookmark to view that page.

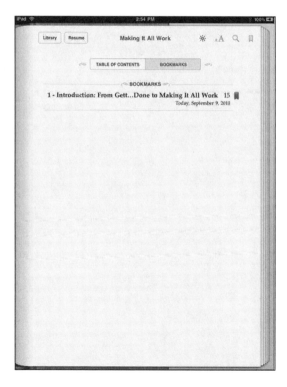

Figure 26.7

The Bookmarks page.

You can also use the page-turner control found on the bottom of every page when you tap the page. Tap and drag the rectangular control to move to the page number you want. When you lift your finger, the desired page will open.

You can use the Brightness and Text controls to adjust the text size and display properties of the iBooks app.

If this seems simple, that's because it's designed to be that way. iBooks is meant to be simple, so you can do the thing you really need to do—read.

Conclusion

When you first opened your iPad box from the Apple Store, you were probably delighted with the ease-of-use and power contained in this handheld tablet device. The possibilities seemed endless.

We are now at the end of this book, but don't think for a second that the complete possibilities of the iPad for business use have been fully explored. We have barely scratched the surface of the many use-cases the iPad can have in your line of work, with more coming each day as new and innovative apps are introduced.

This book hopefully has served as a guide to getting you started on this journey of possibilities, giving you the tools and knowledge to use the iPad effectively in your workplace today and explore additional uses in the future.

Appendix A

20 Great Business Apps

◆ The Top 20

There are so many business apps available now since the publication of the first edition of this book, we thought it would be a good idea to list some of the better apps that are very much worth a look for your business.

This list is going to be ever changing, but it reflects the top apps for most business users today. There is a very healthy selection of document viewers and editors in this list, as well as audio recording apps and remote desktop connectors.

For the iPad business user, getting to your data as fast as possible seems to be the critical function.

The Top 20

PRICES MAY VARY
These prices were accurate as of Spring 2012.

App: Adobe Reader

Developer: Adobe Systems

Description: Adobe Reader is the standard app for viewing and sharing PDF documents.

Price: Free

App: Audio Memos

Developer: David Detry

Description: A professional-grade auto recorder.

Price: $.99

App: Citrix Receiver

Developer: Citrix Systems, Inc.

Description: Connects to any Citrix-hosted system to log into a remote desktop or perform specific tasks.

Price: Free

App: Documents Free

Developer: Savy Soda Pty Ltd.

Description: A lightweight office suite with word processing and spreadsheet capabilities.

Price: Free

App: Documents To Go Premium

Developer: DataViz, Inc.

Description: An office editing suite that works with your email attachments, local files, and cloud storage accounts.

Price: $16.99

App: Dragon Dictation

Developer: Nuance Communications, Inc.

Description: The very popular dictation and voice-recognition program for business users.

Price: Free

App: Fast Company Magazine

Developer: Mansueto Ventures LLC

Description: Regarded as one of the top business magazines in the U.S., this app lets you subscribe on a monthly basis to Fast Company.

Price: Free

App: GoToMeeting

Developer: Citrix Online LLC

Description: Organize and conduct online meetings using GoToMeeting.

Price: Free

App: Harvard Business Review

Developer: Harvard Business Publishing

Description: The Harvard Business Review is regarded as one of the top academic business publications in the world, and this app is your ticket in.

Price: Free

App: Logo Maker

Developer: Laughingbird Software

Description: Design and create a logo for your business.

Price: $2.99

App: Monster.com Jobs for iPad

Developer: Monster Worldwide

Description: A robust job search and employment connection app that works with the Monster.com website.

Price: Free

App: Office to PDF

Developer: Nexscience, LLC

Description: Converts Office documents to PDF. Integration with Google Docs and DropBox.

Price: $2.99

App: Office^2 HD

Developer: Byte Squared Limited

Description: An office editing suite for Word, Excel, and PowerPoint that works seamlessly with your local files and cloud storage accounts.

Price: $7.99

App: PDF Reader Pro Edition for iPad

Developer: iTech Development Systems Inc.

Description: A PDF viewer with large file, annotations, and form support.

Price: $9.99

App: Quickoffice Pro HD

Developer: Quickoffice, Inc.

Description: An office editing suite, PDF viewer, and file manager that works with your email attachments, local files, and cloud storage.

Price: $19.99

App: QuickVoice Recorder

Developer: nFinity Inc.

Description: A digital voice recorder and organizer app.

Price: Free

App: Secure Gmail

Developer: Apps Gone Bananas LLC

Description: Password-protected Gmail client that also handles multiple Gmail accounts.

Price: $.99

App: Splashtop Remote Desktop for iPad

Developer: Splashtop Inc.

Description: Enables remote desktop connectivity by streaming your PC or OS X desktop as a video.

Price: $19.99

App: Square Register

Developer: Square, Inc.

Description: A more robust version of the popular Square app, with more point-of-sale features.

Price: Free

App: Voice Actions

Developer: Pannous GmbH

Description: A voice control system for the iPad.

Price: $5.99

Index

Like the Book?

Let us know on Facebook or Twitter!

facebook.com/courseptr

twitter.com/courseptr

Fan us on Facebook or Follow us on Twitter to learn about upcoming books, promotions, contests, events and more!